Jung and
the Story of Our Time

JUNG and the Story of Our Time

ॐ Laurens van der Post

We live not only our own lives but,
whether we know it or not, also the life
of our time.
The Dark Eye in Africa

 PANTHEON BOOKS

A Division of Random House, New York

All rights reserved under International and Pan-American Copyright Conventions. Published in the United States by Pantheon Books, a division of Random House, Inc., New York.

Library of Congress Cataloging in Publication Data

Van der Post, Laurens.
Jung and the Story of Our Time.

  1. Jung, Carl Gustav, 1875–1961. 2. Psychoanalysis. I. Title.
BF173.V247 1975 150'.19'54 [B] 75–10362
ISBN 0–394–49207–2

Grateful acknowledgment is made to the following for permission to reprint previously published material:

Princeton University Press: Excerpts from pages 31–32, 289, 298, 358, 373, 540–541 of *C. G. Jung: Letters*, edited by Gerhard Adler, in collaboration with Aniela Jaffé, translated by R. F. C. Hull, Bollingen Series XCV (copyright © 1973 by Princeton University Press); short quotes from each volume of *The Collected Works of C. G. Jung*, edited by Gerhard Adler, Michael Fordham, William McGuire, and Herbert Read, translated by R. F. C. Hull, Bollingen Series XX, Vol. 10, *Civilization in Transition* (copyright © 1964 by Bollingen Foundation); Vol. 11, *Psychology and Religion: West and East* (copyright 1953 and © 1968 by Bollingen Foundation); Vol. 13, *Alchemical Studies* (copyright © 1967 by Bollingen Foundation); quote from page 293 of *The Freud/Jung Letters*, edited by William McGuire, translated by Ralph Manheim and R. F. C. Hull, Bollingen Series XCIV (copyright © 1974 by Sigmund Freud Copyrights Ltd. and Erbengeneinschaft Prof. Dr. C. G. Jung).

Oxford University Press: Two lines from the poem "No Worst, There Is None" published in *Poems of Gerard Manley Hopkins*, edited by W. H. Gardner and N. H. Mackenzie.

Manufactured in the United States of America

FIRST EDITION

For

my wife, Ingaret Giffard, who introduced
me to Jung,

and

"T. C." Robertson, for many reasons
inevitably evoked in the course of fifty
years of friendship, but here mainly out
of gratitude for what he has done to make
the earth of our native Africa whole again,
as the example that is the subject of
this book exhorts us also to be whole within.

Contents

Jung and
the Story of Our Time

੬~ Prologue

I HAVE, I BELIEVE, known many of those the world considered great, but Carl Gustav Jung is almost the only one of whose greatness I am certain. Time is relative in more dimensions than those of the continuum wherein Einstein's formidable equation places it. It has a knack of putting the truly great, as it were, well ahead of us, rather than in the past darkening so fast behind. As a result, most of those regarded as great in their own lifetime diminish once dead, and only the truly great increase in stature.

And this increase in stature precisely is what has happened to Jung, although he died only fourteen years ago. Today he looms larger on the scene of the human spirit than he did in his own lifetime. The books in which he recorded his quintessential self and work are more and more to be found in the pockets of the intellectual young. Words that he introduced in new senses into the modern English idiom have lost their élitism and are part today of our ordinary educated vocabulary. Terms like *extrovert, introvert, persona, archetype, anima, animus,* and *shadow,* that we owe him, testify how wide and deep his impact has been.

But what this greatness consists of is almost impossible to define. I myself cannot attempt to do so as a specialist of any kind. Even if I could, I do not believe I would. I am not a psychologist. I was never a patient either of Jung or of any of his distinguished collaborators, or for that matter of any other psychiatrist. I cannot even claim to be a Jungian in the only sense in which I believe he would have approved the term: that is, in regard to someone who has practiced or taught the analytical psychology he pioneered. Used in any larger way and in particular as a label of discipleship, I know he rejected it, and voiced his objections to its use to me on several occasions in those plainest of terms of which he was a master. He did not like the idea of having disciples or blind followers, or even a school, and in his old age agreed most reluctantly to the establishment of the C. G. Jung Institute in Zürich for studies relevant to his own approach to psychology. Indeed, I remember him telling me that the Institute would be lucky if it did not outlive its creative uses within a generation.

Above all, he had a profound horror of "isms," and the adjective "Jungian," which could so easily be a doorstep to "Jungianism," was ruled out in his own discipline of psychology. "I do not want anybody to be a Jungian," he told me. "I want people above all to be themselves. As for 'isms,' they are the viruses of our day, and responsible for greater disasters than any medieval plague or pest has ever been. Should I be found one day only to have created another 'ism,' then I will have failed in all I tried to do."

Ours was, to use the term in its technical sense, a non-psychological relationship. I was in it purely for the love of it. In so far as I could make some small return for the immense amount his friendship gave me, I believe, it came out of this, so that no matter how much my lack of specialist qualifications may limit my interpretation of the man, it is just possible that my view may have a value which is not adequately represented in the mass of material that has been written about him.

At the moment the world knows him almost exclusively as a psychologist and psychiatrist. Yet great and original as his contribution in these fields has been, and unsurpassed as was his gift of healing the abnormal and psychologically sick, his importance to so-called normal man and his societies, I believe, is much greater. It is astonishing to me how this larger aspect of the man has been overlooked by most of the interpreters, who still come from far and wide, like multitudes of dinghies with outboard motors chugging in the wake of a dreadnought, home at last from a sea on which few of us have ventured.

Part of the explanation is that almost all the authors of this formidable intermediary activity have been psychiatrists themselves, or started out as patients either of Jung or of one of his collaborators. Such an approach, of course, is perfectly valid, of great importance, and should not be underestimated. It would be wrong not to recognise Jung for the inspired psychologist and born healer he was. After all, he started out in his career as a pioneer of psychiatry. Psychology and this applied field of it were his medium and led him first to the discovery, and subsequently to the exploration, of a new world within the human spirit greater and in my view far more significant for life on earth than the world Columbus discovered in the world without.

Yet psychology and psychiatry were only a way and not an end in themselves. Had the middlemen between him and the public not all been so preoccupied with their psychiatry, this salient aspect of the man and his work would not have been neglected for so long, and it would not still be possible for another of those books of instant Jung which are increasingly in favour in the Anglo-Saxon world to appear, as one did not long ago, with the final chapter headed "Jung's Contribution to Psychiatry," as if that were both the summit and end of his seeking.

One has only to glance at Jung's *Memories, Dreams, Reflections* to see how the man himself was full and overflowing with a greater concern. There one finds only one chapter, the fourth, entitled "Psychiatric Activities." It is followed by one called "Sigmund Freud." Then there comes "Confrontation with the Unconscious," where, much condensed, Jung gives his own account of a confrontation as portentous for the increase of human awareness as the dark night of exile in the Old Testament wherein Jacob, the father of Joseph the Dreamer, wrestled alone and long with an angel. Only then does one reach the chapter headed "The Work."

Understandable as the psychiatric concentration on Jung has been up to this point, it becomes less so subsequently in so far as it persists in presenting this "work" of Jung also as a mere extension of psychology and psychiatry, leaving the popular concept of Jung

5

confined to what remains, despite the resultant enlargement, still a clinical cell.

Having never been in such a cell myself, I see it differently and, I believe, in the direction Jung himself viewed it, and I may therefore perhaps help in a small way towards another perspective of him. Even so, I cannot do this in terms of pure knowledge or as a product of any profound research, nor as part of a particular discipline. I can only present it in the way it had meaning for me and that was as a living experience in the context of a personal relationship in which I had no professional or private axe to grind. Moreover, since I came to the experience reluctantly, I believe that the difficulties from which it stemmed in themselves are a microcosm of the macrocosm of the problem Jung had in making himself and his work understood and accordingly the problem his own time had in understanding him.

I am compelled, therefore, to begin with myself, not for any egotistical purpose but as the only way open to me if I am to render account of the man and his work as experience, and an act of knowledge rather than another of those abstracts of knowledge already so amply available. Also, I believe that by relating my own long-sustained imperviousness to Jung, I might help to expose in others the same process of negation which, although diminishing, is still astoundingly active in the cultural environment of an hour so much later in the life of our time than we yet care to admit.

Finally, the European context of my life in the interior of South Africa and its extreme Calvinistic mould, owing to its remoteness from the swiftly changing Europe of its origin, when communications were far slower and more difficult than today, tended to be so far behind the accelerating time abroad that although born much later than Jung, I experienced a version of life with a religious emphasis and tensions of mind and spirit that might almost have been drafted from a blueprint of the Protestant Switzerland into which he was born.

੩~ The Time and the Space

And Joseph dreamed a dream, and he told it his brethren:
and they hated him yet the more.

Genesis 37:5

IT ALL STARTED for me as a child in the interior of South Africa. In
the clear light of a certain *esprit d'escalier* that comes to one on the
way down from one's own little attic in time, I seem to have had an
inborn predisposition towards the area of meaning in which Jung's
abundant spirit, without our knowing, was already embattled. I had
always had what seemed to my own family and friends an inordinate
interest in dreams. I was always dreaming, and dreams from the
beginning meant something to me that they did not to the grown-up
pale-faces of my world. The pink marshmallow material they were
in the minds of governesses trained in the Victorian order of these
things became suspect to me at an early age. Even worse was their
dismissal as some sort of poor rich trash of the imagination by the
hearty male teachers of our extrovert society who followed where
wistful spinster ladies left off. They would pass sentence on one's
dreaming processes with a phrase that filled me with dismay: "But,
my dear boy, it was only a dream."

That "but only" of theirs became increasingly discredited when I
saw how it was automatically part of their judgement of almost

everything that mattered to me as a child. Growing up in the European way began to look not so much like a process of growth as a dangerous reduction to a "but only" state, and made me fear it accordingly, so acutely that the fear is still with me.

Like all children of my world, I was compelled to say my prayers every night before going to sleep, in spite of the fact that our evening meal always ended with a long reading from the Bible, an even longer improvised prayer, with all of us kneeling on the hard, polished wooden floor of the dining-room by our rather medieval chairs and their carved frames and high backs, and a final singing of a psalm. Some nurse or senior member of the family was always there to supervise this last ablution of our minds from the stains of the sinful day. They would see to it that one knelt down by one's bed and ran silently through the prescribed formula for invoking divine protection for parents, brothers, sisters, and whoever one's affection wanted on the list, not forgetting a perfunctory plea for one's own redemption from a state of sin, which one did not feel but had been talked into accepting as an inborn element of one's being.

I never minded the occasion and invariably took to my bed afterwards mysteriously relieved and rather startled by the fact that the long, white home-made candle by the side of my bed would look transformed into a lighthouse poised on the rim of the great sea of the African night, lapping at the lip of the shuttered window, and sanctifying my room with a sort of Pentecostal glow. I would stare for a moment at the brass rails of my bed rendered gold, and glance up to see candle and flame stand transparent on the glass within the frame which enclosed, on the wall above my bed, the text stitched in blue Gothic letters on yellow silk, "The Lord is my shepherd; I shall not want."

After that, I could have no doubt of finding safe harbour in sleep, and in such sleep the dream I had secretly placed on my prayer list. But no such dream ever came. There followed some months of agonising questioning and self-examination, when I woke up so often to prod myself on to greater dream exertion that I got up in the mornings exhausted and had my parents thoroughly worried. But somehow, I made my peace with the fact that I could not fabricate dreams myself largely because, far from lowering the process in my estimation, it increased my respect for the dream, since I concluded that it was greater than both I and prayer combined, with a will and a way all its own.

By this time my obsession had become common knowledge. I no longer confessed my dreams or fantasies to anyone, but the damage had been done and inevitably I was nicknamed "Joseph the Dreamer." If I had to choose one moment rather than another in which I first became aware of a deep feeling of isolation in an essential part of myself from the community in which I was born, it was when a fond family officialdom labelled me thus.

Unhappily, this dreaming process had a knack of following through into my waking imagination, in a way judged highly reprehensible by a pioneering society still engaged in a battle for survival which demanded the attention of the keenest faculties of its members on the physical world. Again and again I would be forced to recognise that a recollection of a dream of the night before and a whole train of associations sparked off by it had taken my mind away from the immediate business of the day and that I had unwittingly put myself in a position of being reproved for lack of appropriate attentiveness. The reproof in the beginning was mild and little more than some tart exhortation to the assembled family or classroom, like "Look at him! He's been at it, dreaming again," or, more sarcastically, "Would you be good enough, sir, to step out of your trance?"

Divided by my own private and personal pull inwardly and the tug of the world to keep me focused on the life outside me, I was overwhelmed by guilt and a belief that I was born incompetent in all that mattered most in life. I do not know how this withdrawn and secret dreaming self, so vulnerable, inexperienced, unarmed, and gradually compelled to fall out of love with itself, would have survived if help had not come to it from unexpected quarters.

It first came from my wise, stern, and upright old grandfather. He was already very old when I was very young. Indeed, the difference in our ages was so great and the span of years covered between us so long that I can remember him telling me in great detail of a battle in which he had fought against the English in Africa in 1848. It seemed to me that there was almost nothing that could happen to human beings this side of the grave that had not happened to him, things both bad and good and which his faith and courage somehow had not failed to contain, if not altogether to resolve. The time was to come when, after my first reading of Bunyan, only the best *Pilgrim's Progress* associations were good enough for him and one in particular, Mr. Standfast, stuck firmly to his memory.

Help came from him on a night when I was staying with him alone in the home which he built for himself on his broad farm called Boesmansfontein—"Bushman's Spring." The moment possesses a startling, timeless, Vermeer-like clarity. The great table in the dining-room had been cleared after the evening meal; all the household servants had been summoned to join us and had taken up their positions squatting against the walls. They seemed to represent all the variations of the races of man that made up the population of the interior of southern Africa, and they had a look in their eyes that seemed to me to go back to the beginning of life on earth, particularly so in the light which illuminated the room at that moment.

The light came from a single and immense oil lamp suspended from the centre of the ceiling by three silver chains joined to a bronze hook. The glass of the lamp was always cleaned and polished by the senior servant of the house every morning, since my grandmother was no longer alive and all the daughters gone. The elaborately wrought iron frame which held the bronze lamp had a kind of Near-Eastern look and, somehow, whenever I heard the parable of the lamps in the New Testament, a miniature of this sort of flame always glowed in my mind. Elongated, it would shimmer there in front of the huge family Bible like a reflection of one of our poplars shaking the yellow evening sun flake by flake from its trembling leaves.

It was significant that my grandfather never referred to the Bible as such but always as The Book, and he had such a feeling for this Book of all books, which had been almost his only reading, that he had a special ritual for getting to the piece he was going to read in a strangely halting, groping voice, because he had never been to any school. He would reverently lift the large, heavy leather covers of the Book, with their metal clasps that shone like silver, and open it slowly on the first ivory pages, smooth them out with his long brown hand, and let them lie there exposed on the table a brief moment. I think today that he did this so that he could survey the big green family tree, with its spreading branches painted across both pages, and seek out among the leaves the names of his forefathers recorded there from the time they had landed in Africa as refugees from persecution some two hundred and fifty years before. On this particular occasion, he had decided to read the story of the young Joseph and his blood-stained coat of many colours, which remains for me one of the greatest stories ever told. To my joy it was being read from beginning to end. Suddenly there came the indication that the story had been chosen for my special benefit. My grandfather looked up from his reading, because I believe he knew that part of the Bible by heart, and with his eyes direct on me, declaimed, "And Joseph dreamed a dream and he told it his brethren: and they hated him yet the more." Whenever he came to a dream thereafter, his eyes left the book to seek me out, while he spoke the piece from memory.

Finally, when the text had been read and the last prayers said, my grandfather's favourite Commando hymn, which was my own father's too, had been sung, and the servants dismissed, my grandfather withdrew to his favourite leather armchair by the fire, because on family occasions the dining-room was used in between meals as a drawing-room as well. Beckoning me to him, he took me on his knee. He addressed me by my full name, as he always did when he had something of particular importance to say to me. "Laurens Jan, always remember what the Book says about Joseph and his dreams. Remember that though his brothers hated him for it, had it not been for his dreaming, they would never have found corn in Egypt and would have perished, as you have heard, in the great famine that was still to come."

I could sense that my grandfather had been aware of my dilemma in a manner I was not. He saw dangers in it that I could not possibly foresee at that moment and he wanted to convey to me both a warning and an encouragement. The obvious encouragement was that however much the dream might be suspect for others—most dangerously of all for me, because the others happened to be people I loved—it was as valid for him as it was for the greatest authority he recognised, the Book of Books.

I was much older before I realised how much subtler and wiser my grandfather had been and how through both the subtle seed of a sense of the role of paradox in the meaning of things he planted in my highly impressionable imagination and a warning against taking the dreams of Joseph too literally, he had done much to prevent me from overidentifying myself with the biblical example and becoming what would now in Jungian terms be called "inflated." Indeed, the immediate effect of his concern for me seemed to have ensconced me more firmly for the moment in the state of secrecy about my dreaming life, although it meant that in one vital aspect I was more and more isolated from family and friends.

The first dream recorded in the Bible, the dream of Jacob and the ladder, to me was and remains the greatest of all dreams ever dreamt and the progenitor of all the other dreams, visionary material, and mythological and allegorical activity that were to follow. This dream, I was to realise, was in a sense an absolute existing outside space and time, for it had lost none of its freshness and excitement. Even though I know it occurred in the remote past, it remains one of the great "nows" of my imagination, and I have only to close my senses against the glitter of our electric-lit day to see in the darkness within a ladder pitched on the stony ground of a great waste-land and reaching as high as ever to a star-packed heaven, with the urgent traffic of angels phosphorescent upon it.

I believe the image of the ladder and its positioning between Heaven and earth is intended to convey that through it men and the source of all their meaning will forever be in communication with one another. Angels, as the Greek derivation of the word so clearly denotes, are messengers and visualisations of the means by which the dreamer and cause of dream can speak to each other. No matter how abandoned and without help either in themselves or the world about them, the dream goes on to add—using Jacob's state and the great and perilous waste-land through which he is fleeing in fear of his life as imagery of man at the end of himself and the resources of his world—men are never alone because that which, acknowledged or unacknowledged, dreams through them is always by their side.

For Jacob had not even to ask for help from beyond himself. The necessities of his being had spoken so eloquently for him that the dream brought him instant promise of help from that which had created him, henceforth to the end of his days, and of those who were to follow in his way after him.

All this made the coming of the dream in time appear to me as fateful for life within as the coming of fire for life on earth without. For great as is the service it has performed thus far already, the sum is not complete with only this preamble of intent. It still demands addition of its practical consequences.

The ancient Chinese defined meaning as "that which has always existed through itself." This dream for me too was an intimation that the dreaming process must always have existed through itself, and that when the last secret of nature has been unveiled and the final problem of creation resolved, however opaque the heart of all matter, and swiftly changing as may be the many-faceted and elusive spirit, we shall still find, like stars in the night, images of the dream that always existed through itself.

Although I was moved to tears many years later, I was not in the least surprised, therefore, when one of the first men of life, a Stone Age hunter in a waste-land greater, I believe, than even the waste-land in which Jacob dreamt his dream informed me, "You know, there is a dream dreaming us." To this day I do not know anything to equal this feeling for what the dreaming process is to life and its implication that it is enough for the moment for creation to appear to us as the dreaming of a great dream and the unravelling and living of its meaning.

In the years that followed, I could easily have been talked, badgered, and teased out of my belief in the importance of dreams if it had not been for this dream in particular, and in general for the significant role allotted to them in the stories of the Old Testament we all knew by heart and treasured long before we could be fed on the easier fare of the Brothers Grimm, Andrew Lang, Hans Andersen, and so on. As one moved out of the world of fairy tales and became more vulnerable, and the onslaught of so-called realism on the open, confiding, and naïve imagination of a child grew more sophisticated, one was helped by the frequent appearance of dreams at crucial moments in literature and let the fact carry one's imagination on like a raft on the flood of a great river as, for instance, in Homer's *Iliad* and *Odyssey*, where they are clearly an instrument of the gods themselves.

I remember, for example, the moment I read in an anthology called *The Tales of Troy*, given to me on my sixth birthday, how Zeus decided to inflict a dream on the great foredoomed Agamemnon as the indispensable overture to the sombre orchestration of Homeric men in conflict not only with one another in their overall worldly purposes but above all also with their own selves at odds with their contracted fate. I added all this to the role of the dreams in the Bible I already knew so well and assumed from there on that was how everywhere, and at all times for all men, the dream was some sort of admiralty chart by which their lives were navigated and spread out, like Mercator's epic projection, on a map specially designed for their searching selves. Evidence to confirm this assumption accumulated with the Arab proverb, "Tell me what a man dreams and I will tell you what he is." As significant for me, who wanted to be a story-teller, it made me believe, in a way I might be unable to explain but yet seemed clear, that the art of writing, indeed all art, was a continuation by one's waking daylight self of a process begun in some dreaming process in the darkness of sleep.

I could not see how otherwise events so remote as those that occurred in the world of Joseph or on the great plain of Troy could matter so much to a boy in the interior of twentieth-century Africa that he was already dividing the people he knew into Jacob and Esau categories or, instead of playing "French" and "English" as did everyone else in the towns he knew, organised the boys in his own village into a game of "Greeks versus Trojans." What was it, I wondered even then, that made the whole Homeric world so real to us that some of us immediately were passionately on the side of the Greeks, others as zealously on that of the Trojans, and prepared, with an ardour of an intensity that had to be experienced to be believed, to play at going to war with one another? It was then that I realised that some men were born Trojans, others Greeks, and proceeded, as I do to this day, to see all men either as Greeks or Trojans. And all this somehow suggested a reality not only without geographical and cultural bounds but also outside space and time in which, however rational and egotistical our attitude to it, we participated and found both close neighbours and even immediate enemies.

Nor must I fail to mention how lucky I was as a child to be sustained in this instinctive predisposition of mine by the primitive world into which I was born. Dreams were never "pink marshmallow" matter to my black and coloured countrymen but real, vital and decisive facts, rivalling the reality of any in the objective physical world around them. When I was a child they made manifest to me that for them, as Lévy-Bruhl was to proclaim later, the dream was the real god of primitive people.

My own special Bushman nurse even had a father whose spirit was vivid with manly pride in the name of Dream bestowed on him at birth. With such a progenitor, she was the last to flag in defending an interest in this other world of which the dream was the veiled messenger.

Yet once the need for more schooling drove me from my home, sustaining this particular note in my imagination became increasingly lonely and difficult work. It was not until my last year at school, when a master who had just come from Oxford, and to whom I owe much, lent me Freud's *Introductory Lectures on Psycho-Analysis* that this dishonoured state in myself became reinvested with honour from what I accepted as an irrefutable source.

The excitement caused by those volumes was intense. We all had to work part of the time during our holidays on the farm "The Mountain of the Wolves," which is mine today. I found I could not leave the books at home when I went to work but had to take them with me. On this long, cold winter vacation, my particular task was herding a precious flock of ewes and their lambs in the hills not far from home. I do not think so valuable a flock has ever been better protected by Providence, for I was too preoccupied with my reading of Freud to see to it properly myself. Just the memory of those days brings up the sound of ewes bleating, demented by the disappearance of their offspring, and the far-off, high-pitched quavering replies of lambs who had fallen asleep behind a boulder and so had been left far behind, exposed to the jackals or hyenas we called wolves that might have been on the prowl—a separation of mother and child I was ostensibly there to prevent.

The recollection of that oddly biblical sound remains charged with an agony of nostalgia not just for a golden moment in the blue of southern Africa, suspended, as it were, from on high in a witch-bowl of unclouded time and space, but also for another, infinitely more remote, wherein it accompanied the movement of the human spirit in another waste-land farther and farther away from the Garden that nourished it at the beginning. Africa has always been Old Testament country for me and this was a singularly Old Testament atmosphere in which to be introduced to such an Old Testament spirit as Freud. I may not have been able to articulate it at the time, but I believe I already had an inkling of how, even though unknown to himself, Freud's was an Old Testament temperament, trying with the inspiration of genius to give an Old Testament sense of the overwhelming importance of the hidden world to which the dream was an unique gate, its relevant, scientific, and contemporary idiom. It was my first intimation of Freud as the Old Testament prophet of modern psychology. Jung, I was to find much later, was the exponent of the New. Even so profound a nostalgia, however, cannot hold back a resurge of the excitement which accompanied my reading of those dark blue volumes and which was my salute to them as a great breakthrough in the human spirit. For me they remain the best of Freud and the best of so great a person is incomparable.

Yet I turned thereafter to everything Freud wrote with growing disappointment. He had less and less to say to me, personally. Even the language, which was so simple, lucid, and adequate in the beginning, seemed to become more and more obscure. An urge to invent hideous, lifeless words of his own and abandon the inexhaustible idiom of the European spirit takes over, and his own attitude becomes more and more dogmatic, letting a kind of metaphysics of sex take the place of the gift of unclouded observation and deduction that had excited me so in the beginning. The self-defeat implicit in this, which already many years before, unbeknown to me, had worried Jung all along in his relationship with Freud, was final, as far as I was concerned. Nothing should have made this aspect of Freud more plausible and its appeal greater than the kind of puritanical Calvinist world into which I was born. There in a one-sided, man-dominated world, sex was at its best a necessary evil and the community's attitude invested with an abomination of it and woman, for instance, as great as that expressed by Calvin's fanatical disciple John Knox, whose church really fathered the Dutch Reformed Church of my world and not that of the Holland of which it was ostensibly a branch.

Indeed, the vast complex of the consequence of a compulsive suppression of sex and all associated with it in the mind and customs of man was so great that one could easily see why it could appear the villain in almost every piece of human folly and individual and cultural derangement, as Freud implied, and how the lifting of the sexual ban in life could appeal to men as the one supreme act of emancipation on which the human spirit was waiting as a preliminary to unhampered fulfillment. Even the Victorian dancing, just becoming fashionable in our late-Edwardian colonial day, was regarded as diabolical, and woman's place so much considered in the home and its kitchen and nurseries that one of my own sisters had sermons preached against her in our local church because she had had the presumption to become one of the first of her sex to go to a university and take a degree.

Obviously, in such a world, this aspect of Freud's approach had to have a certain compelling validity. And yet it failed for me, even in its subtlest and most sublime interpretations, because ultimately sex remained to me one part and, however extensive, not all or indeed not even the greatest of the sources of life's energies and seeking. Moreover, Freud utterly failed me because no matter how many dreams he accounted for with his theories—and they were legion—he could in no way explain the greatest of them all, the dream of Jacob's ladder. Sad that someone who had taken one so far could take one no further, I gave up reading him altogether.

By that time, Freud's name was no longer abroad on its own. It was one of the awesome psychological trinity of Freud, Adler, and Jung. Since they were bracketed together by everybody in the same area of the mind, I had no desire to look any deeper into the credentials of the others but assumed that Adler and Jung had to be likewise tainted. With the typical capacity of a child of my time for prejudgement and prejudice, I refused to read them, and so denied them the right, which no one even lesser than they should be denied, of speaking for themselves.

Accounts of how the three had disagreed among themselves convinced me how right I was not to be interested any more. Jung in particular, the commanding heights of the intellectual establishment of my day would have it, had not only betrayed Freud but was really just a woolly, superstitious, and utterly unscientific kind of mystic. I was induced into holding on to this odd belief despite the constant urgings of my own wife. Through her mother, who was a close friend of Jung's foremost English collaborator, H. G. ("Peter") Baynes, she knew more about Jung than most people and had an exceptional right to be heard. Yet I rejected her urging even to read him with an unreason that should have been warning enough of the disproportion implicit in my attitude. I continued to do so until the outbreak of the last world war—that is, for fifteen whole years after abandoning my first reading of Freud. Something happened then which got past the defences of my well-organised prejudices and shook me with doubt.

By this time, what had started out as a feeling of isolation in the midst of a large family I loved had assumed formidable and, for me, dangerous proportions. It had spread to a total disassociation from my own people in their attitudes to my black and coloured countrymen and the whole complex of that subtle and mysterious entanglement of spirit called colour prejudice. I had come to write the first book written by any one of them against racial and colour prejudice in southern Africa. It was something which had been left out of my own make-up and which I was convinced was not natural in any of us. I was certain we all started with as great a love of our black and coloured countrymen as of anyone of our own kind and that we had to be educated aslant into the prejudices that divided us from one another. The violence and unreason of these prejudices seemed to me proof, as it were, of how unnatural they were and how profoundly instinctive, with self-doubt at their source of origin. Others, of course, had observed these things too and had taken them to be peculiarly local phenomena, condemning them as Olive Schreiner had done so bravely and eloquently on purely ethical grounds.

But to me there appeared to be involved something universal and fundamental to all mankind. What we called colour prejudice in Africa I thought could be merely one manifestation of an inaccurate condition of spirit that afflicted human beings all over the world in other forms. For that reason I suspected it was symptomatic of one of the most fateful issues of our time, so fateful that the hero of my book experiences the conflict of spirit at the back of it all as a dangerous sickness of his body. This book was to prove prophetic in many ways, but in that sense alone it was an intuitive anticipation of what I was to find confirmed in the whole range of psychosomatic phenomena taken for granted today.

But equally important was the decision of the hero to detach himself from all the collective prescriptions for the problems of life as I knew it between the world wars and his determination to live them out alone in an individual and natural context of his own choosing. In this sense too the book was prophetic and the hero became, I believe, the first "drop-out" on literary record, reflecting my own growing isolation and antagonism to the mind, mood, and trend of the pre-war world.

So far did it go that I abandoned the literary scene in London and went to live on my farm in the West country of England to practise what my book had preached. Art even then seemed to me a vocation that had not only to be expressed but lived as well. And yet that did not give my isolation the meaning or purpose I hoped it would have done. A feeling of inexplicable and unfathomable evasion grew and whenever between farming and writing I looked into myself, I was appalled by the cataclysmic split in myself between a spirit once so profoundly committed to a dream pattern of its own and the world around him

I had a hunch that throughout all our yesterdays profound elements and energies which had been neither assessed nor acknowledged were at work, and that myth and legend and even dreams were as much historical material as anything preserved in the orthodox archives and on parchment in the offices of writers of history. It was not surprising, therefore, that the first wedge driven into my own inhibitions and resistances against the new psychology was provided by my sense of history.

I had been watching the rise of Hitler in Germany with a terrible foreboding, increasingly dismayed by the inability of so many English and French to see the phenomenon for what I was convinced it was. In the course of the slow, impervious, and sullen pre-war years of ranting out of what seemed to me always a tranced, mediumistic state, Hitler said only one thing that struck me as real, and that was: "I go the way fate has pointed me, like a man walking in his sleep." That and his own account of the dream which purported to have saved his life in the First World War had an alliance of unholy meaning for me.

According to Hitler, he was asleep in an advanced salient of the German trenches when he dreamed that he was about to be engulfed in an upheaval of earth and mud. He broke out of this nightmare with the utmost difficulty. Feeling suffocated and fighting for breath, he stumbled out of the dug-out for air. He had hardly got clear when an enemy shell hit the post and killed all his companions. He himself looked upon this dream as an act of Providence intervening to save him for a greater destiny and from that moment the conviction that he was under the special protection of fate accelerated the process of inflation to which he was already prone.

One could not doubt, of course, that on the literal level in its special context of war the dream had indeed saved his life for the moment. But there was for me another dimension to the dream, even more important. I thought that the dream addressed also the most urgent of warnings of another kind of peril to the dreamer himself. It seemed to be trying to tell him that he was in imminent danger of being overwhelmed, not so much by the physical earth as by what the earth stood for in the imagination.

Always it has been one of the greatest images of titanic forces and urges of life that have their source below the daylight of reason in some dark underground of the human spirit, as great trees have their roots deep down in the blacked-out recesses of the earth. This dream, I felt, could not be warning the dreamer more clearly that he was in peril of being overwhelmed and suffocated in an upsurge of some dark, instinctive, unrecognised collective aspect of himself. Unless he woke up, in the sense that was an image of a process of being self-aware, and removed himself from the mass, the crowd, the collective pressures of whom his fellow soldiers were the image and their sleeping state the sign of their unawareness of their condition, he and they all would surely perish. The dream seemed to stress that his salvation was possible only in finding himself as an individual. But content in the purely literal surface manifestation of the dream, he neglected the cataclysmic warning latent in it. Reversing the deeper trend of his dream, he embarked on a course of rejoining the mass, the great mindless German collective compulsions to rally his countrymen round him in greater and more solidly congealed numbers than even the Kaiser had done.

That one remark of his, read in the light of such a dream, appeared to me all one needed of explanation of Hitler and the Germans swarming to him like bees around their one and only sovereign. It was transformed at once from a dream metaphor into a proposition of a direct and profound scientific exactitude. He, Germany, and by hypnotic induction the whole of Western Europe at that moment, I was convinced, were walking towards unimagined disaster in a nightmare of sleep.

History was written in a way that did not explain history and threw no light on its latent meaning. The legends and myths in which it has its roots and of which the dreaming process seemed so dynamic an element, as I had concluded in my amateur way. There seemed an underworld of history filled with forces far more powerful than the superficial ones that it professed to serve. Until this world was brought out into the light of day, recognised, and understood, I believed, an amply discredited pattern of self-inflicted death and disaster would continue to reiterate itself and dominate the human scene. I had even coined a name of my own for it and called it the "mythological dominant of history." I came to suspect that this area in myself, from which my childhood interest in dreams had come, was connected with it in a way not understood, because it was itself the subject of one of the most dangerous errors in our thinking. We assumed that "without" and "objective" were one and the same thing, as were "subjective" and "within." I believed that they were by no means synonymous and that there was something as objective *within* the human being as great as the objective *without*, and that men were subject to two great objective worlds, the physical world without and a world within, invisible except to the sensibilities of the imagination.

That dream of Hitler, for instance, seemed to me as objective a fact as a cloud in the sky foretelling the storm to come. The lesson I had learned in childhood that no one could subject dreams to his own will or fancy had gone deep enough in me to make that at last clear. Dreams had a will of steel and a way of their own in their role as direct manifestations of this other objectivity. They were incapable of any falsehood; only our reading of them was liable to error, and I had an inkling that they and the prompting of this other objective within, and not even Freud's psychosexuality at its subtlest and inspired best, were the true source of mythology, religion, legend, and art, seeking and reseeking recognition and expression through our several histories. If denied those by fair means, they sought them by foul. Refused admission with a bland "not at home" at the front door of the spirit, they came in by force or stealth at the rear.

Gerard Manley Hopkins had already said it definitively for me when he wrote that there were not only landscapes for us but "inscapes" as well, or, as he put it in one of his greatest poems,

> O, the mind, the mind has mountains;
> cliffs of fall,
> Frightful, sheer, no-man-fathomed.

And he added to those the words, "Hold them cheap may who ne'er hung there." Those words of his should have rung out like an alarm awakening a sleeping aspect of myself, had I not been so much the child of my own slanted and bigoted moment in time. All I can say in mitigation of myself is that I did not accept the statement just as great poetry but also as some kind of scientific axiom.

Germany in the thirties by the day seemed to me such stuff as nightmares were made on, and everyone in the country goose-stepping towards an abyss in a terrible dream of sleep. I thought I saw the new German hordes in the grip of a long, unacknowledged mythological dominant, grown terrible and angry through neglect and about to revenge itself not only upon Germany but an entire culture which had been indifferent to the legitimate claims of the forces of this "inscape" within themselves.

I just could not look for the explanation in the so-called injustices of the Treaty of Versailles concluded at the end of the 1914–18 war as my own contemporaries did. That might well be the plausible sort of excuse in which established history specialised and which made it so superficial an exercise for me. The real motivation came from that underworld of the past of life which is beyond articulation and where our several histories unrecorded, defying articulation, are lodged deep as our own psychology. I held, more by hunch than out of any proved knowledge, mythology excepted, that unless Hitler was stopped and stopped quickly, the greatest of all world wars would be upon us. We had only to study German mythology, I pleaded, to see how the German spirit was fully mobilised for a mythological charade of the most shattering proportions the world had perhaps ever seen.

I failed to convince even my closest friends and in the end began a book to show how a mythological design obsessed the Hitler phenomenon. That was by far the most frightening part of it. German mythology was the only mythology I knew in which the gods themselves were overthrown by the forces of darkness. In Hitler's Germany, I suggested, we were watching precisely a massing of forces of darkness for the overthrow of such forces of light as there were still in the European spirit; we were witnessing, in fact, another instalment of a long horror serial of history like the 1914–18 war, on the eve of which a British foreign secretary pronounced the words, prophetic in more dimensions than he knew or consciously intended, "The lamps are going out all over Europe; we shall not see them lit again in our lifetime."

Although I had a mass of urgent surface duties to occupy me, I worked away at this book in an area of meaning where I had no known guide or example as if the electric light in my own room might be cut off at any moment. Then, suddenly, after an interruption in my writing caused by a journey to Germany to report on the terrifying Nuremberg Rally, more dejected than I had been before, Jung reappeared in my retarded reckoning.

I met a remarkable American journalist, H. R. Knickerbocker. He had just come from Zürich, where he had interviewed Jung for his newspaper. He could talk about nothing else. He kept on saying that Jung was the only man who really knew what was happening in Europe, that none of the statesmen and politicians had any idea of what all this ascending volcanic rumbling on the European scene portended. Only Jung knew.

I listened, oddly rebuked and fascinated. Of the many examples he gave me of precisely how Jung knew, the one that stands out most clearly in my memory happens to be the one most relevant to this wider significance of Jung to which I would like to testify. It emerged from a distinction Jung drew for Knickerbocker between Mussolini and Hitler. Mussolini, according to Jung, could at a pinch be said to rule Italy. In no way whatsoever could one say that Hitler ruled Germany. That, he told Knickerbocker, would be a cardinal and culpable error. I can almost hear the tall, red-headed Knickerbocker saying, "Jung told me never to forget for a moment that Hitler has the power he has, not because he rules Germany but because he *is* Germany. He is more of a myth than a man. He is the loudspeaker that makes audible all the inaudible murmurings of the German soul."

There were, it is true, observations by Jung in this conversation with which I could not agree, particularly his excursion into the political aspects of the problem of dealing with Nazism, like his suggestion that Germany should somehow be induced to spend this archaic upsurge of itself in a war on Bolshevik Russia: that seemed to me an evasion of his own profound insight into the nature and mythological origin of the problem. But these reservations were insignificant compared to the illumination and dawning of confirmation of my own tentative quest conveyed by the account Knickerbocker gave me of his meeting with Jung.

These feelings really overcame all my resistances. I knew

somehow from then on that I had been not just prejudiced but exceedingly silly, rejecting the one spirit that could have thrown light and helped me in an area of unknowing wherein I myself had been groping in a singularly ill-informed fashion. I may have taken steps to correct myself there and then had the war not almost immediately been upon us and I found myself drawn into it as a soldier, my half-written book left behind to be destroyed subsequently by a fire started by German incendiaries in London and what little light there may have been in the writing put out for ever.

And yet I went to war strangely comforted. Whatever the odds against us, I never doubted that Germany would be defeated, because Hitler was going against his own dream. He was doing precisely what the dream had warned him not to do.

Somehow I was convinced that Hitler would be compelled by the force of underground logic of a mythology which demanded so dark and tragic a fulfillment as the Teutonic one to conduct the war in a manner that made defeat inevitable, so that in the twilight hour before the fall of the final night, like the lame god in that turgid myth of the overthrow of Valhalla, the crippled European spirit could snatch some light from the burnt-out ashes of an inadequate pattern of itself to rekindle a greater fire than had been possible before.

In the course of a war that was to last for me three years longer than for most, these and similar preoccupations, whenever I had a moment to give to this world within myself, were, I realised, growing even greater than before. All sorts of things were happening to me during long years of unreason which convinced me that this other dimension, below the manifest pattern of our private and personal as well as our social and international lives, was the one wherein the character of the future was in the main determined. Moreover, my own war, which took me from North Africa, Ethiopia, and Asia Minor on to Malaya and South-East Asia, had given me some inkling of the universality of the phenomenon.

War against the Japanese, and three and a half years in a Japanese prisoner-of-war camp in particular, seemed to reveal how, despite pronounced differences in race, culture, and history, and vast differences of space and time in between the two countries, the forces which impelled the Japanese into war were akin to those that had overwhelmed the Germany of Hitler. The many plausible differences paled into insignificance before the similarities of the equinoctial pull that had drawn the Japanese also like sleep-walkers in an oddly Germanic goose-step of their own, that military *hochō-tori* of theirs, into the nightmare choreography of a similar mythological dominant, culminating in a disaster even greater than the German one. The parallels were not only close but often so refined in detail that the sun, for instance, which is the image of light of reason in man and walks tall as a god in most highly differentiated mythologies, was for the Japanese the same feminine phenomenon it was for the Germans, while the infinitely renewing and renewable moon that swings the sea of change and symbolises all that is eternally feminine in the spirit of man, by some ominous perversity of the aboriginal urgings of both Germans and Japanese, was rendered into a fixed and immutable masculine.

Nor was it an accident that both were fundamentally "father" countries. I had always thought that an important clue to the psychology of countries was to be found in whether they thought of themselves as "father" or "mother" countries. One had only to hear the crowd at Nuremberg as I had heard them, singing of the *Vaterland*, not as some hundreds of thousands of individuals with as many different voices but as one mindless voice issuing from a hungry, man-devouring Cyclops, to realise how much an unyielding father was in charge of the German spirit, and that the bonds between it and the awful Brandenburg sire of Frederick the Great, and his bonds with some submerged Wotan element of the ancient Germans, had somehow by-passed Holy Roman sublimation and remained unbroken.

As for the Japanese, despite the presence of a goddess in their sun, theirs was a similar father-dominated spirit which sent them swarming like bees not around a queen-bee but a king-bee in the person of their emperor. It was no accident that of the three great proverbial terrors of Japanese life, "father, fire, and earthquake," father was the greatest.

But perhaps the main lesson of all for me was that war did not come to us of its own account by some form of spontaneous generation in the human spirit, nor did it come as a design imposed on us by greedy, ambitious men, armament manufacturers, international financiers, Freemasons, Jews, or any of the conventional scapegoats upon whom societies chose to inflict their own inadequacies. It was monstrously born of the way we all lived what for fear of telling the truth and want of a better word we called a life of peace. I felt that somehow, in a way I could not define, we too had contributed to the reaction of Germans and Japanese to the reality of our time. We had to share some of the responsibility in the matter as though we, through our deeds of omission, were the accomplices before but I hoped would cease to be after the fact of the war which we were fighting. Only by understanding how we were all a part, however opposite, of the same terrible contemporary medal could we defeat those dark forces with the true understanding of their nature and origin which was vital if they were to be overcome in a manner to make us all free to embark on a way of peace that would not lead to a repetition of the vengeful past.

I had a feeling that even our capacity for thinking our own thoughts shrank into painfully humble proportions compared with another kind of reality which was, as it were, thinking through us. The typically French "As I think, so I am" seemed to me so much less true, and so static as to be petrified, after the Arabian axiom that as a man dreamt, so he was.

Yet even these reservations about human self-capacity for thinking were trivial set against my conviction that we were utterly incapable of inventing the content of symbols, however much we helped to shape and express them, in the limited means available to us in our own little ration of reality. I was somehow convinced that issuing straight out of our deepest nature, like starlight out of the night, the material for symbols, whether we liked it or not, was inflicted on us as a spur to a widening vision of ourselves. I had never seen so clearly as during this kind of war in which I was engaged how symbolism infected not only the human spirit and imagination, not only expressed something of itself in words, poetry, art, and religion, but when all these and other sources failed it, as ours seemed to have done, how it compelled human beings to act it out in blind, ritualistic behaviour.

I concluded that the Germans behaved as they did to us all in general and to the Jews in particular because we both had become literal symbols and in the process had lost our common humanity for them. We had become mirrors for them wherein they could not separate a reflection of a hidden aspect of themselves they despised and rejected from the mirror itself, and thought they could rid themselves of the enemy within forever by destroying what reflected it in the world without.

I remember so well a particular day in prison when the nature of all this became clear to me. It was a day when one of those strange outbursts of hatred against us exploded among our "hosts," as we called the Japanese, who had us absolutely in their power and made us as vulnerable as human beings could possibly be, with no resources of defence except what we possessed of natural spirit and experience of life immemorial incorporated within us could offer as imponderable means of defence. These explosions were usually unpredictable except that some of us had suspected that when we had done nothing ourselves, however trivial, to provoke them, they were impelled by something connected with the waxing and waning of the moon.

We had noticed that as the moon filled out and the nearer it came to the achievement of its own, incomparable Javanese fullness, the more it seemed to swing a sea of unreason in the minds of the Japanese, drawing it like a great neap tide high up on to the foreshore of their imagination. And as the moon began to decline, a kind of dark insecurity often seemed to overcome our captors, and they themselves would be compelled to inflict the worst and most indiscriminate of their beatings and the most horrific of their cruelties on us.

I had become increasingly aware of this compulsive mechanism in their spirit and was perpetually seeking for a way in which we could mitigate the process but as yet had found no way of protest, verbal response, or silent attitude that did not aggravate it all the more. I could find no response more effective than that of following the example of Job on his ash-heap, accepting all his dangerously unjust afflictions with similar patience, dignity, and an intuition that it was all part of some universal purpose. I had a hunch that if we clung to some such positive acceptance of our fate, the extent to which we served this feeling of purpose with reason, imagination, precision, and patience would give us some protection.

This particular event was just such an occasion when we were all beaten up on sight for no apparent reason. As always when this happened, I noticed a strange, unseeing look in the eyes of the Japanese. It was a look directed not at us but at something beyond us, as if they were afraid that should their eyes focus on us, they would recognise our common humanity and the inner vision which was their authority for the punishment they were inflicting would not only be challenged but extinguished.

There was again something extraordinarily familiar to me about this expression, as if I had encountered it a thousand and one times before, but where? At the same time I would see in the eyes of my men and fellow officers a look not of hurt so much as utter bewilderment and sheer incomprehension at what was happening to them. They certainly were without any means of explaining the process to themselves. And that expression too seemed just as familiar to me as the look on the Japanese faces. And suddenly I knew it all. I had seen the first look so often in the eyes of public prosecutors, magistrates, and judges in the courts of my native South Africa when some poor black native countryman was being tried in a language he could not understand, for a breach of laws he often did not know existed because they went so much against his own instinct of what was due to him as a living human being. And even when he knew of the existence of such laws he certainly had never had any say in their drafting nor had he been consulted over the assumptions that served as their justification. The only surprising thing was that I had not recognised it before, considering how often I had observed also how a judge, in passing sentence, invariably never looked at the uncomprehending accused but past him, exactly in the way the Japanese looked past us. It was as if his eyes too were focused on some abstract of vision of his own, intuitively afraid that one glance at the poor, ragged, and tattered creature in the dock would be enough to cancel out all the plausibilities he had in mind for condemning the person.

The look in the eyes of my men, I realised, was exactly the look in the eyes of the black man in the dock, because their own humanity and indeed innocence were denied their legitimate consideration in influencing what was being inflicted on them. We too treated the black man in Africa as we did because we had abstracted him from his human reality and allowed him to become more of a symbol than a man to us. We were inflicting upon him something of the symbolism that was trying to draw our attention to a part of ourselves of which we were unaware, and punishing him in the world without, in the same way that we were punishing a dark, natural self within ourselves. It was my first realisation of the symbolic role that blackness and colour played in begetting, without our knowing, especially acute forms of racial tensions in my native country.

Out of this realisation, I suspected that both Japanese and Germans were caught up in a similar process, and gradually I became more and more appalled by the collective failure, a failure not only of a single nation but of the cultures of our time, indeed of the whole civilisation that had nourished them, to observe and serve the symbols clamouring for admission into our lives. I had a glimpse of how the same mechanism trapped smaller groups, from parents and children, husbands and wives, lovers and enemies, down to individuals like myself in our relationships with one another. I was appalled by a roll-call of human errors I myself had committed out of the same unseeing provocation in my life.

I reflected in this regard on two strange social phenomena I had encountered in Malaya and Java which, although they went under different names, were identical twins in nature.

In Malaya it was heralded under the cry of *Amok*, which is one of the most frightening I have ever heard. In Java it went under the name of *Mata Kelap*, or the Dark Eye. In both instances some man was involved—I have encountered it only in men—usually at the age of forty, that is, significantly at the beginning of the period of the second half of life. The man was invariably someone who had done his duty by wife, children, and society with the utmost circumspection and dedication to the minute detail of the elaborate conventions governing behaviour in these matters in that part of the world. He would without warning snatch from its sheath his kriss, the Malay and indeed also Javanese dagger, fashioned as if it were an image of the flame of consciousness itself and of the fire that is present so onomatopoetically in the name. Kriss in hand, he would rush out to kill as many men, women, and children near him as he could, though up to that moment he may have loved them and none of them have done him any personal injury.

What made this outburst of individual violence even more significant to me was that both Javanese and Malays individually and collectively set such store by gentleness, grace, delicate and considerate manners. Some of this is implicit in the name Malay, applied to the peoples of Malaya and of the coastal belts of those South-East Asian archipelagos shining like strings of emeralds in their bluest of blue seas, made more profound in the way their sky lagooned by tall, monsoon clouds with opal battlements reflected as deep within the deep below the brilliant surface of the blinding ocean as they loomed high above it. The word Malay, derived as it is from *malu*, gentle, denotes how they think of themselves and how gentleness of spirit is their greatest collective value.

Were they overgentle and hence the relapse into violence? Was there a connection between the two? Could human beings be overgood and was goodness not subject also to the laws of proportion as all else and had to beware of its own excess? From where did these laws issue? What made them reach out with so long, strong, and murderous an arm into the dark around us? Of course, I could not tell, but I was certain that I would never again be at ease with myself until I knew some answer to these and hordes of similar questions.

Nonetheless, the term *Mata Kelap* of the Javanese, and its intimation that the eye of the man who ran *Amok* thus had suddenly darkened, seemed to me so full of potential meaning that it lived with me as a seed out of which grew in time a feeling of a certain understanding through sheer experience of the origin and nature not only of colour prejudice and intolerance in South Africa but of prejudice, intolerance, and other forms of fanaticism in every nation and every human soul on earth. In the end this compelled me to record such conclusions as I could draw from such tentative growth in a book I inevitably called *The Dark Eye in Africa*. Today I would widen its conclusions and call it *The Dark Eye in the World*, so much darker than even in Africa has the single-eyed vision of our time become all over the world.

For the moment, however, I had enough to cope with in my own mind with the realisation that not only individuals had their eye darkened to run *Amok* suddenly but whole nations did likewise, as had the Japanese and Germans against whom we were fighting. I was to find when I eventually came out of prison, to begin another and even stranger round of soldiering in South-East Asia, that the indigenous people everywhere there too had congealed into a great collect as if in possession of only the single eye of a Cyclops so darkened and charged with some strange electricity of injured spirit that they ran *Amok* among the Dutch, who had been their masters for more than three hundred years. I was intimately involved, therefore, for some years with a contemporary example of what happens when a natural, collective value has been rejected and its validity denied, as the Dutch those of the Indonesians, the British of Indians, and the French of their Indo-China. I shared in full the horror of the consequences heaped on us all for having used our power, despite the great benefits we may have conferred in the process, so as to prevent all those peoples with ancient cultures of their own from being their own versions of themselves.

There were not only the riots and murders in the streets I had to deal with in the beginning but more tender occasions, as when I saw Sukarno in Eastern Java on a pilgrimage to his mother, whom he had not seen for many years. As he knelt at her feet to receive her blessing, I found myself profoundly stirred. More, I, who did not really respect him despite his immense charm and what I can only describe in the Elizabethan term "comeliness," was nearly choked by the emotion of the crowd of seventy thousand who had followed him and were sobbing out of relief because the suppressed and accumulated longing of centuries to see someone of their own kind leading them had found a living symbol at last. But again, where did such volcanic forces in the human being come from? What gave them such overwhelming power over men? How and what did one and societies do to contain them?

The extent to which I achieved some understanding of these great non-rational imponderables in what the Japanese were doing to us at the time enabled me to invest our own experience of imprisonment with some of the humanity it so sorely lacked. It enabled me, for instance, to humanise the symbol of the Japanese in us which, even if it did not enable me entirely to humanise what was reflected for them, did by some radio-active fall-out that accompanies any true effort of understanding mitigate more than in any other prison of which I have heard the consequences of the chain reaction set up by so symbolic an interdependence as that in which we were all trapped, captors as much as captives.

What is more important, perhaps, it helped the two of us chiefly responsible for bringing some six thousand men through the experience, not only without any feelings of bitterness for the Japanese but with that extraordinary liberating conviction that their enemies had been forgiven because they truly had not known what they were doing. That New Testament utterance torn out of the agony of crucified flesh and blood nearly two thousand years ago proved to be for me, and thousands with me, one of the greatest scientific axioms of one aspect of the reality of man's inhumanity to man which has to precede our full assumption of liberation from the negations of collective and personal history and set us free to pursue our main vocation of being our individual selves to which we are all from the act of conception, did we but know it, committed.

One and all, we ended up in the main with nothing but compassion for the Japanese that they should have been so unselved as to do what they had done to us. Somehow we had to learn to take the symbols which come at us out of our own natures, like lightning in the dark, for the certain portents they are of great possibilities of new being, preparing to fall upon our arrested and arid lives like rain on desert earth, and accordingly serve and express them with all that we have of light, reason, endurance, and fortitude within us.

I had only to think of the war that was raging all round me. Already I saw how Clauswitz's definition of war as a continuation of policy when all other means had failed it should really be rephrased in depth and expressed as a continuation of the policy of a profundity of spirit trying to be lived when sharply sided men not only failed it but tried to pin it down to one phase of itself wherein they thought they could be more comfortable and at ease with themselves than in any other. This explained to me the strange relief I had observed in thousands of human beings not only in this war but at the outbreak of the war of 1914–18. It was not just relief that what had appeared for so long as a great menace of evil was about to be fought and overcome but a relief that a way of life which had been apparently devoid of purpose had now with the declaration of war suddenly acquired meaning again, and even the most trivial of things and tasks overnight transformed into matters of life and death.

That explained to me how the most exalted of men in the war could suddenly stoop in their own concept of themselves to tasks they would have found humiliating before: the feeling that in doing so they were once more serving a cause greater than any egotistical pursuit of themselves seemed to make the tasks infinitely worth while. War, I concluded, was a kind of terrible surgeon of life called in to cut away some atrophied limb of the human spirit. It was the terrible healer that came out of the deeps of ourselves when we failed to heal ourselves of our own free will. And this war in which I was engaged had been called in because this extroverted, slanted, one-sided process of evolution after the Renaissance, and particularly encouraged by the Protestantism born of the Reformation in which my own natural tradition of spirit had its being, had served its purpose. Outworn, it had to make way for something greater, but since we had not the vision and lacked the vitality to clear the way of our own volition, something within us had called in one more war as the terrible healer to this tragic bedside of our spirit.

I talked a great deal about these things to the men who had been closest to me in prison, as I had done to my friends in England before the war and to my colour-obsessed countrymen in southern Africa, but in vain. I had a hunch I cherished dearly, that repetitions of patterns of history were neither inevitable nor necessary, that indeed history itself sought nothing more ardently than to be delivered forever from the dark negations hitherto implicit in its processes, so that it could freely move on and achieve its ultimate meaning, but it was a lonely sort of hunch. Thus isolated in this whole area of myself, I came back from war more lonely and, as it were, more outnumbered than I had ever felt in life before.

In fact, the day I resigned a permanent commission in the British Army, and rejected tempting offers of promotion within it, to return to civilian life was one of the saddest I had ever experienced. I still had some fourteen months of accumulated leave in uniform due to me, so long and unbroken had my war service been, but I knew that my back was already turned irrevocably on what had been the only true community of men I myself had ever known, a community of men joined, however inadequately and imperfectly, for the service of something all believed greater than themselves. It was almost as if I took off my uniform for the last time like some self-defrocking priest leaving a rare, monastic order charged with the defences of life in a dimension in which it had been nearly overwhelmed.

I soon found myself appalled by the extent to which the war had been forgotten, and the remembrance of the cause for which I believed we had fought it obliterated from the considerations of men. Comparing what I had experienced in the army, I was horrified by the brutality, selfishness, deviousness of civilian life, the disloyalties and the extraordinary greed of ordinary men and women. The army behind me seemed a great, tender, gentle, compassionate order of mercy in contrast to the bitter, competitive civilian world I entered. I was dismayed to see how politicians, statesmen, artists, and intellectuals seemed to have taken up the very partialities of mind and slants of spirit which I thought had produced the war, as if there had been no war at all to warn them of the dangers implicit in such a way of life and no history to provide them with examples of how urgent was the task of correcting the inadequacies of their vision. The loss of a sense of history was almost more frightening than oblivion of the more immediate war. The current civilian prescriptions for the cure of the ills of the day seemed to me just bigger and more concentrated injections of the medicine, the post-Renaissance complex of rationalism and its thalidomide-behaviouristic offspring, that had failed and maimed the Western spirit before, if not actually causing the sicknesses and deformations they had pretended to cure and remove.

I did all I could, as I had done in prison, to correct what seemed to me inadequate and inaccurate in my own way of life and turned to what was nearest to my hand and spirit by setting out, as I had done first as a boy of sixteen, to try to do something to prevent the kind of cataclysmic tragedy which had overwhelmed the Dutch in South-East Asia from overwhelming life in my native continent of Africa. But even in the midst of trying I was aware of the fact that somehow there was lacking the language necessary to unify the Babel of intellectual tongues raised in high-pitched argument over the central issue involved. I was aware that some new language of the spirit, some truly contemporary way of both looking at the reality of an increasingly desperate day and the need for expressing it in terms that the current self-indulgent assortments of spirit could under-stand, was essential if the screaming argumentative horde heading for another disaster were to be silenced and equipped to listen with ears that could hear.

I remember saying to the friend most closely connected with me in the struggle to avoid precisely those disasters which have now overwhelmed the African scene that it would be a grave error if we assumed for one moment that we would be successful in what we were trying to do, and that at the very most we should rejoice if we helped to push events somewhat towards a new and less destructive direction.

I remember a despairing white father in the Belgian Congo saying to me just before the debacle when I was bound on some such mission, "There is another great age of darkness closing in on the life of man and all that we can do is to create little fortresses wherein the authentic light of the spirit can be kept burning so that one day, when men wish to reach out for light again, they will have places in which to find it. But for the rest, we must just accept the inevitability of disaster."

"You may well be right, and disaster may well come," I had told him. "But for me it will always be a point of honour to go on working to prevent disaster, if only to make certain it is the right kind of disaster life needs when it does ultimately come."

Not only did I and what I felt I stood for appear increasingly isolated and I myself alone. I thought I had never known a world so full of isolated and lonely people. This gave me comfort of a sort because I suddenly began to discover that a great deal of this loneliness had its origin in the same area of the spirit as mine. I began to meet people in remote parts of the world and even more, to receive letters from people I had never met, that made me see these lonely spirits as already members in being of a new community which as yet had no institutions to express it. This gave me a new certainty of promise, as it were, that out of the deeps of the disintegrating pattern of my time, a greater community was in preparation and could not be prevented from coming.

Yet for all this so-called companionship, past and present, I was not relieved of the feeling of being more alone in an essential part of myself than I had ever been before. This added to an alarm already great enough, caused by the numbers of people I met who seemed to me not just spiritually but physically sick with an illness which was not their own so much as a sickness of the time in which we all lived. It was as if some new form of Black Death were raging in the spirit of man. But what caused so great and widespread a sickness? And how, when, and where were we ever to be cured of it?

I had never been so without answers, and that set the seal on the loneliness and isolation of which I have spoken. There is no loneliness so great as that which the individual experiences in the face of what is unanswerable, not so much in terms of his mind as in those of the feelings that life immemorial has given him for dealing with all the problems of a questing self confronted with the mystery of the great unknown out in the darkness beyond the farthest horizon of the known. And where had these feelings gone?

It seemed to me as I travelled my well-worn beat up and down

Africa and between Africa, England, and Europe that after many years of arduous traffic I had not really moved far from the moment by lamplight when my grandfather read to me out of the leather-bound family Bible how Joseph had dreamt a dream, told his brethren, and they hated yet the more. What had happened to that great dreaming process I discovered then in me and others? What of the ladder, phosphorescent between a star-packed heaven and stony waste-land earth, charged with angelic messengers ascending and descending it?

When I looked around me it was not only as if the dream had vanished in the debris of war and disaster behind me, and the ladder between men and their greatest value removed, but that they had lost their capacity to dream. If I went by what men in command of the social, intellectual, scientific, and artistic scene said, that wide prophetic soul of the world of which Shakespeare had spoken in one of his greatest sonnets seemed utterly deprived of its dreaming on things to come and civilisation no longer in possession of any great dream to serve. And yet deep within myself the process went on and I knew that I was doing the little I did on account of a kind of dreaming that clothed the memory of my beginnings as with a Joseph's coat of many colours and went on and on providing the flicker of such little light as I walked by tentatively in the dark hour around me. I knew that somehow the world had to be set dreaming again, but what a laugh that raised for being the whimsy and Barryesque sentimentality it was generally taken to be if I ever dared mention the fact to even the most perceptive of my contemporaries.

≈ The Man and the Place

And the slumber of the body
seems to be but the waking of the soul.

Sir Thomas Browne

IT WAS WHEN this feeling was at its height that I came back from a journey to the interior of Africa to find my wife studying at the newly formed C. G. Jung Institute in Zürich, working in particular with Toni Wolff, without whom the great confrontation of Jung with his own unconscious could perhaps not have been carried to so great and creative a conclusion, and Dr. C. A. Meier, who had become Jung's principal male collaborator and to this day holds Jung's former professorship at the Federal Polytechnic Institute in Zürich. Technically I was still in the British Army, a soldier due for reposting and raw with experiences of life and death, unshared and perhaps unsharable with men who had not known them. I could not have been, in one sense, therefore, less prepared for the Zürich of Jung and his fellow workers than I was then, despite the fact that I had never forgotten how just before the outbreak of war, just one remark of his had injected light into a dark, enigmatic moment of time.

However much I felt a fish out of water, I could not refuse to accompany my wife to a celebration over which Jung was presiding.

Somehow Aniela Jaffé, who had been a patient of Jung's and was later to become his secretary and biographer, out of a conviction that the two of us should meet, contrived the seating so that I was on Jung's left at the head of the principal table.

It was an early winter afternoon. The party was in one of those old guild houses founded in Zürich in the fifteenth century. Through the windows, with their stained heraldic designs, I could see the troubled waters of the historic Limmat, with white *Lohengrin* swans blown sideways like down of kapok by a keen, precise wind of early autumn bringing up snow from the Bernese *Oberland* beyond. Grey-green church spires, their bells tolling like medieval peals to summon the knights to congregate in the face of a grave new peril to their city, and the stone attics of tall buildings, aloof as if their heads were still in another day, lined the ancient quay like guards drawn to attention. Just across the disturbed water and white ruffled swans, I could see the walls, grey with history, of the house in which Paracelsus, one of the first frontiersmen of this no-man's-land between land and "inscape" which I have mentioned, once lived, and a sense of the great European past came like an *éminence grise* of the occasion into my reckoning.

The timbered hall had far too many people in it talking far too loudly for my liking, but seemed, as a result of these and other similar associations too many to be mentioned, the right kind of place for a meeting with someone who had so much to do with this other sort of history that burdened my imagination as Jung. He was already deep in conversation with a distinguished professor when I was shown to my place at his side.

They were, I remember distinctly, talking about primitive ways of making fire, and I thought how strange that one should begin such a meeting at a real beginning, not an arbitrary point of departure but the position for a natural leap forward into what came first perhaps in human awareness. Fire, after all, was the great cross-road in the human journey behind us. It was the event that not only set men apart from the animals and the natural world to which he had without self-doubt or feeling of guilt belonged but also removed him one degree further from blind obedience to the gods who previously had had him in their absolute power. It had always been for me the great image of the spirit made conscious of itself and I sat back without a word, eager to hear what they had to say about it.

Jung was not speaking at the moment but listening with great attention. That was for me one of his most moving characteristics. He himself night and day was full and overflowing with ideas. He had only to begin speaking for one to realise that his was a mind perpetually at flood and one would wonder always how he had the power to keep so great a deluge back and spare any part of himself for the ideas of others. Yet he managed to be one of the best, most patient, and understanding of listeners. Listening myself, I had time to observe him because both he and the professor were too engrossed to do more than acknowledge my presence with punctilious politeness.

He was a big man, bigger than his photographs had led me to expect. Physically he seemed to match the scale of his spirit, and to give out an air of such great well-being that one could not help accepting instantly that a body could only be so full of life because the spirit matched it within. From that moment on until his death I thought of him as by far the best physical advertisement possible for his own psychology and attitude to life. His eyes, I was interested to see, were also larger than they appeared in photographs, and exceedingly alert, quick, shrewd, utterly without solemnity, full of spirit and bright, and somewhat puckish with humour and fun. A fanlike pattern of the finest creases at the corners of his eyes clearly came not from exposure to the sun but to the strong light of a continuous and continuing exercise of instant laughter.

He did not look like a doctor, professor, anything at all esoteric, nor for that matter did he strike me as particularly Swiss. His dress was far too casual, almost to the degree affected by undergraduates and dons in love with spirited understatement at Oxford before the war. Indeed, there was something oddly English about his appearance. He wore a brown Harris-tweed sports coat, the sort of lightly chequered sports shirt beloved by English naval officers in mufti, woollen Paisley tie, cardigan, grey flannel bags, and brown shoes. He had a pipe in his hand at which he had long since forgotten to puff.

When he did finally speak, he spoke in English with obvious relish, which suggested somewhere a profound love of the English-ness of the English as opposed to the British in them. This love, I was to discover, went very deep in him, and my memory of my experience of it to this day makes it impossible for me to think of him as the unmitigated Swiss phenomenon he is held to be. This, even then, was so clear an intimation and constitutes so important a nuance in the character of the man, particularly for those of us who belong to the English-speaking world, demonstrating as it does part of the proof of the universality of his being as well as of his work, that however anachronistic an interruption of the moment of our meeting might appear to be, its orchestration belongs in spirit to that time and place which gave it birth. For I was not alone in this reaction to the man. I was to discover, for instance, how someone so utterly English as Hugh Walpole, the novelist, shared my impression and had tried to define it in the terms natural and most evocative to persons of his generation.

"He looked like some genial English cricketer," he said, describing Jung at their first meeting. I have no doubt that although left unsaid, this comparison was supported in Walpole's imagination by all the positive associations with cricket which dominated the popular vocabulary of his day. These included so wide a selection of the literary élite that English poets wrote poems about cricket and one constantly heard phrases borrowed from it—the definition of an upright, honest, and fearless man as a person who "wielded a straight bat," for example, or the application of that most dismissive of all English phrases for condemning what was unfair and underhand in life, "not cricket," or worse, "not playing the game."

I only regret that Jung himself may never have known Walpole's comparison because although he and I had discussed the novelist and his work in detail he never referred to it. Had he known it I am certain he would have been highly amused if not gratified by it. For contrary to the fashion of my own day, in which games and what they represented set most great intellects in a rage and almost every artist and writer I knew boasted how he had loathed games at school and declared roundly what a barbarous practice he thought them still to be, Jung regarded them as of the utmost importance to the sanity and well-being of men and their societies.

"Civilisations at their most complete moments," he once told me, "always brought out in man his instinct to play and made it more inventive." He would point out how in the Greece he loved, games had a religious origin and were held to be sacred ritualistic performances. In fact, he was even to give me a long exegesis on the origin and meaning of tennis and how the modern game, derived from Real Tennis, began in the quadrangles of medieval monasteries as religious exercises. If one looked closely at Real Tennis even today, one would see within it the impact of its original monastic design.

"One of the most striking testimonies to the quality of the English spirit," he told me once, "is the English love of sport and games in a classical sense and their genius for inventing games. One of the most difficult tasks men can perform, however much others may despise it, is the invention of good games and it cannot be done by men out of touch with their instinctive selves. The English did it and, by heaven, they even taught us Swiss how to climb our own mountains and make a sport of it that made us love them all the more. And their Wimbledon, did they but know it, is in sort a modern version of an ancient ritual."

Not only was the instinct clear in him also to play in his own way; he could when relaxed indulge in an almost schoolboy playfulness and at times harmless sense of childlike mischief. But at this particular moment I did not need the support of Walpole or anyone else to search for my own English equivalent of the man.

My own impressions of him were flitting like a butterfly between two flower-beds, not knowing on which of them to settle—one as some sort of Fellow of All Souls, and the other an English squire, dressed with a nonchalance which was natural as it was also a product of an imaginative concern that the tenants gathered for his harvest festival should feel utterly at their ease. I was ultimately to settle for the image of the squire, not in the contemporary sense which has made it almost a pejorative but in the heraldic concept of the term.

So there was, I believe, a very dear and special part of him that was also a kind of England. He had even, I was to discover, long ago got friends to teach him to sail in the English Channel and he became a dedicated wind-and-canvas man. Even his way of speaking English, apart from a slight Swiss accent, had an unusually light, easy, casual, familiar, almost schoolboy flavour to it.

"It is hellishly difficult," he was saying in a deep, animated voice to the professor, a smile forming on his face, "to know what you are trying to get at in all this unless you can tell me what fire means not to primitive people but to you yourself. It is its meaning for you, not to others, that matters."

The professor seemed taken aback at what appeared to him a

question too obvious for answer and said, I thought rather perfunctorily, as if assuming that fire could only mean one thing to all men, "Why, it means energy, of course."

For a moment I regretted I had come, so blank and aridly intellectual did the answer sound. I thought, dismayed, "Dear God, how unnatural and unreal these bloody European intellectuals have become. It's worse than before the war. You wouldn't think to hear him that fire was a divine gift stolen from the gods, that Prometheus suffered the cruelest of punishments, and that what he and fire stand for in all of us still suffers because of that precious theft. Besides, it is light in darkness, safety against the beasts and animals that prowled and threatened life in some long-forgotten prehistoric night; it is warmth against cold; it is what brought us from an age of ice, gripping the earth from pole to pole, to this privileged moment in time, cooking the food we are to eat, warming this room against the winter which that cold wind outside is bringing up so fast. It is all these and many more things before it becomes an abstract of energy in the mind of a professor, however eminent."

All this flashed through me not as words but as one searing feeling, and I heard the voice of Jung with great good humour teasing the professor in similar though far better and more gracious terms than I had used to myself. Indeed, the professor looked so abashed that instinctively I tried to change the subject by saying that I had listened with immense interest to their discussion of the various primitive ways of making fire, but that there was one way which I had encountered which they had not yet mentioned, and I wondered whether they knew of it.

For the first time Jung turned to give me more than a polite look. I was amazed to notice how his face possessed what I think is permitted to the faces only of those who are naturally and permanently filled with wonder and reverence for all the multitudinous detail of life, however drab, for whom there is no frontier between what is ordinary and extraordinary, great and small, but where all are equally charged with their ration of universal wonder. His face just then, and he was in his early seventies, looked truly young and innocent, as if he were still some kind of child in a nursery of time and had just been offered some new brick necessary to carry out his first essays at building.

I told them quickly then how during the war in a jungle of

South-East Asia I had encountered a small yellow aboriginal people who lived forever in a world of green leaves, sodden moss, dripping tree-ferns, and perpetual rain, where making fire by friction in the classical primitive manner could not possibly work. They had accordingly developed a method of making fire I had seen nowhere else. Each of these little men carried, suspended from a leather thong tied round his naked waist, a longish square block of wood. This block was divided into two sections. It had a solid hardwood lid, out of the centre of which protruded a long, tapering rod of wood with a deep niche carved into its end. This rod fitted tightly into a narrow, tapering cylinder bored into the main block of wood. When a little man wanted to make a fire, all he did was to undo his leather thong, extract the rod from its cylinder, take some very fine dry moss from a leather satchel he carried over his shoulder, insert the moss into the niche at the bottom of the rod, fit the rod into the opening of the cylinder, and then with his hand slam the rod hard and fast, as deep as it could go into the cylinder. That done, he would quickly pull the rod out and one would see that the moss was on fire. And, I added, before either of my listeners could comment, that the first time I saw fire made in this way, a very senior RAF engineer officer on my staff was standing beside me. As he saw the glowing moss extracted from the cylinder, he turned to me a face comic with amazement and exclaimed, "Good God, Colonel! The diesel engine!"

I was about to add that this, of course, was precisely the principle on which the diesel engine worked and that here, unbeknown, in one of the greatest jungles of the world, primitive human beings who had never had any contact with our own civilisation, which we thought so superior, had for centuries been applying a principle of ignition which we had only recently discovered and whose application to the diesel engine we regarded as one of the brightest of our inventions. But of course Jung had already grasped this point and for the first time I heard him laugh.

That laugh of his was one of the more memorable events of that afternoon, as far as I was concerned. It was both Olympian and intensely human at the same time. It came out of that big man sheer and immediate, with no inhibition at all between the impulse to laugh and the laughter itself. I had only heard such laughter before among the Bushmen, the first people of my native country, whose brightest possession it is and whose capacity for laughter had impressed and moved me so much in the past that I had felt that if I myself could acquire the gift of such laughter for the proceeds of the sale of everything I possessed, I would not hesitate.

"How can you do it?" I was to say to him often. "You are the only person I've met who can laugh like a Bushman." And he just laughed all the more.

Later, when I met Olga Fröbe-Kapteyn, the remarkable Dutch-woman who organised the Eranos meetings, where Jung delivered some of his most momentous lectures at her home at the Casa Gabriella on the shores of Lake Maggiore, she told me more about Jung's laugh. She said that in between lectures, Jung and other distinguished speakers who came there to talk on a common theme would sit in the open at a great round table under the trees in the garden of her house and there, from time to time, this laughter would break out from Jung. On one occasion, she told me, a tourist travelling on the main road between Italy and Switzerland, which passed hard by her house and only a little above the garden, came down the stone steps with a look of amazement on his face and said, "Signora, please forgive my intrusion, but we could not go on without asking who it was that laughed just now in so wonderful a way, and whether we could not just for a moment be allowed to set eyes on him."

Later, when I had to speak about Jung at a memorial service held in New York after his death, I begged everyone there who was thinking sadly of more tangible and possibly greater things that had vanished forever with Jung not to forget the laughter, because it was a laughter possible only to those blessed with some of the insight of the gods themselves and their feeling at some new indication of their laws.

If I had still any doubts about the quality and calibre of Jung, his laugh on that sombre and sombring autumn afternoon settled it, all the more because it affirmed that the continuity had not been broken between it and the first laugh of an authentic child of life, laughing because the policeman who for him represented the desert in the human spirit which the grown-up world creates and calls law and order, had been brought low in the common dust by a mere banana peel.

He could laugh as he laughed then because in this story of fire I had just told them the despised primitive, the rejected child of civilisation, had tumbled the police imperialism of knowledge and values European culture imposed on others to a far greater extent than even its territorial and political dominion, and restored it to its place in the heat and dust where no flesh and blood has pride of place, where men are compelled to accept their common fallible and groping humanity equally and are forced to struggle humbly for such meaning and fire as their brief and impartial ration of time permits.

There are many ways of laughing, but the greatest is that which comes from the joy of seeing disproportion restored to proportion. Few men, I was to find, had so great a reverence as Jung for the forms of life and mind which the established and powerful world despises and rejects. Were I compelled to select one great text for introducing the main theme of Jung's life and career in his own spirit and for those of others, it would have to be a text taken from the Book of Common Prayer: "The same stone which the builders refused: is become the head-stone in the corner."

And all this came out of a profound love of the ancient proportions implicit in the original blueprint of life. His laughter was delight, sheer and uncompromising, in the triumph of the significance in the small over the unreality of excess and disproportion in the established great and so a pure rejoicing in another enlargement, however minute, of the dominion of proportion. I never knew him to laugh at anyone or anything so much as with them and with life. It was inevitable that from then on he made me laugh, not only by the infection of his own example but because of his wit, sense of fun, and spirit, more than anyone I have ever known.

The detail of the conversation that followed does not matter. It centred on the determination of the professor to maintain that such a method of fire could not have been possible unless somewhere, sometime, my jungle people had had contact with a superior civilisation. Jung winced at the word "superior" but held his peace. It was obviously for him one of those classically futile exercises of attempting to explain a unique phenomenon of life, and indeed life itself, purely in terms of cause and effect. Jung clearly had little interest in promoting it and, when he decently could, decided to leave the party.

He bent down, picked up a knobby walking-stick of rough wood which had been lying beside his chair and which added more than ever to the impression of the country squire in his appearance. For a moment he stood impressive and tall against the slanted light streaming in through the windows, where the heraldry of the guilds of Zürich had now been blazoned with a pattern of the abiding heraldic sun going down between burning rags and tatters of wind-torn cloud.

A feeling of disappointment assailed me. I was full of things I would have liked to ask him and full of resentment at this part of myself which had prevented me from meeting him many years before, as I could so easily have done. But this, I thought, would be the end; soon I would be launched on another round of exploring Africa for, at the best, partially comprehensible ends.

Then, unexpectedly, he asked me to go home with him, and not long afterwards we were sitting in his library, where we talked for five hours.

We talked, to my surprise, a great deal about Africa. There is a kind of conversation I have hardly ever experienced except in Africa, when one is alone in the bush or desert with the minimum of civilised contrivances to diminish the impact on one of that great swollen sea of land, its skies, winds, and clouds, and abundance of vivid and infinitely diversified natural life. Its subjects come up fast in one's senses like a dawn of thunder when over and above the voices of one's African companions, as a rule pitched singularly low out of the instinctive reverence induced by that natural surround standing like a vast cathedral over them, one overhears one's first intimate conversation of nature—the voice of the lion, the passionately intense cough of a leopard, the sound like pistol shot of an elephant tearing a strip of his favourite relish of bark from a tree, the night-plover's sea-pipe call, the bush-buck barking to keep its courage up, a baboon whimpering in some unfathomable nightmare of the tangled bush, the croaking of frogs by some precious star-filled water and the sustained Gregorian chanting of the cricket priests of the night, and overall the smell of the incense of the devout earth evoked by the first fall of dew. It is a kind of conversation one certainly never hears in Europe. However interesting and exciting the theme, the voices themselves remain unraised to the end.

And yet on this occasion, although I was sitting in comfort in a historic city, in a library full of books not there just for show but with the almost threadbare shine on their covers which is the consequence only of long hard use over many years, and although it had gone black outside and a hungry European night was pressing against the window like the muzzle of a great bear on the prowl, I had a most extraordinary feeling that he and I were only technically there, and in reality were back in Africa in the way I have just described. It all reached such an intensity that again I had another enigmatic variation of the feeling at the party, a feeling that I was actually warming myself by one of the first fires with one of the first people to promote its discovery.

Part of all this, I am sure, came from his own attitude to fire. He never took it for granted; it always seemed to remain something of a miracle for him, and always sacred. He had a way all his own of laying and lighting fire, except in so far as his way had a touch of the primitive people I had seen making it with great precarious difficulty, preparing it with infinite solicitude as if it were a matter of life and death that, once made, it should not die.

He did it instinctively, as if performing a religious rite, and as the Hindu flame leapt up the light on his face would show an expression devout as of that of an archaic priest.

The impact of the coincidence that we were there continuing a conversation begun at such a beginning and in such an atmosphere of first things first was too striking to be ignored, particularly when it was reinforced by another. Until that moment I had not known of his love for Africa. I had not known that he had gone on a long, far safari through it and had even lived among the ancient Elgonyi of Mount Elgon in East Africa in late 1925 and early 1926. This last was the year in which I myself first left my native country and had also gone to that very same East Africa.

Coincidences have never been idle for me, instinctively, but as meaningful as I was to find they were to Jung. I have always had a hunch that they are a manifestation of a law of life of which we are inadequately aware and which in terms of our short life are unfortunately incapable of total definition, and yet however partial the meaning we can extract from them, we ignore it, I believe, at our peril. For as well as promoting some cosmic law, coincidences, I suspect, are some sort of indication to what extent the evolution of our lives is obedient or not obedient to the symmetry of the universe.

Coincidence is nothing if not an expression of a symmetry of meaning, and that symmetry of meaning, I felt that night, had demanded not only that we should have been to the heart of Africa I loved at a similar moment in time but also that fire should have been my first introduction to the world of his mind and his nature.

Also, my experience of Africa and above all what it evokes in human imagination have been the source of almost all that has concerned my imagination. I have walked through vast areas, from the Cape of Good Hope to the baroque mountains and deeply wooded valleys of Ethiopia, and travelled in other ways through yet more of it. I thought that if I came near to knowing and understanding anything, it was Africa and its peoples. Yet I was finding as we talked that Jung, although he had not walked literally so far and wide as I had done, understood African aboriginal patterns of life even better than I and, if anything, revered them more. The whole tone of his speech became warmer and more animated and his turn of expression more poetic and almost lyrical when he spoke about it. He had always, as I came to call it, a special "African" voice.

Although there were moments when I felt a little abashed that a Swiss, however eminent, should know my native continent quintessentially better than I did, any possibility of resentment was cancelled by the confirmation and support he gave to my own intuitions and feelings about it and their wider significance for the life of our time. It would warm me like wine to hear him too imply that the balance between the primitive and the civilised, the Jacob and Esau of which I have spoken, had never been honourably struck, and that a great deal of the troubles of modern man came from the fact that he himself had a deep, warm, caring, trusting, instinctive, primitive self from which he had not only allowed himself to be divorced but had gone on to despise and repress with a deadly ruthlessness.

Africa, it became clear, meant so much to him not only because of itself. He called it, always with a note of awe in his voice, "truly God's country." From his lips the term ceased to be a cliché stuck to some technicolour concept of nature out in the blue but recovered all the power of a great and aboriginal observation delivered for the first time. He loved Africa, among other things, also because it had finally settled whatever doubts he might have had of the validity and universality of an area of the human spirit shared by all men, no matter how different their cultures, their creeds, and their races and colours, an area for which he had coined the term "collective unconscious" but of which I was yet unaware. It was almost as if the basic imagery of that untravelled region itself had been made visible for him by Africa in all its abundance and extravagance of vegetable and mineral being and flamelike animal and human flesh and blood.

But there was for the man himself something more specific and significant to it than even as much as all that. Africa in a profound sense had been the most subjective of all his journeys in the physical world. All the others had an overriding objective concern. He travelled, as it were, well protected in the coat of armour of the purpose of his main work, so much so that I am struck how in comparison with his other journeys, India had no great impact on him and gave him perhaps least of all. It seems in retrospect to have been almost irrelevant and a redundant exercise in what had already been foresuffered, foreseen, and established. But Africa penetrated to a deeper subjective level of the man where only a complete submission to the experience for its own sake enables a person to achieve a relative objectivity. The journey itself, he told me, was the most impulsive he ever undertook and came out of a sense of having been challenged to a personal confrontation with the reality of primitive Africa.

So deep did this anticipation go of having to meet this other Africa face to face, as it were, that thorough as he was in everything he did, he prepared himself with greater thoroughness than ever before. In the voyage out, for instance, he spent most of his time learning Swahili, so that when he landed at Mombasa, he told me, he surprised the black porters and stewards by addressing them in this ancient Esperanto of East Africa. His instinct about his own inner motivation for the journey was confirmed immediately because the next morning, when he woke up in his train in the interior of Africa and through the red dust of a scarlet dawn had his first glimpse of the land, a lone Masai warrior leaning on his spear, a great Euphorbia candelabrum lit like a Byzantine cathedral light by the fire of a new day, and a prodigious, volcanic surge of animal life soaring over the long yellow grass, he had the most extraordinary feeling of a remarkable certainty that he had seen it all before, so certain that he gave a cycle of time to it out of conviction that it had been some six thousand years before.

He always claimed with justice that outer events and their

physical detail of matter and men were relatively unimportant to him—hence the lack of physical and human detail in his *Memories*—but in Africa the "without" and the "within" were so interdependent that he spoke of it and remembered it all to the end of his days with astonishing detail. Perhaps the most convincing single testimony of his identification with Africa came towards the end of his stay on the frontier of Uganda and the Sudan. There one night he became so excited by a dance of African warriors, organised by a local young chief he liked, that he could not resist jumping up and joining in the dance. It was, I gathered, some sort of a war dance and, swinging his rhinocerous whip over his head as the nearest thing to a weapon he possessed, he leapt and stamped around with a horde of men whirling spears, swords, and clubs in ascending rhythm of some archaic possession of their spirit.

At this high point of the dance there emerged an aspect of himself of which he had not been aware before. Despite his involvement in the accelerating pattern of the frenzied dance, he felt the danger inherent in it and saw himself in a position of special responsibility towards it. Over the chief's protests, he immediately called off the dance and tried to disperse the roused warriors with gifts of tobacco, and when that failed, leapt at them again, swinging his whip with a laugh that concealed an urgent truth in the jest it pretended to be. His eyes would brighten and he would wave his arm again up and in front of him, simulating the long-vanished action, as he spoke of the tensions of the moment, then relaxed with a gesture that affected one strongly when he went on to say that to his relief the crowd dispersed.

It was the turning point in his relation with Africa. Soon after that he had a dream which is recorded in detail in his *Memories* and which warned him in unmistakable imagery how close he had come to "going native," how Africa in a sense had been the primordial matter not just, as I have already suggested, of man in general but specifically of his own untravelled self, with which he had to deal within himself and not by a proxy of a life on a dark and alien continent.

I told him that night of a book I had just written about Africa, which had as its text a quotation from the Elizabethan Sir Thomas Browne: "We carry with us the wonders we seek without us: there is all Africa and her prodigies in us." He was deeply moved, wrote it down, and exclaimed, "That was and is just it! But it needed the Africa without to drive home the point in my own self."

Africa had thus given him final confirmation of the universality of his theory of the collective unconscious in man. Three other personal values, self-mined and deeply extracted from Africa, came first with me that night. One was how he stressed that his and everyone's first duty was to his own culture, place, and moment in time, and the material on which he had to work always what was nearest and came most naturally to hand. The second was that it confirmed his suspicions of the motive behind the growing habit of the European to travel the physical world as communications became easier and faster. There was for him an element of profound evasion involved in all this and without denying the validity of travel for specific ends, travel always for sheer travel's sake was another matter. He saw it more and more as a substitute, *Ersatz* journey for a far more difficult and urgent journey modern man was called upon to undertake into the unknown universe of himself.

Finally, as far as Africa itself was concerned, his own experience had shown him how the Dark Continent and its aboriginal peoples attracted Europeans because it provoked through its own physical character and example what was forgotten and first and primitive in themselves. He generalised at length from his own experience in this regard that night, impressing on me how it inevitably provoked in the white man a great temptation to revert to an utterly uncontemporary version of himself, all the more powerful and difficult to resist because in most cases it was unconscious. As a result the resistance of the white man in Africa to "go black," or "native," as he put it, produced so powerful an undertone in his spirit that it brought tensions which were almost unendurable and caused him either to succumb utterly and become a pale, effete version of the primitive or to reject and hate the dark man who had served to evoke it. The farther from his own instinctive self, the greater the temptation and the greater the fall, or the more intense the rejection in the European we call prejudice and hatred.

The task of modern man was not to go primitive the African way but to discover and confront and live out his own first and primitive self in a truly twentieth-century way. Not the least of Africa's services to him personally was that it had confirmed and emphasised the reality of his own primitive nature which had already caused that conflict in him in his student days to which he referred as a clash between his "country or natural mind" and the "town mind" he encountered among professors and fellow students in the nineties at the University of Basel. This experience seemed to me to have blown into full flame the fire of the love necessary for transcending two extremes that had long burned in him, not vicariously through an Africa but at home in his own context and directly with whatever turned up on his own doorstep.

It happened to be a moment also when Schweitzer and his work in Africa were beginning to attract worldwide attention and approbation and his name inevitably cropped up in our talk that night. I noticed first that concern of Jung's never to denigrate any areas of thought or ways of life that gave meaning to the lives of others, for he was not once reductive about the achievement of a Schweitzer he had briefly known—an example which might well be followed by the rest of the world. Yet since Jung had profound reservations of his own on the subject, he felt compelled out of respect for his own truth to allow himself the general comment that there was an element of some evasion of an urgent personal task in Schweitzer's choice to live out his life in Africa.

He had to say this also out of a clear conviction that Europe and European man had no longer moral energies to spare for others. They needed all they had of these for themselves. According to Europe's success in dealing with its own divided self, its resources of moral and other energy no doubt would increase out of the living example it set, enabling it to reacquire a real capacity for service also to others. But for the moment the precept that charity, in its Greek sense of being an expression of a truly objective love, began at home was never more relevant and urgent for the West. Only an example lived truly and fully out in the life of our time could help and save. Preaching and continuation of efforts to convert others in our own confused image would only imperil both ourselves and those we presumed to serve.

Nonetheless, the regret and a clear love and gratitude and a living nostalgia for Africa were always humanly there. Writing to me once about a book of mine which had brought back to him, he said, the sights, sounds, and smells of unforgettable days and nights spent in the bush, he declared that he would never cease to thank whatever gods had woven the pattern of his fate that they had also included Africa and all its wonder within it.

He longed to go back and had his heart been less responsible may even have done so, but he felt he had little enough time for the work he wanted to do to go back over a page already turned. Once, when I thought I had almost persuaded him to come back with me, he said with the only laugh that ever sounded sharp and sided, "You see, after hobnobbing for months with witch-doctors and delving into their witchcraft, I was amazed on my return to Zürich how many witch-doctors and how much witchcraft there was in it and the Swiss mountains and beyond; and until I have learned all I can about them too I do not feel I have the right to go back."

Always he could be both amused and oddly gratified that yet another neighbour or critic had referred to him as "that old witch-doctor," or tried to dismiss him as "that old male witch by the lake." And always too from that moment on I never went to Africa, as I was doing just then three or four times a year, without calling on him first at Zürich and on my return dropping in on him again, hoping that thereby I was keeping something of his concern and wisdom in the mind of my kind of Africa and something of Africa's being in his. By some curious process of synchronicity, these visits of mine invariably coincided with an aspect of the work he happened to be doing and added some nuance rather than substance to a particular point he had reached in his own quest. He often referred to me laughingly as a sort of messenger boy between him and Africa.

What was of overwhelming consequence to me was that as we sat there talking, something was communicated to me more out of what Jung was in himself than out of his ideas, and in the process this feeling of isolation and loneliness in a vital area of myself which had haunted me all those years vanished. I was no longer alone; I had company and company of a noble order. I was having my first elementary lesson that men, women, ideas, and the causes which are singularly our own are often those we reject, even to the point of a kind of mental persecution as ruthless as that of Paul's persecution of the very Christians for whom he was to become the greatest and most poetic of voices.

It is as if there were something in all of us that demands a journey to a Damascus of our own before we can discover in a single, blinding, forever decisive flash the light that we are in the innermost nature of ourselves contracted to seek, so that this is perhaps one of the first things to say about the Jung whom I myself had for years rejected.

He was a born, great, and inspired neighbour. He had a genius for propinquity. He was a neighbour to all sorts and conditions of men and women, from the most despised and rejected forms of life, ideas, and attitudes to those overcome with a kind of nausea and vertigo of the wordy heights they have achieved. He is a neighbour to millions that are yet to be born. His gift for propinquity brought him near to all the most hopeless forms of being locked out from the norms of life and concern of his day, no matter whether it was a deeply disturbed spirit shut away in some asylum, some cast-off and mentally deranged woman, or some despised and oppressed and, by all civilised standards, ignorant primitive, a humble Negro barber in Chattanooga, the chief of an almost vanished American Indian entity, or a Swiss lakeside wine-merchant. They understood and felt near to him when the great minds of his own day without having read him dismissed him, as I had done, as a woolly and treacherous mystic.

I find that just as he gave me the feeling that there could be a valid meaning to this loneliness about Africa and this other dreaming area of myself which I had carried about with me for forty years—that my life, however apparently single, was in procession—he performed precisely the same service for countless others.

For example, he did it for the distinguished scholar Richard Wilhelm, the translator of the work we call *The Secret of the Golden Flower* and the *I Ching*, or Book of Changes, which is one of the oldest books in existence today. Wilhelm carried about with him a loneliness of an experience of China and its ancient culture which he neither could share with others nor knew how to integrate with his European self. He had a concern and understanding of the first experience of an immense proportion of the human race which not only made no sense to the Germany and the Europe of his birth but was rejected by them as incomprehensible Orientalism and occultism.

As a result, deep as it patently was, the loneliness vanished when he met Jung. He found that his experience could immediately be decoded and rendered into an idiom which made sense to Europe and became, as introduced by Jung, a source of enrichment of its own culture to such an extent that the *I Ching* alone, which some fifteen years ago was known only to a few, today sells annually by the tens of thousands.

I mention Wilhelm first as another example of how great a spiritual neighbour Jung was because when Jung heard that first night of our long meeting how I had gone to the Far East as a boy and what a great impact it had on me, he asked me instantly if I knew of Wilhelm and his work. Alas, or perhaps fortunately, I did not know, because Jung proceeded to give me in words that came out fountain-wise the best possible introduction and preparation I could have had to a Wilhelm I had never met. I realised how Wilhelm had opened up a great new world to him, even as Columbus did for his own restricted day, the ancient civilisation of a China already a thousand years or more before Christ, already at home in a dimension wherein Jung himself was a lonely, exposed pioneer and on which the culture of the West had turned its back for so long, to its impoverishment and peril. It did not matter to me that the excitement caused by this re-entry from the outer space of European abstractions into this organic world of China led Jung to generalise somewhat naïvely about the East and West as two definite and clearly defined opposites of spirit and culture. I knew that though one could at a pinch regard Western cultural projections abroad in the Americas, the British Commonwealth, and Europe as one and the same complex of spirit, however splintered politically— a loose sort of union called the West—one certainly could not do that to the East.

China, however, was truly a new world, a unique and infinitely meaningful universe of its own, and when Jung spoke of the East, as he often did, the East he had mainly in his mind was that represented by China, into which he was conducted by this rare German scholar whose son has carried on the exacting work. He was himself so very much enriched by Wilhelm, he put it to me one day, that he felt as if he received more from him than from any other person he had ever known. And Wilhelm had so enriched the meaning of our time as to provide perhaps a kind of Archimedean support in the European spirit from which it could be levered out of the dead weight of itself.

I was moved by another special note, different from the African one, that came into his voice whenever he mentioned Wilhelm's name. It was a note of delicate, grateful, loving remembrance of someone and something that was incorruptibly precious to him and which never entered into the mention of any of the many other human names that also meant a great deal to him. I was not surprised to see later in his letters to Wilhelm how this feeling presided over them as a concern for the man's well-being, tender as that of a woman for an injured child, because he already feared that Wilhelm was dying, as surely as any soldier in battle in the war, for bringing greater meaning to the life of European man. For Jung's own primitive, intuitive self knew as clearly as any African witch-doctor in charge of the "soul" of his tribe how perilous if not mortal a task the absorption of a whole new culture could be to the men and people called upon to promote it. He knew that a culture so fundamentally alien to all Wilhelm's own European values could be interpreted not just by translating the words in which this ancient China fashioned it but only by becoming so organic a part of Wilhelm's own imagination that the whole flesh-and-blood idiom of himself would have to be translated as well, and the basic image of the man transformed into a reality for which he had no historical and cultural immunities. The experience, he feared, would be a kind of fire that could burn out all Wilhelm's energies: hence his ever increasing anxiety over the physical well-being of Wilhelm and his constant pleading to the man to take greater care also of his physical self. The immensity of Wilhelm's endeavour, its dangers, and Jung's fear of their consequences found verification, alas, in Wilhelm's untimely death.

I realised how a Jung, out of a profound loneliness of his own despite the close support of a unique circle of friends around him, could so recognise and understand the nature of the loneliness in Wilhelm and provide the companionship needed for completion of the tremendous task heaped on his sensitive and bowed-down spirit. I have yet to meet in history or my own life the person who has been able to find and evolve himself without an act of recognition of this kind from another he respects in the world without. Jung did it for me in a lesser way that night as he did for Wilhelm in a greatly more significant field. I can only say that I have never felt that particular form of loneliness since, because from then on I felt profoundly confirmed and accompanied within.

Then, when that storm-battered book of Jung's, *Answer to Job*, first appeared, he had a most moving and tender correspondence with a white nun in a convent in the Black Forest of Germany because she found that for the first time someone had enabled her to see meaning in the concept of the Trinity. Shut out for so long by her doubt of a vital concept of the faith to which she subscribed, she had suffered a form of loneliness of guilt that made her feel an almost unique untouchable in her community. But long before this correspondence was ended, she saw herself peopled again, part of a living human procession. She was, as the Kalahari Bushmen say, walking with the moon and stars again.

Again, a doctor with a practice in a remote mountain district of Switzerland asked Jung to see a simple girl of the hills who he thought was going insane. Jung saw her and realised at once that she had neither the intelligence nor the need for a sophisticated and intellectually demanding analytical treatment. He talked to her quietly in his study and came to the conclusion that all she suffered from was the fact that her community, in a sudden enthusiasm for what was thought to be modern and progressive, had poured scorn on all the simple beliefs, ideas, customs, and interests which were natural to her. Her own natural state, her first, as it were, primitive self, had lost such honour with herself and others that her heart wilted because of a lack of incentive in the kind of prospect life held out for her.

Accordingly, he got her to talk to him at length about all the things she had enjoyed and loved as a child. As she talked, almost at once he saw a flicker of interest glow in what had appeared to be burnt-out ashes of herself. He found himself so excited by this quickening of spirit of a despised self that he joined in the singing of her nursery songs and her renderings of simple mountain ballads. He even danced with her in his library and at times took her on his knee and rocked her in his arms, undeterred by any thought of how ridiculous if not preposterous would be the picture of him in the eyes of orthodox medical and psychiatric practitioners when told of what he described with a great laugh to me as "such goings on."

At the end of a few days the girl was fully restored to a state of honour with herself and he sent her off in high spirits to her home. She never again regressed. Indeed, the result appeared so miraculous that the learned doctor in the mountains wrote to Jung and asked him how it had been achieved. Jung wrote back to the effect that "I did nothing much. I listened to her fairy tales, danced with her a little, sang with her a little, took her on my knee a little, and the job was done."

But the doctor was never persuaded, Jung told me, that his leg was not being pulled, although the girl stayed what the world termed "cured."

I myself remember a beautiful, unusually sensitive girl not yet in her twenties whom Jung at the age of over seventy, at a time when he was trying hard to put analytical treatment well behind him, had reluctantly taken on as a patient. I still recall vividly the wonder in her voice when she talked of how in all the years she worked with Jung, he never once took her outside the range of what she could understand, how always he respected her own limitations and capacity for experience. Through his own respect for what she was she recentred herself and thereon followed, as a plant grown from a small seed, an enlargement of herself out of her own desire and volition.

Finally, I knew a remarkable woman who was so terrified of herself and of Jung, so ignorant of analytical psychology, although she was a person of great culture, that she went to see him three times a week for six months without being able to speak. Yet on each occasion he just talked to her about all the things he thought could matter to her as much as they mattered to him, and suddenly at the end of six months she found her own voice within her and spoke out more and more confidently. Soon her isolation from a vital part of herself, and therefore from others too, vanished, and she became what she is today, a person with a unique creative voice and meaning all her own.

This sort of approach to his practice was not without its embarrassments. Almost all his life he was confronted with misunderstandings as much among scientists and theologians as philosophers and psychologists who confused Jung's method in the practice of analytical psychology with its scientific aspects.

"I had to point over and over again to pompous asses," he told me once with a laugh, "that I obviously drew a firm line between psychology as a science and psychology as a technique. I shocked a great scientific Excellency once by telling him that when cases seemed to warrant it I had no compunction in speaking to them of spirits instead of complexes and archetypes, with the reservation, of course, that what appeared to them as spirits could merely be personifications of something unconscious in them and sooner or later, when truly made conscious, might vanish. I was compelled always in the beginning to respect my patients' own truth and idiom and never treated two patients exactly alike."

He used even the word "patient" with great reluctance because he felt that people in trouble with themselves gave him precious insights he could never have obtained any other way, and preferred to talk not of patients but of persons working with him. It was because of the artist in him and his dislike of inventing technical words with no historical association to give them life that he had no great liking for the American substitute, "analysand."

I could multiply these examples a hundredfold, each with a significant nuance of its own. I could elaborate how this gift of propinquity and respect of his for what I called the essential "otherness" of all persons and things enabled him to enter into the spirit of a form of life so remote from his own as the aboriginal life of Africa, to extract from its customs, its rites, its witchcraft, black magic, and all that was universally dismissed as sheer superstition, meanings which he told me were more valuable than any learned from his exalted professors at Basel. But the real point of the occasion for me was that it was a passport into a new world which suddenly made all the questions that had pursued me, apparently so irrelevantly, suddenly valid and at home in my spirit.

My interest, arrested through disillusionment in my first tentative reading of Freud many years before, began to flow and gather momentum again. The "inscape," "mythological dominants" and "underworlds of history," and impact of dreams on everyday life which had perturbed my imagination for so long could no more be dismissed with that "But it's only fantasy," which is the favourite missile of our reductive day, but were increasingly broadened by his empirical demonstration of their validity as facts of natural science.

Not psychiatry, not even his enlargement of the field of psychology, it struck me, were his major achievements. They were by-products of a discovery and evaluation of an as yet unmeasured potential that followed his breakthrough into this great new world within. It was as momentous as the breakthrough into the nature of the atom, and again the fact that both coincided in time suddenly seemed significant.

Indeed, it is almost as if the synchronicity of the two developments imply that they are concerned with two aspects of the same reality, or perhaps even that the atom, nuclear in its fission, could be regarded as a physical metaphor of the "inscape" of man nuclear in fission of a conscious and unconscious self. It seemed to me almost as if they were one and the same thing, relative to the position from which we view them, one seen utterly from within, the other made visible from without.

The relationships between spirit and matter, world within and world without, are transcendental and incapable of total expression in non-transcendental terms. These two great objectives to which we are subject play on us like some great symphony which we can describe not directly but only through its effect on us. We are condemned to know them in part and only through their consequences in us, even though they circumscribe us in full. Yet this much seemed certain to me: less and less can we maintain what men have tried to uphold with a fanaticism of a wilful rationalism which should have suggested grave inner doubts of itself from the beginning, that there is a cast-iron division between the two, and more and more do even the most rational of scientists incline to consider the possibilities of them being aspects of one and the same greater whole. For someone compelled to live by hunches, as we all do when in unknown territory, I never doubted that the physical world is spirit seen from without and the spirit is world viewed from within.

It does not surprise me that in the final analysis, at the point where our dreams vanish over the rim of our own round of sleep, we meet matter receding fast over the horizon of the most powerful electronic microscope, and in the process behaving less like solid, predictable, dependable, inanimate material but more and more as of the swift-changing texture of living thought. We pass from one to the other, as it were, like Alices in Wonderland through a looking glass, to find with both mind and matter within that the objective mystery which faces us macrocosmically in the night skies above confronts us microcosmically in reverse. There in the depths of our own mind, beyond those "cliffs of fall, frightful, sheer, no-man-fathomed," of which Hopkins spoke, symbols, images, patterns of meaning, all with immense energies at their disposal, are constelled and in orbit strangely akin to the minuscule solar systems, planets, Milky Ways, comets, nebulae, and black holes of anti-matter, dynamic in the heart of the physical atom. How could two such discoveries coming at the same desperate moment in time, therefore, not be another of those strange affirmations of the symmetry of meaning, intruding on our vision like those old signs at dangerous railway crossings in remote country exhorting us to "Stop, look, and listen"?

Happily, physicists like the great Swiss scientist and Nobel Prize winner Pauli did stop, look, and listen, but neither a physicist nor a psychologist myself, I cannot pursue parallels which in any case by definition cannot meet this side of infinity. I can only follow Jung on his dangerous and long journey of exploration into the world within and describe its fateful, still strangely misunderstood relationship and interdependence with consciousness as manifested in the course of my own life, the life of my time, and such history as I know.

And immediately one faces the common misconception and cause of one of the commonest errors in contemporary thinking about Jung, even in the thinking of men and women who consider themselves his followers and disciples. Jung's breakthrough and going down into this Dante-esque underworld was a result of his overriding concern for consciousness in man or, to make a metaphor of the subject of conversation at the beginning of our meeting, of kindling more fire for greater light on the darkness of our mind, and to determine, among other things, what it was in man that so often arose to extinguish such little light as he possessed.

Great as the mystery of so vast an unconscious area in life obviously is, there is a far greater mystery involved and that is the mystery of consciousness, and beyond that the ultimate wonder of how and for what purpose these two in one or one in two, according to our own inner point of departure, are directed. The mystery is not lessened because it is articulate; the light the fire throws does not diminish the aboriginal mystery because of its power to illuminate some of the night. On the contrary, the plot thickens; the mystery grows with the growth of consciousness. Consciousness could not have the importance it possesses for life, nor could it have survived the onslaught on it which is symbolised in the flood of the Old Testament or made visible and active in all the war, disaster, revolution, and social and individual tragedy inflicted on the human race, including the Wagnerian cataclysm of the war from which I had just come, if in some way consciousness had not had the support of the collective unconscious.

All that is unconscious in life must aspire to consciousness. It is so meaningful, I imagine, precisely because in some way it serves the greatest longing of the collective unconscious. It is, as it were, the deepest dream of greater spirit in this underworld of life, and it is only when consciousness betrays the longing and the dream which gives it birth that it is overwhelmed and for the moment destroyed. I say for the moment deliberately because always hitherto the dream and the longing have never failed to return and consciousness be refashioned as on the anvil of some great blacksmith to flash keen, two-edged, sharp, and shining as a sword heraldic in the hand of some new advanced guard of man. Yet there was a lesson in all this as portentous as it was difficult to declare.

The mystery and the unknown, before and after, are not the synonyms many take them to be. Mystery includes the known as well as the unknown, the ordinary as well as the extraordinary, and once the feeling of mystery abandons our travel-stained senses in contemplation of the same well-worn scene, we have ceased in some vital sense to know what we are observing. What that mystery is, of course, is beyond verbal definition. We know only that its effect on us is either positive or, as in the spirit of our time, negative, but for me it is perhaps most creatively of all the feeling that in the midst of my own partial knowing and experience of things, there is a presence of a something else far greater than I can comprehend which knows me and all I perceive already in full. Reality, no matter how widened and heightened our perceptions, never ceases to be anything but the effect on us of an infinite mystery.

Again, Shakespeare expresses it better than anyone else when he makes the doomed Lear speak to Cordelia, his soul, his daughter crying in the night about to fall, as they too, like Francis Thompson, cling Heaven by the hems: "We shall take upon us the mystery of things, as if we were God's spies." In other words, awareness of the mystery of things acknowledged and revered, though inexpressible and utterly non-rational, is also a vital form of knowing which enables the human spirit to pass through the lines of the defences of what he knows, and as a spy enter the territory of an embattled unknown to prepare the way for the mobilised forms of consciousness to follow and extend the area of his awareness. And it is in all these senses that this ever recurrent process of the dream and the longing in its keeping and the consciousness which emerges from them are the most moving and life-giving aspects of the mystery that impinges on our lives.

In this great abysmal underworld, on which Freud had opened the gate and through which Jung had passed and gone on to become the first to penetrate in depth, the dream and the longing were never permanently discouraged out of their role but always rose phoenix-like out of the burnt-out ashes of a conscious expression which had failed its unconscious motivations, and soared up again and again to compel life anew for another effort at greater consciousness than before.

It is odd, or perhaps not odd, that Jung's family had had at one time a phoenix in its coat of arms and that he was so young, both in person and name, the youngest, and most childlike wise, old man one could meet, as if to leave no doubt that he was uniquely charged to make what was oldest in life young and new again. In this manner he was the very first great explorer in the twentieth-century way. And to understand what he was and accomplished and the immense hidden distances he travelled, I myself go back not only to what others close to him told me over the years but most of all to the little he told me about his own beginning and the feelings it evoked in me. Without these feelings and the impact of the man such knowledge and statistics as the world already possesses could not have lived as they still live and shine for me like a fire of my own in the African night.

✒ The Lake and the River

Lakes resting on the other,
The images of the joyous.
Thus the superior man joins
   with his friends for discussion and practice.

I Ching

JUNG WAS BORN on July 26, 1875, at Kesswil on Lake Constance but when he was barely six months old his father, who was a clergyman, poor even by the standards of a poorly paid vocation, moved to Laufen, almost at the edge of the great Falls of the Rhine. Some four years later his family moved again to Klein-Hüningen, a small hamlet just outside Basel but still on the Rhine, and for the next twenty-one years he went on living there, so that for nearly a quarter of a century the presence of this great river, the view of its swollen, thrusting, forever on-flowing water, and its sound as of the wind and stream of time itself, was in and around his senses. It was not until December 1900 that he left the banks of the Rhine to settle in Zürich on the shores of another great inland sea, where he remained until the end of his days.

I always begin my contemplation of the man as well as his phenomenal achievement by reminding myself of these apparently sober geographical facts of his beginning and his movement from childhood into early manhood. I stress them to myself because they were of immense importance to him physically, as well as being, I

64

believe, a dynamic element in the evolution of his character and work. He himself was fond of telling everyone, as he told me over and over again and indeed recorded in that last will and testament of his called, with a profound non-egotistical and modest precision, *Memories, Dreams, Reflections,* that already as a child he was convinced that no one could live without water. He did not mean, of course, the physical fact that without water people died of thirst. He meant the presence of water as he had experienced it in lake, river, and lake again, and its significance within his unfolding awareness. He would recall how as a small boy on a visit to the Lake Constance on whose shores he was born, its water to him was a vision regained of an incomparable splendour ringed with a bright circle of certainty that one day he would have to live near a lake.

He told me repeatedly, as well as recording the view in several of his books, essays, and letters, that the nature of the earth itself had a profound influence on the character of the people born and raised of it. He could not define it and there were no scientific means by which he could prove it empirically or even produce historical statistics to give fitful illustration to his conviction. Yet he remained unmoved in a stand that, for instance, the German national character could not have developed as it did had it not been an expression also of the nature of the dark soil of Germany. Any other race who migrated to Germany, he believed, even without any definite cultural process to encourage them, would have acquired in time some of the fundamental aspects of the German character because of their nourishment and participation in the nature of the earth of Germany.

He held, using the most improbable parallel accessible to him just then, that even the remotest Siberian aborigine brought to settle in Switzerland would change out of all recognition and in time become a good, solid, respectable Swiss citizen. He would say this not only in private but also in public, with a certain indulgence of the irony and humour native to him, knowing how such a thought would tease his more stolid countrymen, rooted in the assumption of their own unique and inalienable Swissness.

He declared himself thus without doubt, I believe, because nature in all its forms possessed for him not a cold, impersonal, impervious, objective reality but was itself an expression of symbolic form, evocative of all that was symbolic within the spirit.

The symbol within is in a condition of thrust and movement and the energies at its disposal highly kinetic. That is why a contemporary artist like the sculptor Henry Moore, for instance, has so great an impact; he has a genius for joining the symbolic in nature without to the living image of its symbolic equivalent within us all.

For these reasons I always found it necessary as a preliminary to understanding what I experienced of the man to look as precisely as I could into what lake and river have tended to represent at all times and places in the imagination of man.

The lake is one of the most telling images of a great universal made specific, the macrocosmic sea microcosmically contained in the earth and so made a comprehensible source of nourishment to the life and spirit of man. It reflects and draws down into its own deeps and so into the heart of the earth all that its opposite, the sky, represents and possesses of illumination and height, becoming a kind of mediating factor between two great poles, two opposites of reality: a dark, earthly principle and another of light and celestial sky and all the values they stand for. In other words, the yin and yang of Tao, the ancient Chinese concept of the one and only living way as set out in the *I Ching*, the Book of Changes of Wilhelm that was to give Jung so much. It is for me the most comprehensive, precise, and authoritative study of living symbolism and its role in time, space, and the evolution of creation and being which is its purpose.

The Book of Changes personifies the lake and makes it the image of the feminine value with the greatest future and possibilities of increase, calling it the youngest of all the daughters in a house of many mansions, describing it as a source of joy as expressed, for instance, in the extract quoted at the beginning of this chapter. But the river is another matter. It is an image of water already in movement, finding its own way through great ravines, carrying all over cataract and rapid and through conditions of external danger, to emerge intact and triumphant for union with the sea out of which it rose as vapour at the beginning. It succeeds in doing so only because it finds its own way without short cuts, straight lines, or disregard of any physical impediments but in full acknowledgement of the reality of all that surrounds it, implying that the longest way round is the shortest and only safe way to the sea.

As a result, the *I Ching* emphasises that water represents the nourishment that comes from above for life on earth, where it is transformed into an element which leads the heart of men to the soul locked up within the body, reflecting there a light that is enclosed in the dark. Above all, the water which the river conducts so untiringly to the sea itself, this ancient book stresses, is a master image for what is abysmal in life.

That Jung's chosen river should have been the Rhine seems to me among all the facets of these almost supernatural preassociations the most portentous of essentials if the child Jung were to succeed in becoming the kind of man he was. I say this because the Rhine is one of the great mythological rivers of the world, a dark and angry stream, as dark and in as strange a rage and passion to get to the sea as the Congo issuing straight out of the darkest centre of the heart of darkness of my native Africa. I have travelled the Rhine as I have travelled the Blue and White Niles from source to sea and never found the ease on it that I felt on the Nile and its tributaries. It was for me too a river with its source in the heart of darkness of the history of Europe.

Jung, one should not forget, was born as part of the Germanic complex of culture and religion as expressed in its unique Swiss annex. Above all, he was raised on the banks of the unconverted and unrepentant Rhine. It is only when set against this uncomfortable inheritance that one can measure how remarkable was Jung's metamorphosis of a Swiss-Germanic self into one of the greatest universal personalities since the Renaissance.

Jung himself stressed to me more than once how profoundly symbolic his native land was to him always, from the moment when as a child at Laufen on the Rhine—so far back in time that he could not be certain who it was except that it was the voice of a woman, probably an aunt—someone firmly anchored in the sea of his memory his first glimpse of the distant Alps by pointing out the storm-tossed waves of hills also to him and observing how red they were.

"I never looked at the Swiss scene again," he told me, recalling that moment, "without feeling myself in the presence of a great mystery. I never could look at the mountaintops without also looking at the valleys and their rivers and lakes and thinking of them all as a great and mysterious whole."

In plants and trees, perhaps the most intimate issue of the earth's own nature, Jung felt himself closer to the act and deed of creation than in any other physical manifestation of life. It was as if through them, he would say in a voice resonant with awe, that he looked into the mind of the Creator at work on his creations. They were never just trees, plants, or flowers to him. He was to call them thoughts of God, expressing not only the mind of the Creator but also the magnetic beauty of the instant of creation.

And the older he became, the nearer his own physical end, the closer and clearer his own green thought and the thought the trees expressed in their own green shade drew together and comforted and endeared one to the other.

I remember one evening at Bollingen when he referred to this. A wind was raising a remote Merlinesque sort of moan from the trees he had planted thickly around his tower. The lake was lapping at the shore hard by as the waters of Avalon might have done the night a dying Arthur forced a reluctant knight to toss the great Excalibur back into the deep out of which the image of the shining and dedicated sword had been born. He could never, Jung said, go along with the concept that man alone was created in the image of God. That wind, those trees, that water we heard, those contemplative plants and flowers outside, the valleys and the great mountaintops with their fall of snow, reflecting sun, moon, and stars underneath, all seemed to him as a boy an expression of the permanent essence of God more true and wonderful than any in men and their societies. It was to them that he turned when the world for the moment defeated his questioning self.

Animals, much as he loved them, were already one dimension further away in their ability to move at will. They were, to put it symbolically, in both being and spirit already uprooted, and cut off from that which had made them. He hastened to add that it was God's Will that moved them and not their own, but even with this Will they represented a step towards the exile that men today call consciousness.

There was, for instance, their reappearance in the dream which came to him in a moment of great irresolution when, his schooldays over and entry into a university before him, he did not know what course to follow. He was at his wits' end, with argument and counter-argument continually raging within, when out of himself there came a dream which put him back in a dark wood on the banks of the Rhine by an ancient burial mound. He dug into it and turned up the bones of prehistoric animals. He interpreted it as a sign that he must get to know nature and the world in which he lived. That, coupled with another dream in which water played a great role, made him settle for science and so on towards medicine. Taken at its manifest level, he was no doubt right. At another level, however, it showed how the manifest interpretation was only the servant of a deeper process and that the dream looked at as a whole showed him already contracted by life to dig into the long-forgotten feminine earth of the human spirit. But for the moment the point was that a dream associated with the Rhine put him back in the midstream course of himself.

Yet in the beginning it was as if this life by the river in its externals were bent on casting all that was dark, negative, doubtful, and problematical at him. Until he was nine, when his sister was born, he was an only child and had no companionship of his peers to share with him the strange impact of life by this uncomfortable river and in the process to lighten it. His earliest memories of it seem to have been of the dead it threw up and how it made him face death with his eyes and senses wide open at his most impressionable years.

I myself have sat in the garden of his father's old vicarage on the brightest, hottest, and most fulfilled of summer days, the trees in the orchards around heavy with fruit, the scent of hay drifting like incense over all, and the noise of the urgent river drowning the humming of the bees struggling sap-laden through the air so thick and sticky with a honeyed light of its own that they seemed to be swimming in it rather than flying through it. I should have been uplifted by it all but I was profoundly uneasy all the time and glad to get away, wondering how so lonely a young boy as Jung could have endured so busy and fecund an earth. It was all just too much, I thought, and yet he made his peace on his own terms with such a natural impact on his personal evolving senses, but not without sacrifice to the gods, who had seemed to have prearranged it all with such profound and meticulous a detail of purpose aforethought.

Already profoundly introverted, he was turned inward upon himself more than ever. From what I knew of my own much milder isolation in a great natural surround, there was evidence of this for me in the fact that he was always having accidents and once narrowly escaped falling into the river. It was, he would tell me, borrowing from the vocabulary of his own theory of psychological types, all a result of the fact that he had been born with an inferior "sensation function," an underdeveloped sense of the reality of his physical here and now. Good and true as the explanation may be, there is no doubt that he was encouraged by the circumstances of his boyhood to be more preoccupied another way and that, as my African countrymen would say, his soul was more than ever not really in his body. In other words, whatever supervised his sense of physical direction in the external world was only too often just not at home when called upon.

I know that Jung often said himself that although his life outwardly was uneventful, inwardly it was overwhelmingly eventful. This picture of a person rich in inner eventfulness with a poor relation in the external world is greatly heightened by the fact that when Jung at last took time off from his urgent work to look back on his life, he was already an old man who by the most exacting standards of measurement had achieved almost too much. When he talked to one of his beginning, therefore, it was almost as if one were looking at the child through the wrong end of a telescope.

Indeed, this applied not only to his childhood but to his beginnings and progression as a young psychiatrist, and constitutes a formidable factor that has coloured and perhaps even slanted current judgements of the man and his work. When I met him, for instance, he was already in his seventies, the shape of his major work perhaps not totally filled in, yet clear in outline as a mountain range in a Japanese woodcut. Almost all his early contemporaries and collaborators were dead or about to vanish from the scene and the men and women who surrounded him, with a few exceptions, much younger and without any knowledge of the pioneering Jung, let alone the boy, and so naturally inclined to see his achievement only in its most mature form, neglecting the almost incredible flights of intuition and as yet unconsolidated landing grounds in the dark by which he had arrived at the stage where they encountered him.

All of us therefore have been proscribed in our valuations by a lack of knowledge of the younger Jung, and even his most loyal and deserving followers tend still to ignore the urgent need there is to go back to his earlier points of departure so that what his inspired and swift intuitive vision uncovered, relatively in passing, can be consolidated and expanded. It is of the utmost importance to realise that most current interpretations are of the older Jung and his work in its most mature form. However true, they remain somewhat partial.

Yet even allowing for the built-in obsolescence, as it were, of our current perspectives, there is a far more fundamental cause of our difficulties to discover the man in the child and the child in the man, as we must if our vision of him is to be complete. Even in those few lines of his *Memories* devoted to his early life at Laufen, it is obvious that a great deal did happen to him also externally but did not remain in his memory because it was singularly unimportant to him.

He was born so introverted that it would seem almost as if he had been only technically a child and in reality almost always very old and very wise. I know that this in a sense can be said of all children. I have always been amazed by the fact that, for me at any rate, the newly born child does not look either new or young but extremely old. At the moment of birth it still belongs utterly to all the life that has ever been and not to the world so young in time in which we who brought it there appear so briefly. We forget that it is our own life on earth that is so painfully new, young, and short and that what we bring with us into it at birth is already as old as time and that our own progress from there on is an act of increasing separation from that organic and idiomatic antiquity of our being at our earthly beginning, leading towards our own personal and private moment of birth through adolescence into the world of today.

No child at birth is so young to me, so poignant and unarmed for what is to come, therefore, as the boy and girl born into their own contemporary selves in adolescence, particularly now that all the aids designed by a wise and infinitely experienced nature in rules and ritual of initiation for just these occasions have been universally discarded by our rational selves, like demented persons finding themselves in a desert without water-bags because they had jettisoned them as an unnecessary encumbrance in a moment of plenty.

But in Jung, what is a natural endowment in us all seems to have been bestowed with another dimension added and an extra pull of gravity to it. It was almost as if something in him knew from the start that this personal birth in a contemporary idiom was irrelevant because that dimension of reality was already a spent form, a burnt-out and discredited pattern of being and an increasingly wintry illusion of the senses devoid of any protracted meaning, and that he would have to accomplish it altogether in another way.

So in a very real way he was never young as we were, and was incapable of having equals in his own time and place to keep him company. In the deepest meaning of the innocence of the image evoked by the term, he never had someone of his own kind to play with. It was no wonder that at school, where he was considered strange, odd, unpredictable, and hardly ever popular either with students or teachers, this old, old atmosphere about him was felt instinctively and he was nicknamed "Father Abraham." This had a singular unconscious aptness, considering how Abraham himself was preoccupied with God and was to accomplish a significant break-through in man's relationship with his own highest meaning that burning Old Testament day when he abstained at the last moment from sacrificing his own son to the voice of his inner calling.

Something of this, I imagine, played a part, which though it must not be exaggerated was nonetheless real, in the apparent lack of concern in his own analytical approach to the psychology of children. Although he was to write a most impressive study on what the child in all of us means, his greatest interest was always before and after childhood in the world we know. So that when one considers the great emphasis of the initial Freudian approach on the rediscovery of an inevitably traumatic pattern in the child, and a return to a kind of psychological infancy in the belief that it would free the maimed adult for a new fulfillment of himself, the difference of nuance in Jung's own approach was most striking. Of course his concern for the child in life was as great as any of his contemporaries, but the problem of the child, he held in the main, had to be dealt with through the parents, so that whenever asked to help with disturbed children he would say, as he once told me, "Bring me the parents and I will deal with the problems of the child through them." It was not for nothing, therefore, that he discovered almost immediately how even the companionship of other children in the limited extent possible to him "alienated" him from himself. It accounts for a certain bleakness and the thin wintry wind which seemed to preside and blow over the scene of his unpeopled youth, and gives one an inkling into what would have been an unendurable loneliness of spirit for anyone else to endure for a lifetime as he did.

And he would not have been able to endure this, I am certain, had he not discovered strange companionship within himself. It started in a Promethean instinct to have a fire of his own and to allow no one else to tend it, as if this were a symbolic enactment of a realisation of personal awareness in himself, seeing how fire always has been the image of consciousness in life. It was soon confirmed by his first sustained dialogue not with other human beings but by something more *other* and permanent than himself or any of the human beings with whom he argued and talked. Awareness is nothing if it is not also a dialogue between oneself and what one feels *other* and greater than oneself; between what one knows and does not know; between what one is and what one is not and yet dimly feels called upon to be and serve, where the last horizon of a known self meets the mystery which encloses it as the universe the earth.

Indeed, one does not begin to discover oneself as an individual until such a dialogue breaks in on a hitherto undivided self and some great *forever,* as it were, outside space and the time and change to which we are all so irrevocably subjected ourselves, presents itself to one for a relentless process of enigmatic question and answer that is going to run to the end of one's days. And that other *forever* in the beginning at all times and places has had one of its most authoritative representations in imagery evoked through stone, which to the inner eye of the candidate for initiation in self-awareness is the naturally divine in its most lasting and incorruptible physical form.

I myself have seen this awareness as a child most movingly enacted in terms of stone by the almost vanished copper-coloured, Nilotic-cast Hottentots of my native Africa, of which they are after the Bushmen the oldest inhabitants. It seems, alas, an irrefutable law of life that for most of us the new meaning clamouring in us always has somehow to be acted out, has to be lived before it can be known. So I have often watched breathless and seen how at the ford of some river whose crossing is natural parable and allegorical material to the mind of man, or near some great tree whose presence bears witness to the seasonal changes prescribed for all in the wheeling courses of an unfolding creation, the Hottentots would in passing add a stone of their own to the little pile already there. And when I asked them why, they would invariably reply that it was out of respect and gratitude to Heitse-Eibib, their god-hero, as I already knew, who came back to the day bleeding in the dawn from the wounds he had received in another victorious battle for light against darkness in the night, and whose breath was in the wind stirring the leaves of the great tree with a strange, virginal apprehension over their impending consummation, to remind those despised copper-coloured men as they sat there in the heat of the day that Heitse-Eibib himself was breathing through them and urging their spirit to rise and be on its way. They chose stone, those persecuted men, to mark the presence of Heitse-Eibib thus because he himself had marked with stone the place of his first resurrection from his first death.

So it seems to me only too natural that it should have all begun with a stone in the garden of Jung's home at Klein-Hüningen. He would sit on this stone day after day wondering whether he was the one sitting on the stone or the stone that felt it was being sat upon. The problem raised by the speculation that followed was not solved there and then, but he had no doubt that he was in some secret relationship with the stone. The dialogue thus begun about what he was in terms of a greater, more permanent, and irreducible reality as represented by the stone, and its intimations evoked of a mysterious interdependence of his own world within and the specific world without, went on and on, only to yield its answer, I believe, within hours of his death.

It is not surprising, therefore, that all his life he was to love stone especially and that the moment he had broken through the wall which had separated himself and this immemorial past from the present to give it a truly contemporary place and form, at this moment in which he had accomplished, as it were, his own Renaissance, his own rebirth, his dialogue with stone took on a more active and outgoing form, and was conducted until the end of his days when his spirit so moved him on the stone itself with hammer and chisel.

It was to be particularly so when he was about to embark on another stage in the journey of himself. He would seem compelled then to mark the exact time and place of arrival and departure by carving on stone images and personifications of the new forces motivating him. For instance, when the death of his beloved wife Emma hurled him into a totally new phase of himself towards a fresh encounter with the reality of his time, he took up this dialogue and hammered and chiselled the honey-coloured stone at his lake and woodland retreat of Bollingen, never in a rush but with a kind of devout absorption, patient, calm, resolute, and of a certain marble measure that seemed more akin to the Olympian than the demonic element in himself to which he so often referred, using the term always, of course, in its original, classical sense.

But at the moment of his first intercourse with stone in the garden of his father (it was significantly always his "father's garden," never his "parents' garden," "the garden at home," or even his "mother's garden"), he was launched on the way to self-discovery, leading to the disconcerting realisation that not only were he and the stone a significant twosome but that he was strangely paired within as well. He appeared to himself to be two distinct persons, to whom he gave the sober, empirical baptism of personalities No. 1 and No. 2.

The first was the awkward, inadequate schoolboy and young, underprivileged, and, in a worldly sense, inexperienced person that he felt himself almost overwhelmingly to be; the No. 2 was an old man of unchallenged authority and power, at first thought to have lived as a "manufacturer" in the eighteenth century but later seen to have been a relatively provisional experience of an even more profound pattern than he suspected, with its origin in remotest antiquity. For all the paradoxical imagery in which it and the relationship between its two ambassadors were to be expressed, it was a relatively undifferentiated and personalised dress-rehearsal for something far more complex, ultimately to be integrated into another and much more mature personage, to whom he was to give the name of Philemon. He did this, as we shall see, because of a special meaning he read in the Greek myth and legend in which Philemon and his wife Baucis were the only people on earth to welcome and shelter Zeus and his winged messenger Hermes when they came down from Olympus to examine men for their piety. No. 2 therefore, even in this first eighteenth-century personification, was a manifestation of the archetypal pattern of the wise old man who has at his disposal experience of all the life that has ever been.

Most human beings discover him as a resource within their natural selves, if they are lucky, only in maturity. They begin by feeling they share his company in the reflection they find of him in other men in the world without, and perhaps the greatest majority of us are content to do this, following others we consider wiser than ourselves, without ever acknowledging the need of separating what is reflected either from its reflection or reflector and turning to the original image itself and the mirror of it that we are in ourselves. But it is significant testimony to the natural antiquity of the young Jung that he discovered his old man within so early and kept his company so faithfully from then on that he became not a hindrance but source of purpose to the No. 1 personality, for all its love-hate relationship with this ancient other, causing such acute tensions at times that Goethe's great cry of "Two souls, alas, are housed within my breast!" might have been Jung's own.

All tensions, contradictions, and paradox could ultimately be contained because No. 2 was in the final analysis a source of enrichment for the tentative schoolboy—indeed, as Jung's first immediate personification suggested with such precision of symbolism, was a "manufacturer" for him, a producer of the meaning which the world without so markedly failed to provide. I myself always give this element, for two reasons, a priority over other factors that might have better claim to it when weighed in purely ponderable chronological terms. Without the company first of this eighteenth-century old man who evolved subsequently into Philemon, Jung could not have accomplished what he did. He may indeed have been so injured by his absence as to have become one of the number of casualties proliferating at such a terrifying rate in the world today in the battle of the individual for a meaning of his own, instead of a person who was to heal and make whole fragmented beings on so spectacular a scale.

There were to be moments, it is true, when it would appear as if No. 1, the aspect of Jung in the world and of it and its immediate necessities, had taken over the whole of him; others when No. 2 overshadowed No. 1 to such an extent, as a dream forewarned him later at Basel, that it dwindled to a single fluttering light, in danger of being extinguished by gusts of a wintry wind in some titanic shadow looming over it. Yet in the main the interplay between No. 1 and No. 2 kept Jung always in a state of balance and always brought him back to the heel of striving for fateful proportions. Asymmetric as the interplay of these two personalities was, it was the kind of asymmetry which a great Zen Buddhist priest told me once in Japan contained the dynamic implication of greater symmetry to come and without which life would become petrified in one inadequate expression of itself. No wonder Jung was later to tell me with a laugh that he could not imagine a fate more awful, a fate worse than death, than a life lived in perfect balance and harmony.

Although Jung's critics today hold that his confession of being two people in one is evidence of an unbalanced if not pathologically schizoid personality, there was nothing but sanity and not a trace of the pathological in this double allotment of responsibilities within the emerging Jung. It is true that there were moments, particularly after his first reading at Basel of Nietzsche's work, when seeing how the doomed writer projected his own No. 2 personality on Zarathustra and tried to raise himself to superhuman heights, Jung slammed the door of his mind for a long time on his "old man" out of fear that he might be a similarly morbid phenomenon. Jung's fear did not vanish until he realised that Nietzsche's hubris had put this natural phenomenon to a morbid and excessive use and he was free to rediscover the *ancient* in himself in a much more meaningful and more highly differentiated form.

The play and counterplay of his No. 1 and No. 2 personalities was to run through the whole of his life. It is a pattern, though observable in every human being, he was to tell me with an unusually sad resignation, of which only the very few, alas, were at all aware.

Finally, I believe this activation of the pattern of the "old man" within himself started long before he was capable of forming any image of it, let alone being sufficiently aware of it to be capable of putting it into words. Apart from his own natural disposition in that direction, it was all a consequence of the extent to which his father and mother failed each other and the father in particular the son.

Jung knew at a very early age that he could derive no comfort from his parents' relationship with each other. The word "love," almost from the moment of self-awareness, made him acutely uncomfortable. He was, it is true, devoted to his parents and he never doubted their devotion to him. His mother in particular, he often stressed, was extremely good to him and in the long run contributed more to his development than his father. That she was, as he would say with a tender, ironical smile of remembrance, "also a bit of a witch" and had also a No. 1 and a No. 2 personality was to prove an advantage and helped him no end to honour his obligation to his own No. 2. Though he found her disconcertingly unpredictable and unreliable in terms of his own No. 1, she was a great source of strength and support in his own unconfessed self, through the natural mind, as he called it, of the No. 2 that dominated her being.

His father, on the other hand, though unerringly predictable, seemed to him powerless in all the areas that mattered most to Jung, and in which a father is delegated by life to exercise some of the function which personality No. 2 was evoked to assume at so unusually early an age in Jung. Even in the area of religion, which happened to be the father's speciality since he was a priest, he utterly failed his son. Unfortunately, it happened to be an area of life to which Jung was born with an absolute commitment. Almost from the start, as we shall see, he experienced what men call God as a mighty activity within himself. He experienced it with such a clarity, totality, and certainty that he never himself had need of any proof of the reality of God. Moreover, from the age of three his imagination was assailed as a result of this activity by symbols and images of the most vivid and disconcerting kind. They seemed to fall like showers of shooting stars streaking through the dark on his perplexed and at times frightened senses or, like volcanoes erupting, shook the known ground on which his mind stood and glowered with fire high in the night above him.

Yet his father in all other senses was an exceptionally good and honourable parent and I for one see no justification, as Jung saw none, in blaming him for failing his marriage and his son. The whole trend of the age was against his being anything but a failure to such an extraordinary son and almost to any woman, let alone so formidable a wife. He did his best and I find myself moved to follow the example of those pre-war Indian university students who, despite all their futile efforts to secure a degree, nonetheless felt they had achieved something which other men who had not tried likewise had not done, and indicated that something by inserting after their names in their applications for work "B.A. (failed)." I would not hesitate to put in the lists of the university of life with all possible respect after the name of Jung's parent the honour of "Father (failed)."

However much Jung made his peace with this failure and never bore any resentment but felt only the most heart-rending compassion for his father, it would be wrong to overlook the depth of the wound it inflicted. I believe this failure of his father to be a parent to him also in the sense that his No. 2 personality was, made it inevitable that in a boy so introverted, nature rushed in to fill the gap and introduced the theme of the universal old man long before it was normally due. Also I believe that as a result of this failure, his own sense of the "father," in the much needed worldly aspects of the immediate reality, always remained underdeveloped. I think he was permanently deprived by this lack of a natural example in his childhood of what it means to be father to the man in him, and so perhaps more influenced than he would have been by his powerful, admiring, warm, confident, and strangely ambivalent mother. I suspect it was all the better perhaps this way for his ultimate development and for us, living as we do in a world where the masculine can be taken for granted but in which there is such desperate need for a rediscovery of a lost feminine half. In terms of Jung's No. 1 personality, however, it did create a certain imbalance, as economists now say.

As a result, there was in the economy of his own spirit a negative balance of exchange in this facet of himself. I think this is one of the explanations of why he was to get on better, on the whole, with women than men in life. It explains, I believe, his strange relationship with Freud as nothing else does, and a certain kind of archaic authoritarianism that surged up in him at times in his dealings with other men. I believe that some of the unreliability he came to attribute to men in general was encouraged by an inability to rely on a part, however small, of the man in himself.

Of course, what was remarkable were not these upsurges but their rarity, and the fact that Jung was never tempted to hide behind the failure of his parents. Similarly, he did not hide behind the failures of history, his teachers, his generation, his time, culture, and indeed whole civilisation, but took the consequences of all these elements within himself from an early age as the raw material or base matter, to paraphrase the alchemists he was to rediscover and honour as pioneers in his own field, out of which to make the philosopher's stone of his own greater being.

I think that not the least of the measures of the greatness of his achievement is implicit in the fact that in an age when men and their societies increasingly used the failures of parents, society, and history as excuses and justifications for not being fully responsible for themselves and their reactions, he always spoke of his parents with gratitude and love and referred repeatedly to his "dear and generous father." However sad that his father could never give him a positive light to go by, Jung would go back as if it were the seal of the pure metal of memory to a moment at Laufen when he had been restless and feverish at night and his father had walked up and down, carrying him in his arms and singing to him in a voice not only audible above the waters of the impassioned Rhine but still to be heard clearly and of value to him despite eighty years and more in between.

It was inevitable that as a result of such a direct personal experience of all that men mean by God—such a mighty personal attack, I am tempted to say, because of the power and density of the onslaught on his awakening awareness—he had questions of an unusual, urgent, and original import to ask. Whenever he turned to his father, he was cruelly disappointed and dismissed with the exhortation that he had to believe and trust first and then he would know and understand. It seemed the wrong way round to Jung; one surely had to experience first and then one would know and could learn to understand. Belief and faith in the mind of the schoolboy were already impediments to the pursuit of knowledge and understanding—a conclusion that would seem strange in so naturally an intuitive imagination, where belief of what intuition inflicts on the spirit is evidence of what is to come, a report on things not yet seen but still to be observed and proved, were such a conclusion not provisional and really a symptom of the great hurt done to Jung's spirit at so early an age by the insistence of his father and his time on a total dogmatic loyalty to a rigidly prescribed religious belief. His father refused utterly to accept the pre-eminence of experience in Jung's approach, the son suspected, because of unacknowledged and profound doubts of his father in his own faith and its power to provide a living answer any more.

So almost from as early as he could remember, Jung resigned himself to the fact that he could get no help from his father—a fact that saddened him all the more because he was convinced that a real interchange of honest question and truthful answer between them would have helped the father too, and perhaps prevented his dying in a way which Jung found all the more tragic because it was the end of a living death rather than a life. Indeed, his father's death, in Jung's twenty-first year, was for him his first and most intimate demonstration of the consequences of the conventional Christian insistence on a blind, unthinking, and literal imitation of Christ.

Yet all this was redeemed in a way by one thing the father had done for the man Jung was to become which, trivial as it may have appeared to his generous soul at the time, was of an abiding polar importance in the life of the son. Nothing could have been more timely, or performed half so well a service badly needed by the boy facing this lonely personal birth through adolescence which I have defined at length before, than the father's action one morning at the foot of the Rigi in Jung's fourteenth year.

The Book of Changes lays much emphasis on the importance of the small in the accomplishment of the great and implies that in the infinite, small and great are one. It is as if the father, in giving all that it was in his power to give that morning, gave everything in terms of the fullness of life when he sent his son alone by rail up the mountain of the Rigi because he did not have enough money for two. Few other episodes in the life of Jung move me more. Looking at his rounded life now in a way he himself never could, and as a result being more and more overawed by the absence in it of anything that can be dismissed as truly accidental, I think part of the reason I am so moved is because both father and son were united at that predestined moment as they never were at any other time in one and the same expression of greater meaning, the meaning which the Book of Changes says, in a phrase John of Patmos could not have excelled, is that which has always existed through itself.

It was a turning point in Jung's career because as he came out on top of the Rigi he had his first glimpse of the mountains of his homeland from above. He found himself looking deep into Wilhelm Tell country, into the mythological heart of Switzerland. I myself have often stood where he stood and as a foreigner found the view almost supernaturally awe-inspiring. I can understand that for a moment he was overwhelmed not just by the beauty and scale of the externals of the scene but because it was home to him as nothing had been before, and roused in him a nostalgia that was a summons as on a distant bugle to some unimagined prodigal return. It was, he told me, not only a vision of the world of which his No. 2 was so disconcerting an emissary but also in its solemn, white, prophetic summits, dark valleys, and cataclysmic gorges, a staggering visualisation, a relief map almost of the hidden life and mind and spirit of man. It was a moment as of initiation and confirmation in a great natural temple to which he would return henceforth again and again in his imagination for a communion that was total as it was sacred. It was the most wonderful thing, he would say, ever given to him by his father. And after such a gift, how relative all that Jung and all of us who write of the father have been compelled to call his failure, since, for all its inadequacy, it is the only word available.

From his remarkable mother, on the other hand, Jung received a totally different response. Part of her supported the social and spiritual conventions of the time, but the boy soon discovered that in the heart of her feminine self she was without qualification on the side of his own No. 2. She supported him in an unpredictable and completely non-rational manner out of her own instincts and intuition. Jung would refer many times, not without a certain awe, to how active in her was what he called the natural mind, a mind concerned not with ideas, ideals, and any moral evaluation and other ethical fall-out of the spirit and religiousness of man but with world, men, and things as they were, deep within themselves, or with what I have called to myself the "great thuses" of life. Meister Eckhardt, the fourteenth-century Dominican mystic whom Jung was to study intently, somewhere called them, with far greater precision, *istigkeit*—the "isness" of life and time.

This natural mind of his mother gave Jung no direct food for thought in concepts and ideas but confirmed and sustained his own inner sense of direction at all sorts of critical stages. I have already indicated how his father's failure brought his development more and more under feminine influence. But there was far more to it than that. His was above all an inspired, intuitive spirit and in this he was nearer to women than the generality of men. As intuitive as the most intuitive of women, and all the better equipped to serve his intuitions because of his possession of an intellect to match them, he was even more at home in this dimension of life than his mother was, and able to share the apprehensions of her natural mind, not in the partial archaic way she experienced them but in a totally and utterly contemporary idiom.

There were many examples, small and great, of this positive interreaction between them, but of these perhaps only two are necessary to illustrate the effect on the main theme of the evolution of the boy into the man. The first was that it was not the father, on whose library shelves a splendidly bound edition of Goethe stood and in whose sphere of influence such a matter should naturally have fallen, but his mother who out of sheer instinct told him he ought to read *Faust*. The advice was as timely and sent Jung to as lofty a summit of his "inscape" as his father's act of generosity on the great Rigi had done in his landscape.

Apart from the all-important cause that he was born so profoundly introverted and so naturally tended to withdraw into himself, many things had happened to the boy within and without to keep his inner life a secret from both his parents and his world. Indeed, if I were to review his life in conventional chronological sequence I would have had to touch on the main causes of this long since, because one of the main incentives came from a great dream which was inflicted on him when he was little more than three years of age, as well as a daytime vision some nine years later. But in view of the fact that this is an account of a personal experience which for me began in his old age, and so is inevitably concerned more with psychological dimensions of time and space than the more obvious and conventional level on which these great twosomes act, I am forced to turn to those moments not at their emergence so much as at the point, many years later, of their acquisition of meaning in the spirit of Jung. All that mattered at this particular phase was the realisation of how his real person was growing, as it had done almost from infancy, like a pearl on the bed of the sea around a grit of secrets held inviolate within the outer shell of a mere boy doing his duty as best he could by his parents, environment, and school.

Every instinct of his insisted that he was in possession already of facts and forms of knowledge that it would be most unwise to share with others. He knew that he was not in possession yet of the valid, properly informed and differentiated self to understand fully and contain all that was being inflicted from within, let alone to defend it against a world whose values these events challenged or contradicted outright. What is more, it was perhaps not so much that he knew all this instinctively at so early an age but had the courage in full measure of his as yet untried instincts.

He seemed to know in a non-rational and utterly non-conceptualised way that such secrets were in a sense holy secrets, vital for the living of an individual life uniquely his own. They were part of the living mystery whose worldly manifestations all great religions hide from the eyes of the generality of men and women and only the highest of their initiates are allowed to perceive and serve: for instance, the Jews ordained in the holy of holies of their Tabernacle and the Japanese in their greatest shrine at Ise, where the sacred mirror is screened from vulgar view by a simple white, unstained cloth hanging between columns of plain wood, on which the grain of the seasons to this day is apparent like finger-prints of God and his time.

The keeping of such secrets, either collectively or religiously, is not to be confused with secrecy. Such secrets are the only forms of protection possible for experiences of the infinite and living mystery which cannot be broadcast in a way that will render it capable of being understood or save it from popular destruction. They are like seeds that need the darkness, isolation, and cover of the earth to germinate unobserved before they can emerge and grow in the light of the day for which they are destined. So it was undoubtedly with the boy Jung, charged already to bursting point with secret growth of an unprecedented density and power.

His No. 1 personality must have done its work far better than either he or his No. 2 suspected, for it is remarkable how little parents, teachers, and schoolboys were aware of the volcanic world it hid from their view. Of course they had their suspicions, like the teacher who gave vent to them by falsely accusing Jung of plagiarism and lying when he wrote the best essay perhaps ever written at the school. Had the teacher been worthy of his vocation, he might have reappraised his judgement in observing how the boy took the punishment so unjustly inflicted on him. The natural indignation over such unfair treatment fell from Jung with unusual swiftness and was reduced to insignificance in a great calm that came over his spirit as he discovered he was far more interested in what it was both in him and the teacher that had produced such a collision than in the pain and injustice inflicted. The discovery of this was of immense importance to him as an act of spiritual emancipation, for it proved him already no longer a slave to mere action and reaction as the generality of men and their societies were. It proved him to be in possession of an acausal element in himself and he was to put this discovery to the most creative use later in many other ways, particularly in his parting with Freud.

Then his schoolfellows too were full of suspicion and strange distaste of what they felt they did not know in him. When they had named him after the patriarch Abraham, they set some four thousand years between him and them. One afternoon they ambushed him on his way home from school. They had a glimpse then of the volcanic temperament of Jung which kept them at bay from then on. He seized one of them by the heels and, using him as he was later to use a rhinoceros whip on a mob of frenzied African dancers in Uganda, threatened the others to such effect that they all fled. The discovery of such an aggressive temper surprised him too and was at rare intervals to surprise him to the end of his days. So at least I am told, for I never saw any trace of it myself in the man I knew.

Neither father nor mother knew how he lay awake at nights in an agony of spirit over his total inability, again a consequence of his own direct experience through dreams, visions, symbols, and fantasy, to accept the conventional view that God was purely good and loving. He accepted already, as Meister Eckhardt had scornfully proclaimed in the fourteenth century, *quod erat absurdum,* that if God were good he could be better. He did not doubt, it is true, that God could also be loving and a great bestower of a grace, which he too had experienced after admission of the as yet undeclared vision, but there was implicitly more to it than that. Somewhere and somehow God was terrible as well and stood in a relationship with darkness and evil, indeed perhaps had need of them as an instrument of grace and redemption, that frightened all the carefully conditioned Protestant wits out of him. During the three-quarters of an hour it took him to walk from his home to school, which he had to do often in worn-down shoes, he was as a rule aware neither of the time nor the distance because his imagination was entirely possessed by problems of this nature and the fantasies they inspired. The journey back, despite the intervention of long, concentrated school hours, was spent likewise, the dialogue within as alive as ever and ready for taking up exactly where he had abandoned it when he entered the gates of the privileged Gymnasium at Basel.

Indeed, so possessed was he by speculation on problems concerned with religious material issuing out of his own aboriginal nature that it came between him and the study of mathematics in a way no one would have expected of a boy with so good a mind and capacity for concentration even in the face of formidable opposition from his inborn preoccupations. He himself made little of his difficulties in his *Memories* but remained somewhat puzzled if not outraged by them for the rest of his life. For me, because of the benefit of hindsight and, I believe, no other presumption, these difficulties seem a direct consequence of the naturally profound religious nature of Jung and therefore merit far more attention than they have yet received.

They were all in the realm of the applied religion we call ethics. Such statements as "If $a = b$ and $b = c$, then $a = c$" seemed terrifyingly immoral to him. The view, of course, is partly evidence of that instinctive respect he always had for "otherness" in men, things, their dreams and imagery, and which he held to be inviolate even in such algebraic symbols. But at heart the difficulty was more mysterious and far greater.

Axioms in the minds of those who first formulated them, particularly that of Pythagoras, whom Jung numbered among the greatest of men, were launched more as religious statements than scientific pronouncements, however great their applied scientific potential was to prove. To define the mathematical concept of infinity, for instance, as that which is so great that it can be neither increased nor diminished is as good a definition of a God as one could possibly get. And when Jung in his eighties one day remarked to me that God was so great that it was utterly impossible to add to or subtract from his greatness, he smiled when I called it a profound mathematical proposition. He himself later lent support to this interpretation by trying to explain the concept of the Holy Trinity algebraically and in the process showing a firmer grasp of equations than one would have thought possible after his early struggles, and as the years went by suspected more and more that each number represented an archetype of its own.

Then to say that the one divided by the nought, or the zero which was the invention of ancient Indian philosophy, produced infinity, was another way of saying what the mystics proclaimed in their assertion that if God had not created the universe out of nothing, he would not have created anything at all. So that the *one* as measured in mathematics against the *nothing,* or the anti-one, could only produce the *infinite* as answer.

Finally, to turn to an axiom which bothered Jung particularly, the statement that parallel straight lines met only in infinity. It was not only a religious but a great psychological truth, for the great opposites in life, man, things, and even inanimate matter where body and antibody, through their opposition if not contradiction of each other, form a common substance did steer a strange parallel and irreconcilable course until forced to join each other by some transcendental agency which was an expression of infinite meaning.

Yet with all this and so much else besides at war within Jung, the complacent, unobservant world could see in him little more than an awkward, at times disconcerting boy without any apparent inkling that they were in the presence of one of the most inspired natures of all time. Jung repeatedly referred to his questionable popularity at school and university and to the mistrust he seemed to arouse, not so much even by what he said or did as just by what he was. Small wonder that there appears to have been no single teacher or professor who really had any decisive influence on his development and whom he thought important enough or just humanly close enough to merit specific retention and acknowledgement in his ultimate *Memories*.

Only his mother, without any cloud of idea or mind to dim her reaction, instinctively knew this *other* in him and its needs and out of instinct introduced him to *Faust*. It was as if the "witch" in her, to pursue the word in the idiom of the pre-Arthurian world wherein it had its positive meaning, recognised that there was a "Merlin" in the son in need of the protection of the magic she sensed in *Faust*.

The encounter that followed, as a result, was one of the most momentous of his life. Although he could report on it and explain its repercussions for the moment only in terms of what he was then and of the needs the meeting served, the consequences continued to the end of his days and never failed to enrich his spirit. Of course, he was in a sense already a ploughed field ready for the seed of *Faust* to be sown in its soil. As a German-Swiss he was sufficiently part of the Germanic complex of European culture to be wide open for the impact of *Faust*, which, as Jakob Burckhardt observed, was fundamentally a German myth. He was, to use another Burckhardt phrase which Jung himself was to employ for a time as proxy for the term "archetype," a primordial image, but an image with a peculiarly German relevance. He was, of course, a great primordial universal as well, but nowhere in post-Renaissance Europe, the Europe of Jung and even my own later day, was the pattern of *Faust* so active, charged, and concentrated as at the heart of the German cultural complex. He experienced it first only at a personal level. He found himself utterly absorbed by it and both uplifted and relieved for the most significant of reasons.

It was not because of Faust himself. "That fellow," he told me, "made very little impression on me at my first reading. I could not guess how important he was to become, so great a bungler, such an awful amateur and fool he appeared to me. My real interest was in the devil. I hated the way Faust tricked him. I thought it unworthy both of Goethe and Faust to resort to such barefaced deceit. For although people in my world spoke a great deal about God, Old Nick was hardly ever thought worthy of a mention."

And of course, Mephistopheles meant so much to the boy Jung because it was proof at last that his own experience of darkness and evil personified in Goethe's Mephistopheles was real. The coming of Christ had not abolished them or him; they existed still active and valid as ever in life and as in *Faust* they played some mysterious role in what theologians call redemption but which he already was beginning to regard as some sort of metamorphosis or transfiguration of individual man. Over at last was the great initial battle he had fought alone and in secret against a feeling that in finding God's world not all light and love but also full of old night and unrepentant evil, he might be either mad or hopelessly in error, which shocked his love of truth even more than the prospect of partial derangement. He had the company of one of the greatest of German spirits from then on to confirm the sanity of his awareness of darkness and evil as living elements of reality.

The comfort this gave him could never be underrated. It was true that one such victory did not mean that the long campaign was over; it had barely begun. He still had a long way to go before even the full meaning of Faust's pact with the devil burst in on him, let alone disclosing its immense prophetic import for Germany and the world in the collective meaning brought into an individual focus in Goethe's drama, but the book had already become one of his great formative experiences.

"People would ask me whether I had enjoyed *Faust*," he told me with a certain indignant bewilderment. "They might as well have asked me if I had enjoyed an earthquake which had changed a familiar scene for good. Enjoyed it, my foot! But it did give me a certain uncomfortable comfort."

He was to read it again and again and was to tell a journalist years later that it was for him a pillar in the bridge of the spirit which spans the morass of world history, beginning with the Gilgamesh Epic, the Book of Changes, the Upanishads, *The Secret of the Golden*

Flower (also translated from the Chinese by Wilhelm), the fragments of Heraclites, and so on to the Gospel of Saint John, the letters of Saint Paul, Meister Eckhardt, and Dante.

The other great service rendered him by his mother, though less specific and spread over several years, often more as an atmosphere than active participation, was that she stimulated and helped him to honour his interest in the non-rational, at times, parapsychological phenomena of life so despised by the intellectual establishment of his day. The interest again came to him so naturally that he could not understand the lack of curiosity of intellect and science in such matters, quite apart from the scorn heaped upon them. It made him more aware than ever of the great divide between the natural mind, or "country mind," as he called it when safely studying medicine at Basel, and the "town mind."

He acknowledged the help science was to him in providing him with empirically established knowledge and facts. He was forever indebted to it for the discipline and method it gave to his urgent, inquiring spirit. But he was appalled by its inability to give him any real insights either into the nature of the truth it served or the material bombarding him in this preoccupied area within into which he had been born.

Much as the need for concentrating on his studies at school and university had pushed his No. 1 personality into the foreground and driven his No. 2 apparently out of sight, seen or unseen it remained at work in his imagination, and this schism he saw all round him, between first and last, primitive and civilised, science and religion, lived on as his great preoccupation. At the most the change in him for the moment had been in a reallocation of the forces of his mind and spirit between the two. He had learned no longer to speak to people out of his intuition alone. That in itself was a formidable step, considering how continuous an assault intuitive perceptions made on his attention and how much intuition was his medium. He accepted that he lived in a world where intuition had to be supported by facts and did all he could to develop his empirical faculties.

As a result the difference between his and his mother's instinctive appreciation of the non-rational aspects of reality was that he approached them also empirically. As so often when some inner crisis was coming to a climax within, chance introduced the appropriate circumstance to redirect him towards his natural course.

At a moment when the clash between his natural and cultivated selves was at its most extreme, and he may well have been seduced into the pursuit of an orthodox medical career, three totally non-rational phenomena burst in on him from the world associated with his ageing mother. In his *Memories* he gives these explosions in a different order than the one in which he mentioned them to me. Since the order is irrelevant, I relate my own version as more in keeping with what, after all, is not a study but an account of a personal experience.

He came into his home from the garden one day, he said, to find that a bread knife had exploded inside the sideboard with the sound of a pistol shot. He extracted the knife, which was broken into four neat segments. An expert who examined it was convinced the break must have been made with considerable and deliberately applied force to produce so clear-cut a result since the steel itself was flawless. Within a few days, and again in the vicinity of his mother, a walnut table, seventy years of age, split right through the top with another resounding retort, despite the humid atmosphere of the room in which it was housed.

These were non-rational intrusions on his everyday reality which his natural mind just could not ignore, and he found that for no obvious reason he connected the events with a mediumistic young girl of fifteen and a half, whom he had recently met and with whom his new empirical self was determined to experiment. Why and how had knife and table been shattered? What forces were made manifest in such a fashion? Although those were his only direct experiences of such things, he knew from history, literature, folk-lore, and hearsay that they were but two of a great legion of such occurrences. And what was at work in the spirit of the young girl connected with these events to send her into a somnambulistic twilight state and practise what were dismissed as spiritualistic phenomena? He just could not understand how persons like his mother could take so disconcerting a phenomenon for granted, or how teachers, professors, and fellow students were utterly uninterested in it.

He took it upon himself, therefore, despite the exactions of the university, to study the contents of what the girl produced in trance and other twilight states of herself. In due course he learned, he thought, how a No. 2 personality could enter a child's awareness and become an extraterritorial influence in her character capable of an autonomy and courses of action all its own. Already he had taken his first conscious step away from the mainstream of conventional science and medicine. And he was to return to the precept and question she induced in him again and again in later years. What had made her in a tranced state so good, confident, and elegant a lady of fashion, talking in an educated German totally alien to the dialect of her class, when in her natural state she appeared so ordinary and simple a girl? One cannot stress enough here how significant it was that in taking even this tentative step towards his destiny, his guide was already what one is compelled to call, for want of a better word, the abnormal and unrecognised in the feminine spirit of his day. She helped to prepare him beyond all his own expectations or the dreams and fantasies of his by now well-equipped No. 1, to be totally at the ready when the decisive catalyst appeared on the scene of his aspirations.

He came across the textbook on psychiatry by Krafft-Ebing. He had left his prescribed course in psychiatry to the last, so neglected, disdained, and remote a subject was it to him and his professors. The psychiatric case material quoted in this book, even to me reading it in a much less inhibited day, seemed almost too startling, too highly charged and powerful a stuff for even the strongest of Protestant stomachs to digest. But Jung took it all without any discernible difficulties, perhaps because it was not the case material in the book that interested him so much. Although already strongly tempted to accept a most promising offer to practise medicine from one of his more esteemed professors, he needed hardly more than a single sentence in the preface of Krafft-Ebing's book to change his mind completely. It was Krafft-Ebing's observation that madness or "psychoses are diseases of the personality." Jung had hardly to read further, for he knew at once that his future field had to be psychiatry. There alone, he was convinced, did biology and spirit, science and the demands of the soul, the discipline without and the call within, have common living ground. He believed that no one at the university would understand this step and that once more he would isolate himself from the generality of men, but inwardly he had never felt happier or more confident than when he reached this conclusion. The *two* in him at last were one.

One wonders, however, whether the others at the university

really had as little understanding as he thought and whether far more good wishes did not accompany him than he allowed his inverted senses to realise. I say this because I met in a train once in Switzerland a man whose father had been at Basel with Jung. He told me that according to his father, Jung was always "the life and soul" of the student fraternity to which they both belonged. And I myself feel always compelled to remind myself of this aspect of him when considering the book of his youthful past, so closed against the human warmth and immediacy of the man, but so open and exposed to the claims of the eternal and infinite. For among the many heroic achievements of which he proved himself capable, not the least for me is the fact that alone as he always was, wintry and bleak as the scene of childhood, youth, and coming to manhood appeared to be, he never allowed those years to become a winter of discontent but kept a midsummer night's festival of delight aflame in himself. I find it not at all strange, therefore, that sudden as the decision was, he celebrated it and the end of his university career by giving himself first a night at the theatre and then at the opera, followed by a journey to Germany, all just for the fun of it.

He enjoyed himself enormously, particularly at the opera, if enjoyment is the right word for an experience of such intensity. He saw a performance of *Carmen*, which so impressed him that the music and theme stayed with him for days. Here already there was evidence that he was not, as often alleged, indifferent to music. It was intimation only of the fact that always music meant almost too much to him.

"I listened to music only sparingly," he would tell me, "because it made me almost unbearably sad and upset me far too much, when I had enough to be upset about already."

Even if it is not on record and the detail inaccessible, I am certain from this and all I knew of him that the fun and incorrigible sense of humour, the love of life for sheer life's sake went with him also in his translation to Zürich and the staff of its great Burghölzli mental hospital. Indeed, although he was leaving Basel and the banks of the Rhine for good, it was as if he left then on a note of music discovered for the first time in himself, to go out at last a young man on his own in the external world as he had always been on his own within.

৯ The Vigil and the Summons

Naturally nature has so disposed me.
Leonardo da Vinci

JUNG LEFT BASEL for Zürich as poor as ever in a worldly sense, except, of course, that he had employment and remuneration guaranteed for the first time in his life. His baggage must have appeared extraordinarily light but yet he travelled rich and almost overloaded in spirit, so that I always feel compelled to examine the nature of this load before accompanying him further on his dangerous journey into unexplored country. As far as general possessions were concerned, I would put first the profound sense of history with which Basel had equipped him. It had done this not just by what he learned at the university itself and out of the books which he devoured there in his spare time as a famished person devours food, or from the history extracted in his intensive reading of philosophy out of a hypersensitive and highly charged interest in the subject, but also from what the city out of itself conveyed by silent implication more eloquent even than the chosen historical word. Whenever I heard him speak on a subject I was always astounded almost to the point of unbelief by his knowledge of its history, just as I was in conversation by the evidence continually

93

showered on one in relevant asides of the breadth of his reading of the humanities and indeed the literature of the world.

How he found the time to do all this among the pressures of studies, which at Swiss universities are greater than most, as well as in the midst of the proliferating demands of his inborn preoccupation and the many other calls of his family, community, and life as a student would have been a total mystery did one not know by now his overriding tendency to be solitary and his natural endowment of abundant energy.

Moreover, his energies were never exhausted, not only because he was physically strong but because he was somehow always following the mainstream of himself. He was therefore not in the position in which so many of the men and women of our time find themselves, living on the capital of their energies because, pitted as they are against their own natural selves, they do not earn new allowances of energy for themselves but merely exhaust the supply which nature had originally bestowed on them. He, on the contrary, seemed to generate more and more mental and spiritual energy for himself as he went along. Living, as it were, on interest and far from touching on the original investment of nature, he saw both volume and value grow rapidly in an age of increasing inflation of mind and being, to a point at times where one wondered whether in him energy had not accomplished the impossible of spontaneous generation.

These energies had enabled him to read widely in the philosophy most relevant to him and enabled him to find in its history some anticipatory support for his prevailing interest in dreams, symbols, fantasy, and their mechanism, all of which both contemporaries and university establishment dismissed with scorn. He had weighed his values on the scales of philosophy ancient and modern, from Heraclitus to Hegel and the Schopenhauer who gave him also a scent of the contribution the Far East one day might make to his own private and personal quest. Philosophers like Heraclitus, Abelard, and Kant excepted, his conclusions were not flattering to them because he found that like theologians they would go on delivering themselves of resounding solemnities and plausible profundities when they, as he told me once, "should have shut up and closed their big mouths until they were in possession of the facts to support their thinking."

Nonetheless, his intensive reading of philosophy and religion had provided him with a knowledge in depth of the climate of spirit in which history unfolded which few professional historians could have excelled. He knew the history of antiquity, particularly Greek and Roman antiquity, as though it were not some remote subject of academic study but an urgent and highly relevant contemporary reality. He knew it not just as the history of proven facts, statistics, and a chronological progression of external events but also through the myths and legends which it came trailing, like clouds of a forgotten dawn, glory from what had once been home for the spirit of European man.

Moreover, he would read his philosophy and history and the literature which breathed life into the facts also in the original Greek and above all Latin, because thanks to his father, he had accepted at the age of six the necessity of mastering Latin and had devoted himself to its study so ardently that he read it still at the age of eighty as if it were native to him. He knew the history of the Renaissance as well as anyone who made it a special study, and cherished it because it was a great reawakening of the spirit and its reunion with an arrested European culture, to make it a fateful turning point in the life of man. In the process, his grasp of the humanities became as great as his grip on the disciplines of science and he drew inspiration from the humanists of that great reawakening as experts in the awesome business of the decline and fall of great cultures, and examples in how the human spirit responded most creatively in such terrible moments of crisis and transition. Above all, he felt himself close to the Erasmus whom his contemporaries called Desirderius but for whom as a child I preferred the original Dutch name of Geerard because, illegitimate as he may have been born, he seemed to embody, as his Dutch name implies, not only someone utterly born of the desire of those who begat him but also out of the legitimate longing and valid need of a whole age for someone just like him, as we in my own arid day seemed to need and desperately to desire his spirit still.

There was the most moving proof of Jung's love for Erasmus as well as of the priorities of his spirit in that poor as a Basel Cathedral mouse, he spent money he could not spare at the age of nineteen, he told me, to buy in a second-hand bookstall an old copy of Erasmus in Latin. He was still reading the book with its worn leather covers when I saw him last just before he died.

All these particular aspects of his interest in history were stimulated by the fact that history at the University of Basel in Jung's day tended to be dominated by Jakob Burckhardt's illuminated passion for it. The man himself still walked the university alleyways when Jung was there, with the spirit of that other great Basel phenomenon, Bachofen, in close support. And no one could expose himself to history there without encountering the impact of Burckhardt's attitude to it, and in particular his interpretation of the volcanic phenomena of the Renaissance, the Reformation, and so on to the story of Greece, so logical and inevitable an outcome of the historian's obsession with the first and a work, alas, published only after his death. Jung had reservations about Burckhardt because he could never plunge deep enough below the surface of antiquity for the young man's needs. Yet Jung did not fail to recognise that Burckhardt had plunged deeper than most and so never ignored the new perspectives of history he made possible.

No one has portrayed the Swiss's relationship with his history and earth better than Jung. For instance, in an address on Paracelsus, the strange, early sixteenth-century physician and philosopher who had a prophetic vision, however clouded, of where Jung was to stand some four hundred years later, he defines all this with a poetic intensity which seized his pen far more often than those who read him only in translation can conceive. He does it all the more convincingly, I believe, because from what he told me, he is describing also a reflection of himself.

"The great peaks of the Alps," he wrote of Paracelsus, "rise up menacingly close; the might of the earth visibly dwarfs the will of man; threateningly alive, it holds him fast in its hollows and forces its will upon him. Here where nature is mightier than man, none escapes her influence; the chill of water, the starkness of rocks, the twisted, jutting roots of trees and precipitous cliffs, all this generates in the soul of anyone born there something that can never be extirpated, lending him that characteristically Swiss obstinacy, doggedness, stolidity, and innate pride which have been interpreted in various ways, favourably as self-reliance, unfavourably as pig-headedness. 'The Swiss are characterized by a noble spirit of liberty but also by a certain coldness which is less agreeable,' a Frenchman once wrote."

So much of history was at first almost too much for a young man so eager to press on into the future as Jung and he felt a certain relief at leaving it all behind. Zürich at a first glance related to the world not through the history and intellect but vulgar commerce and seemed a freer and more modern city, which excited him, but an invisible Basel made a city of history inviolate within his spirit and to the end of his days was there to support him at all sorts of decisive moments, so that he was never delivered of a strange, persistent nostalgia for the place that fashioned it.

Yet even more important than this wealth of history, he brought with him Niebelungen treasure straight from the bed of the Rhine in the form of two inner experiences which constituted the greatest among the secrets around which his robust spirit had grown into early manhood. They were of immense importance to the hopes he had that his new calling would enable him to understand this cataclysmic rift he had observed widening and deepening in the spirit of man between the religious and scientific needs of his being. Just as he had found theology and organised religion in their contemporary form bankrupt, science had brought no real comfort to his spirit, and it was almost as if he felt that a plague had been called down on both those houses of the spirit of man and from there made the world the pestilence-stricken place it appeared to be.

Yet poor and inadequate as they both were in their respective ways, the importance of bringing them back into some contemporary form of well-being seemed greater and more urgent than ever as he packed his bags for Zürich. He knew he was leaving a city which was a privileged law and rule to itself and where the citizens considered themselves lights of civilisation compared to the barbarians scattered among other cities, villages, valleys, and Alps of Switzerland. In particular, it was scornful of Zürich, with which it existed in a state of great rivalry if not enmity, and regarded the city on the lake as an ignoble opposite of itself, a place of gross and vulgar materialism.

Indeed, Jung himself felt there was a great deal of justice in the charge and knew that in a sense Basel was closer to his No. 2 as Zürich in the first instance might be nearer to his No. 1. It would not be without meaning to class them respectively as the No. 2 and No. 1 cities of his life, particularly as he referred to the Zürich of that day to me once as the most materialistic city in the whole of Switzerland. He confessed that ostensibly he could not have gone to a place in Switzerland less likely to provide the ideal human material for his purposes.

"Zürich taught me a valuable lesson," he would tell me. "If you waited for ideal human material in my business, you would never start. Always you must take what is nearest at hand, no matter how unpromising, and accept it as the only and therefore the best thing you can do and by sheer hard work transform it into the thing you need. You would be as surprised as I was in Zürich what can come out of the most unpromising human earth when you really try, and keep at it."

Yet I wonder whether he would have reached so mature a conclusion in Zürich had he not possessed these two great secret experiences to steer his life by and so prevent himself from becoming a victim of this great rift cleaving the human spirit in two. The Chinese say that the journey of a thousand miles begins with a single step. Jung had already taken his first recognisable step when he was barely an articulate child, just over the age of three, and as a result was further on the way than even he knew or suspected when he arrived in Zürich, thanks to the first of these great secret experiences. This was a single dream of a blinding illumination and undeniable authority, in which he went down into the earth, that great, overwhelming symbol of the everlastingly fecund and procreative feminine, and found there deep underground a monumental phallus set on a golden throne.

One of the outstanding characteristics of the Jung I came to know was that indifferent as his attitude was to the externals of his past, obedient as he was to the natural law of remembrance to which we are all subject and which compels us to recall before all else what we value most, his memory of his own dreams and fantasies was as circumspect, fastidious, and reliable as it was well-nigh incredible. He never forgot a detail of his encounters with the inner world in dream or fantasy that mattered to his development either in himself or his patients. Dreams, symbols, spontaneous imagery, and fantasy were permanent features of his real and natural world and, just like a born guide I knew in the bush and desert of Africa who would not fail to recognise a tree, incline, or dune that had marked a journey done only once forty years before as a boy of five, Jung would never forget the smallest detail of significance in the dreams and fantasies and other features of his movement through this inscape of his remotest past. I would listen to him telling me, perhaps for a third time, of a dream dreamt some sixty-five years before, as children do to the retelling of a favourite story, fearful that some cherished detail might be forgotten or changed, but his accounts never varied and, even more remarkable, lost none of their original vitality in the repetition so that one's own growing familiarity did not breed contempt for them but rather added to their wonder and meaning.

And he would tell one of this dream in a voice that even in his eighties seemed to have lost none of the awe felt over the event at the time. The phallus, he stressed, was not an organ of the human body, because it was utterly disembodied and had a large eye in it. Many years later he was to recognise a prototype in an illustration of a mythological deity of the long-forgotten past. This dream made such an impression on him that he could not speak of it to others until he was sixty-five years old, and this fact, when first he told me of it, made me recoil with horror that the world of nature could inflict so strange and cruel a vision in the silence and blackness of night on a child who could barely walk. I was not at all surprised that he could not speak of it to his elders and betters, knowing from my own experience of a Protestant culture closely resembling his how great an unmentionable sex and anything to do with it must have been. What astounded me was that so young and vulnerable a spirit could have endured all on its own so horrific a vision, until I realised that nature seldom inflicts on us, unaided and alone as we may be, anything for which it does not also provide the relevant immunities.

It takes not nature but man, his slanted societies and savage intellectualism, to force us to bear the unbearable. Somehow he took the dream upon himself alone, great a burden as its secret was for the child to carry, seeing that from then on he could never be confronted in his mind with the conception of God of his father and his world, without the dream of the phallus presenting itself, as if to say, "That may be all very well and true, but look and beware, I also am here and I too have a meaning that is not in their reckoning at all."

None of this prevented the dream from becoming a master compass of his spirit, almost an automatic pilot keeping his life on course. Even at the age of just over three, the dream directed clearly, I believe, as the other lesser dream of a burial mound on the Rhine had so timely suggested at Basel much later, that his main interest had to be, as it were, underground; that far below the solid, opaque surface of things he would find the greatest creative energies; and that it was in this collaboration of male creativeness, of which the phallus was the image, and the great feminine elements represented by the earth, that his destiny would be found.

From then on the dreaming process had become increasingly important to him, whatever the incapacity for decoding their secret intent. He told me how, more and more, dreams and visions at crucial moments in life came to keep him on the way he had to go, like those few examples already mentioned. But the real parallel, the other great secret equal to this first dream, was not another dream but a vision, another terrible imposition from within, in which he saw the cathedral of Basel on a day of unblemished sun shattered by divine excrement dropped from a golden throne on high in a bright blue sky.

Once again I recoiled at the apparent brutality of the way nature inflicted this vision on a boy only twelve years old and at the refinement of the cruelty of its timing. Heaven knows, life at school for Jung was difficult enough. There were not just the agonising difficulties of being poor and looked down upon, and in any case by nature the odd child out in a school like the Gymnasium, full of the richest and socially most privileged and conformist of children in the city. There were troubles at home and troubles within and yet for once he had left school on this particular afternoon oddly contented and reassured to the point of exultation, but as he came out of the wide gates of his school, just opposite the vast cathedral, to see the blue of the steep-angled roof all aglitter against the blue of a sky without remnant of cloud, filled with such rare feelings of well-being and confidence that God was there on high well in command of the universe and all below for the best in the best possible of moments, this vision struck like lightning and entered his mind with imagery full of unmistakable physical detail. Even to this day such a vision could hardly be the favourite intrusion on the privacy of the freest and most eclectic of imaginations, but in the nineteenth century of Jung's Switzerland its impact must have been of a ferocity incomprehensible to us today.

Yet in the years I have lived with Jung's account of these two great secret experiences, this aspect of their intrusion has been redeemed for me by the realisation of how indispensable they were to what I call to myself the great necessities of his being and of life. The first dream, in terms of these necessities, seems to me the only thing that could have protected the chosen flesh and blood of Jung against corruption from its purpose by the values of an outworn and spent world, and ensured that it should already be firmly in position in Jung's imagination before external values could entice him for themselves. Only such an impact at so virgin a moment could give a dream the authority that would make all other influences by comparison powerless and so hold the needed emerging spirit safe in its keeping.

This secret vision nine years later too in the manner of its coming seemed to me justified in the same way. It is true that one is forced never to forget how such visions were abhorred by the orthodox intellectual establishment and even regarded as highly blasphemous if not a danger to normality and sanity. For this is the means whereby one can realise the inborn courage which allowed the young Jung to admit them to himself and hold on to them. It is our only certain intimation that something in him already knew that the vision too was a continuation of the dream process, more imperative than the dream itself. I say this because I think there is an important difference between the two processes. I believe that the dream is part of the unconscious made accessible to our waking selves in sleep—a form, as it were, of unconscious consciousness. The vision, I believe, is a dream of the unconscious so charged and powerful that it breaks with startling clarity through the watchful barriers of our waking state to become a dream experienced consciously. Somehow Jung knew this, or rather allowed it to know more for him than his upbringing allowed him to know for himself, so that both vision and dream could, with an extraordinary accuracy, combine to keep his imagination in its own natural way which the whole trend of the age and all its organised knowledge not merely rejected but refused even to investigate.

Not surprisingly, with no conscious precedent to guide him, there was a stage when he took the sense of direction in which his imagination was being so impelled literally, and interpreted this kind of prompting purely on its manifest level. This is why he had been induced into believing that his most ardent wish at Basel was to become an archaeologist.

It was years before he realised that the latent meaning of this urge was indeed archaeology, but not of the physical world, not digging for lost and vanished cities of antiquity, but some archaeology of the mind aimed at uncovering amid the ruins of the modern spirit the foundations of the authentic city of the soul which once stood four-square and complete with circle of moat against the chaos and old night, wild, dark, and unformed, before the coming of the Word in the beginning and that trumpet moment when the first spirit could deliver itself of the greatest poetic statement I know: "Let there be light: and there was light."

"I was," he told me at one of our earliest meetings, "often amazed to the point of despair at the presumption of the organised knowledge and discipline of my day and their common attitude of all-knowingness which I encountered everywhere among men in command of religious, scientific, and philosophic heights. I was enraged by their lack of just ordinary, natural, healthy curiosity in what they did not know and their instant dismissal as irrelevant, superstitious, or mystical rubbish of what seemed to me pointers towards increased knowledge and new areas for investigation."

I was prompted to tell him that first evening how moved I had always been by the first people of my native country because of the feeling they gave out of utterly belonging to life and time and nature, how I found that even though they themselves may not know much, they had no doubt of being fully known wherever they went, whereas in this world and this war from which I had just come I felt that for all our pose of knowing everything, of being the greatest know-alls in history, we ourselves had utterly lost the feeling of being known.

And he slapped his hand on his knee and said, "That is precisely what I felt as a student. I started out in life with the feeling of utterly belonging, of a most wonderful sense of participation in the beauty and wonder of my surroundings, and then found myself pushed by the life of my time in a direction where the feeling was seen to vanish over the horizon and seemed permanently lost. And I knew that somehow, however necessary that separation might be, for the moment it must not be allowed to last and that if this separation was to have any meaning, I had to live life in such a way that one day I was reunited with the sense again of that all-belonging I had had in the beginning, in a greater and more meaningful measure than before."

Jung had a quality which only the greatest of intuitives possess. He felt in honour bound to stand fast in his hunches and not move on until he had proved their validity. No matter how far forward his hunch pitched him in time, he brought it back into the heat and dust of a common day and worked his way back to it empirically, with all the conscientiousness and thoroughness of a Swiss watchmaker fitting a new and infinitely complex timepiece together.

It made the charge of "mysticism" commonly hurled against him so preposterous. He told me, for instance, that he worked through 67,000 dreams with his patients and helpers before even attempting to theorise about them. He avoided theorising and attempted none except when the necessity of doing so was imposed on him by facts, and he remained all his life as in love with facts as he had been born in love with intuition.

One of his earliest hunches was that this dream he had had as a child and his vision of the shattering of the great cathedral at Basel were somehow interconnected and had a great deal to do with a mortal split in the Western European spirit which manifested itself outwardly in the increasing conflict between science and religion. Since he was the son of a minister himself, the offshoot of a long line of parsons, with a bishop or two thrown into the lineage, Jung's interest in religion had been encouraged by his inner and outer environment to be even more profound than in the science to which he was apprenticed and in whose discipline he was so highly schooled.

Yet intuitively he was convinced that the division was unnecessary as it was lethal. Both, after all, were dedicated ostensibly to the pursuit of the same truth. He expressed the dilemma in words to me which are as real and applicable now as they were in those broad, ample nineties of the last century of a Switzerland still secure in its own long summer of the mind with the harvest still to come. "In religion, even as a medical student," he said, "I found that I had utterly missed the factor of empiricism; in science I found a total absence of considerations of meaning. Something had gone terribly wrong to bring such impoverishment about and I was frightened for all of us as I had not been frightened before."

The interdependence of the two is implicit in this observation and it was a clear indication of how much more pre-prepared he was than he realised for the call to Zürich when it came. For the day he arrived at so firm a conclusion it was inevitable that sooner or later he would make it clear to all, for the first time in history, that meaning could be restored to religion only by enabling it to become the living experience for all men that it had been to him since childhood. At the same time it was only by a rededication of science to the service also of meaning that religion could receive an essential empiricism and the two join in an overall purpose wherein they should never have been allowed to divide against each other.

Since science and its method dealt with what was demonstrable, Jung hardly needed intuition to perceive what was inadequate in its approach. He had only to use those perceptive eyes of his to recognise it immediately once he started his medical training. It was another matter with religion. There his conclusion was the result of the long and painful growth which started with that first dream at the age of three. One can trace today from that remote point with an extraordinary wealth of detail the acceleration in the mind of an increasingly isolated boy, the irrevocable estrangement from all that was religiously acceptable already hinted at, until reality from within burst in as a painful boil in the vision Jung had of the shattering of Basel Cathedral.

Taken literally, of course, the vision was either blasphemous, and I have heard it denounced on many sides accordingly, or comic, and I have heard it raise the nastiest kind of laughter I know among as many others, leaving me dismayed for the persons who laughed at it. But if taken as a dream, accurately decoded the message of the vision was already plain on the day it sent the schoolboy Jung running in vain for the shelter of his father's vicarage. The excrement of the vision is an image of food which has fulfilled its function of feeding the body that has consumed it and is, therefore, expelled as waste. What the vision is telling Jung and us is that whatever the Christian church, as represented by the great cathedral on a hill overlooking the Rhine, has given as food to the religious spirit of men in the past, it has exhausted its powers of nourishment. In that shape and form it has served its purpose and ceased to be a source of living religious experience.

As remarkable as the content of the vision itself was the effect on Jung when once he admitted it into his imagination after struggling against it for some days and nights. Relief and joy over at last allowing himself to think the unthinkable was almost indescribable. The effect and meaning stayed with him always. It was, he told me, the unfailing source from which he drew the courage later to go on admitting greater and even more terrifying unthinkables into his imagination. Provided he always obeyed the will of what he thought God had precipitated unsolicited on him, however incomprehensibly, he would have the power to pursue it with the comfort of unimagined grace such obedience conferred. Indeed, the feeling of relief and joy was so great in the months that followed that he longed to share it with his parents, particularly his father, but knew that any effort to do so would fail.

Few of us to this day recognise the imperative of courage in the life of the imagination and how only courage can make it free from fear and open to the fullness of reality. Its "cliffs of fall, frightful, sheer, no-man-fathomed," demand a heart as brave as that of any soldier going into battle or that of any mountaineer pioneering a new way up Everest. Only those who have never hung over the cataclysmic abyss of their own spirit hold such exercises of the imagination cheap. Had we the means to calculate it, I believe the casualty list of individuals lost in the exploration of the untried and unknown in themselves would read like one of a world war.

From that moment on, it was inevitable that his choice of a profession would never be a partial or sided one. And it could only be the one on which he had decided because he hoped so ardently that in them alone, these divided ends, these estranged opposites of his day, were active and could be made to meet. When we consider how easily he could have become the doctor for which he had trained so long and followed a vocation for which he was exceptionally endowed, or again why he did not just turn into the philosopher or the priest which natural preoccupation and the kind of dreams and visions inflicted on him showed him also to be inclined, we can only make a respectful obeisance to the power and clarity of his intuition and determine to work more on what we and others have of it as he followed and developed his own.

For just as the instinct of the physicist was compelling men to explore the nature and nuclear tensions of the atom as a gateway into the mystery of matter, Jung was propelled into walking an untrodden way towards the meaning of which the science and religion of his day appeared so deprived, just by a hunch that it might be found in the tensions and disturbances of the rejected and despised atoms of humanity locked out from so-called normality of life in the lunatic asylums of his day.

So on the 10th December of the year 1900, at the beginning of our desperate century, Jung reported for work at the great Burghölzli mental hospital situated on a woodland fringe of Zürich. It is almost as if the symmetry of meaning of which I have already written wanted to demonstrate thereby that a new era was beginning also in the mind of man. Besides, there were other parallels to give this symmetry a substance, more concrete than those summed up in the aspirations of the apprentice that Jung still was, however gifted and unusual for his years.

It was first of all the year wherein Freud had published *The Interpretation of Dreams.* Many years later when Freud died, Jung used the cliché "epoch-making" to describe this work, because for once there was no other phrase, no matter how inventive, to better it. All one can do perhaps is to extend the phrase, to bring out into the open what it merely implies, and add that it was also an epoch-shattering work. It would be hard to say which of the many areas of the great Victorian world still so sure of itself and its values was the more outraged by Freud: science, philosophy, religion, or all the complex vested interests of mind, morals, and conventions of the entrenched, apparently idealistic and rationally conditioned spirit of the time. Almost every level of educated society felt itself oddly insulted, perhaps because, to use the new word from which it recoiled, it was unconsciously aware that it was irrevocably undermined and could never be the same again. Much of what was hypocritical, Pharisaic, and unreal in its pretensions could no longer even plead ignorance as an excuse in the new court of law of the spirit Freud's findings constituted.

The gloomy Dean Swift once wrote that you could tell a man of genius by the sign that the dunces were all in confederacy against him. One could, alas, have measured the originality of Freud's achievement even more by the numbers of the highly intelligent, best informed of men instantly mobilised to attack him because the world of appearances in which they had their self-importance, and which their mind and imagination had served as if it were the only permanent and worthwhile dimension of reality, was suddenly shown to be only one aspect of reality, and a rather shallow one at that, and they just had had notice duly served on them that there was a far greater world underneath of which they had never had the faintest suspicion. Ironically enough, the time was fast coming when even this first historic penetration of Freud into an unconscious of man—or "subconscious," as it was first called—was to be seen for the prospector's shaft it was, sunk only just deep enough beneath the skin of appearances to prove that there was much more to be mined below of infinite depth and width and wealth of meaning.

But for the moment, it was more than any establishment at the beginning of the century could take, particularly as the greatest driving force in this underworld, according to Freud, was sex, so savagely repressed in Victorian man and the object already of some two thousand years of either total denigration or at the best lofty condescension and patronising tolerance from the Christian heights of European culture. The implications of Freud's findings, moreover, were all the harder to bear because they made highly respected values of ethics, behaviour, knowledge, and science villains in the piece of their own history and implied that mental sickness, derangement, and disorder of spirit could originate in their own wilful repression of age-old impulses in man.

Nor was Freud's revelation of disturbances in the human spirit caused by unconscious forces, the only portent of decline and fall and change they had to face. The suspect German concept of a *Zeitgeist*, a specific of spirit universally valid in a given moment of time, has a far greater meaning than our rational-oriented world is prepared to concede.

Similar portents were gathering everywhere in fields other than those of science and religion, like that vortex of black crows which Vincent van Gogh, in whom a prophetic unrest was already present as a fever in every stroke of his urgent brush, painted into the corner of his most disconcerting landscape of a piece of Provence yellow with the corn of some last, rich summer as of spirit fulfilled and never to recur again. Jung himself had read the portent as accurately in art and literature as he had in science and religion. The natural processes of examination of his own self and his time, encouraged by Goethe and Goethe's *Faust*, were converted into an early warning system by his encounter with Nietzsche, who had also been a brilliant if outrageously controversial professor at Basel. Unfortunately, like *Faust*, Nietzsche's *Also Sprach Zarathustra* failed to have the significance for the English-speaking world which it possessed and still possesses for the complex of German culture.

Zarathustra, written years before Dostoevsky's work, had already been almost too much for Jung. Its impact was profound, more because of the unfathomable depths of unexplored forces in man it revealed than because of the inhuman heights to which Nietzsche aspired. All that Jung had inherited so richly of the values of the earth protected him against any temptation to emulate this soaring vision of superman which Nietzsche evoked and which was already present like a virus incubating at the heart of the German nation which had produced him. Grateful as Jung was to Nietzsche for this new perspective in depth, he saw the disproportion, the pathological morbidity in Nietzsche so clearly that he slammed the door firmly on his own No. 2 personality, which might have tended to identify with this ambitious modernised projection in fiction of the constantly recurring ancient in the primordial spirit which *Zarathustra* represented in such perilous excess. The door was not to be opened again for a number of fateful years, during which Jung devoted all he had of heart, mind, passion, and thoroughness to his new calling as a psychiatrist at the Burghölzli hospital.

To this day the Burghölzli is one of the great mental hospitals of the world. It is impossible to visit it even now, as I have on occasion had to do, and not be moved by what is done there with compassion, imagination, and dedication for those who have found it impossible to endure the world on the exacting terms we who live in it not only endure but encourage and maintain.

But it is not so exceptional today, I believe, as it was on the day when Jung first arrived there to work under the remarkable Eugen Bleuler. Jung never ceased to stress how much his own development owed to Bleuler. Over and over again, when accused of ingratitude to Freud and betrayal of the Freudian school, of which he was popularly regarded as a graduate, he would assert not without indignation that he was never of the school of Freud.

"Eugen Bleuler and Pierre Janet were my teachers," he would tell me, and stress that to Bleuler in particular he had always felt grateful for the encouragement he gave him as a young man and for the example he set of total respect for his vocation as a psychiatrist. Above all, Jung felt indebted to the exacting methods of observation of all forms of hallucination and derangement he acquired from him. His own work was destined to take him far away from the world of psychiatry but the method of accurate, unflinching observation he learned from Bleuler at the Burghölzli never failed to keep him company. "It helped me more than I can say," he told me, "in dealing with the totally unanticipated and the unknown."

Yet Jung could not have acquired this much had he not arrived at the Burghölzli utterly prepared to give it and its methods every conceivable chance within himself first. He went there, as I have stressed, with the door firmly shut on his No. 2 personality, which since boyhood had the disconcerting, one is inclined to say infernal, knack of intrusion into his daily round, weighing in the scales of experience of life's primordial past everything that his worldly No. 1 self had done, or was intending to do, and in the process finding the boy wanting. Jung could therefore say for the first time almost since that moment without stain in the beginning at Laufen on the Rhine, some twenty-three years before, that for the time his life appeared to have taken on an undivided reality. He surrendered himself entirely to what was best in his No. 1 and entered the world of so-called normal men and the kind of no-man's-land which they in their normality based on averages and externals called the region of the abnormal, like someone, as he put it later, entering a monastery dedicated to the commonplace and banal.

His interest in all these strange, non-rational phenomena and the dark, unexplored areas of the spirit which his No. 2 was already bringing to his attention were put firmly almost like some diabolical temptation behind him. He was henceforth determined to be, he declared, "all intention, consciousness, duty, and responsibility." For six months he locked himself within the limits set by the Burghölzli to get to know the life and spirit of the asylum. Yet with that incredible thoroughness of his he found time among other things to read through some fifty volumes of the *Allegemeine Zeitschrift für Psychiatrie* right from its beginning. But unseen and locked out as it was, his No. 2, through these two master secrets of dream and vision and other subtle means, was always near and as active as ever.

Indeed, the fact that its subtle magnetic attraction, beneath the surface of the activities of the young psychiatrist, was still very much a force in being seems to be apparent in both the motive for this self-imposed incarceration and the consequences of his half-year of monastic dedication to the world of appearances and its barren and unending routine. The motive stemmed from a firm belief implicit in him already at Basel after his reading of Krafft-Ebing that delusion and hallucination could not just be dismissed as symptoms of a disease of personality but somehow, somewhere, must have an important human significance. He wanted desperately to know how the human mind reacted to the sight of its own destruction. And as he moved through the wards so full of people who had either rejected or been deprived of normality, he was increasingly tormented by the question: what really takes place inside the mentally ill?

He was so amazed how little this question and all it implied bothered his colleagues that he found himself observing them almost as much as their patients and began to suspect that there might be some strange interdependence between what passed for normal and what was condemned as abnormal. He began to suspect that there could be a pathological element in what paraded so confidently as normality around him. The conviction grew that no knowledge of the problem confronting him would be complete which did not include the study of both, so that at the end of some six months the vow was not broken so much as absolved by some inner dispensation of the rule of truth. His life at the Burghölzli ceased to be monastic and took on increasingly the nature of an apprenticeship to something immeasurably greater to come.

Were one to give this new period the name it would have merited in the Arthurian age and its Round Table, the legends and stories of which had been one of the great formative influences of his imagination as a boy, and of which he was to dream again at a cross-road of himself at the appointed time and place, these were years of vigil during the long night of the initiation of the esquire into knighthood, before the coming of the day in which it could set out on its first chivalrous errant as armed in spirit as it would be properly equipped and horsed in the world without. That is why I have felt compelled to call this chapter of his life one of vigil and summons. And this heraldic parallel is for me all the more accurate because the summons to come was to be from the imperilled feminine to whose service the original knight was pledged, and for which he had been rehearsed already, as it were, by his meeting with that young girl near Basel who, though born to a modest station in life, had possibilities of grandeur and nobility so great locked up in her that in moments of trance she became articulate in a German of the most impeccable and elegant kind.

Jung turned to all this discredited human material in the Burghölzli from then on not as someone who knew any of the answers for them or for himself but as someone hoping to learn some of the answers from them. Unlike his colleagues, he no longer set

himself alone or apart from the inmates. He did not regard himself
as a repository of the one and only, the final and absolute concept of
sanity. He went to work conscious of agonising conflicts in himself
between two apparently irreconcilable poles of the spirit which he
had experienced ever since the age of three when he was first locked
out from that sense of everything being totally and utterly
wonderful which he had felt in his pram in the garden of the
vicarage on the banks of the Rhine. He approached the community
of the mentally disturbed more and more as someone who was a
mere acolyte in what Saint Paul called the "priesthood of the
suffering."

Encouraged only by an unproved intuition that if somehow,
somewhere, he could find an intimation of the causes of all that
suffering and a hint of its meaning, he would come to some
understanding of both his own conflict and that of the deep and
increasingly dangerous split in the contemporary spirit which either
kept him awake or appeared as a nightmare in his sleep. It was
almost as if in derangement and suffering there were an as yet
unlived meaning crying out for attention to its need of being
allowed to live in the life of the sufferer and his society. But how did
it come about? He was certain it was due in part to the fact that his
and their time too were out of joint but, unlike Hamlet, did not
curse the spite that he was born to it. His one concern was what
could he, Jung, do to set it right.

He was certain now that mental disturbances and even the most
profound derangement of the human personality were not mere
diseases of the mind but, like the dreams and visions, behavior of a
human meaning, as it were, in code. If only he could break the code
and transcribe it in a contemporary idiom, making it accessible to
himself and others, much of the problem would be solved. In all this
he was much closer to the patients than he was to his own
profession.

He could not make his peace with the blindness of his colleagues'
assumption that there was no sense to be found in the condition of
their patients and that what was needed was more of the medicine of
the very forms of normality which had failed them and had played
no small part in the shattering of their personalities. Much as the
Burghölzli gave him of method, therefore, it would be wrong to
imply that he did not find it lacking in insights. The more he

marvelled at the fact that his colleagues looked on the symptoms of derangement as if they were the disease itself and remained utterly disinterested in the content to which the symptom tried in vain to direct their attention, the less could he feel himself secure in what passed for normality. So for all his training in a great scientific discipline and his own increasingly well-adapted social personality, he felt more and more involved with the sick than with colleagues who administered to them from the height of a presumption that all was well within themselves.

How right he was in this and how much he gained thereby was ultimately evident in the fact that these lost souls so rejected by the normality of his time were forever remembered each in his, or more often her, own disinherited right and figured almost as fairy-tale characters in his recollection of the emotions and labour of that time in the tranquillity of his old age at Bollingen. Here he could say to one, with the assurance of someone who knew that his only armour in the encounter with death so near was sheer unmitigated observance of truth, that the men and women who had given him most in life were not persons whom the world considered great, and of whom he had met more than most, but the unrecognised, unacknowledged, and anonymous of his and their own day.

There was, for instance, the case of a woman who had been declared totally insane. To the end of his days, Jung still spoke of her with an animation as if all had happened only the day before. She would make remarks like "I am the Lorelei." The doctors would take this as conclusive evidence of her insanity. But Jung, so he told me, thought immediately, there must be some reason why she calls herself the Lorelei. What can it possibly be? And he went on to recite the lines of Heine's poem to himself until he realised that he already had her clue in the opening line: "Ich weiss nicht, was soll es bedeuten" (I do not know what it can possibly mean).

Obviously the woman was not so mad that she had not registered with some despair how these lines described precisely what the great specialists thought of her and her condition. She would reiterate the remark "I am Socrates' deputy," which appeared even more meaningless to Jung's colleagues, but following the same instinct and using the same sort of mental procedure that was soon to become part of an established method, Jung concluded that this woman was telling him and all around that, like Socrates' deputy, she was falsely accused and that this label of insanity was wrongfully applied to her, hinting perhaps that there might be no form of madness so great that it did not have some sanity disguised within it.

Most remarkable of all, she would declare extremities of the seemingly absurd like "I am plum cake on a corn-meal bottom," or "Naples and I between us must supply the world with spaghetti." Such remarks raised many an amused if not derisive smile even more frightening than those smiled over the vision I have mentioned. But to Jung they were the most significant of all her utterances, because it was evidence of some law of creative compensation still at work in a profoundly troubled spirit; some sign of a feather still stirring with the life of a desire at heart to raise itself above this lack of recognition and unknowing experienced in a despised, abnormal state; a longing to put itself back once more in an important and useful role in the world of ordinary men and women. It was as if behind the dark, opaque screen of derangement there stood another woman longing to join in the life of her time, observing and deploring the tyranny of spirit standing between her and her desire.

Over the years Jung spent many hours with her and I was always impressed how what must have been his compassion for her in the first instance had been transformed into genuine affection if not love for her, judging by the clarity and warmth with which he remembered her in his own old age. Though he came to her too late to cure her, he told me he learned far more from her than from any of his colleagues. She was to provide also an indication of how fundamentally Jung's and Freud's characters differed and how it was inevitable that they would not go on long together. When Jung took Freud to see her after eight years at the Burghölzli, Freud declared at the end of an expression of somewhat perfunctory interest in the patient that he could not understand how Jung could have spent so much time with such "a phenomenally ugly female," a remark which surprised as it shocked and dismayed Jung.

The fault of not understanding the deranged like this old lady, Jung was now convinced, lay with the psychiatrists and their failure to realise that even in the most gravely disturbed of spirits, there was embedded something fundamental also of themselves. As a result, he threw the whole of himself into the task of understanding the estranged, averted, wounded personalities confronting him, committing himself to as total an act of participation as possible.

No fantasy, statement, gesture, or remark was any longer dismissed off-hand as meaningless but was treated as if somewhere in Jung himself it would have a particle of itself to echo or reflect, so that he would be able to recognise it in terms of "reality" as he knew it. He told me that even faced with persons who had not uttered a word for years, he would refuse to accept defeat and would watch them closely. When he saw a frown or other expression appear on their faces, or even just an unwarranted gesture accomplished with their hands, he would repeat as best he could the expression and gesture himself, trying to think at the same time of the first thing his act of imitation brought to mind. He would then put it in words to the patient and was amazed how often thereby he established contact, broke the silence, and in time established a dialogue that led to a cure more often than he had hoped for, and certainly at a rate that the Burghölzli had never experienced. All of this, of course, needed not so much confidence—for how could anyone have been confident in so strange and unexplored a region—as the rarest of courage of his untried and unproved intuitions and courage also, I hasten to add, of a unique and distinctive moral kind.

I think always in this regard of a case he was fond of quoting, which he discussed once at length with me, referred to in many of his writings, and described in detail during a series of seminars in London organised between the wars by Hugh Crichton-Miller, who was one of the first psychologists of real distinction as well as great originality to recognise Jung's work in England. The case for me has been of singular importance, not only for what it taught me about the quality of Jung as a young man but also for what I believe it revealed of the nature and origin of moral necessity in the spirit of man. Far from being merely a pragmatic expedient of man and his societies or the expression of religious principles in social codes and conventions of human behaviour, an imperative pattern seems to me exposed in this case as if it were a basic element in the nature and structure of the universe itself. It seems one inalienable aspect of the law and order creation brought to chaos and old night in the beginning. However provisional and imperfect a particular ethical pattern in a specific culture may be, however relative its historical significance and however constant the need for scrupulously reappraising and changing it, nonetheless it represents one of the great, natural, indestructible necessities of life, time, and the universe without which no culture, society, or individual can achieve any given state of meaning. It seemed to me from that day on when Jung, in the deep, sonorous voice that rose up in him whenever he was speaking of anything that had particular meaning for him, first told me the story, as if there were a reflection deep within the life of man of all the universe had of law to keep sun, moon, planets, and stars in motion on their appointed courses, and that without such a condition of law and order, both stars and men would be thrown into disorder wherein all would be shattered in a collision of irresistibles, great and small, with equal and opposite immovables.

Inevitably, therefore, this story was of a moral disorder which challenged Jung's own moral order within. He had not been at the Burghölzli long when he was presented with a woman who was classified as schizophrenic and given the poorest of diagnostic hopes of a cure. Jung put all he knew of fantasy, dreams, and his new evolving word-association system into his encounter with this woman. In essence, the woman's immovable depression was a consequence of the fact that while deeply in love with sociably the most desirable of men, she had married another. She had two children by her unloved husband when five years after the marriage she learnt that her first love would probably have returned her own. This knowledge plunged her into a profound depression. She lived in a district where the water was notoriously impure and yet, while bathing her children one night, allowed her young girl, who was her favourite, to sip up the bath water from a sponge without attempting to stop her. What is more, she gave her little son impure water to drink although there was pure spring water kept for drinking.

As a result the young daughter died of typhoid; the son was not affected. It was clear to Jung from all he learnt that the woman, unconsciously or half-consciously, by deed of omission or active participation, was accomplice to the fact of murder of her daughter and the attempted murder of her son. Obviously she was not schizophrenic at all, but weighed down with a burden of guilt and outrage of natural law. What was he to do?

He had no precedent to guide him. He knew he could not consult his colleagues. He had to solve the problem on his own with the chance, judging by the assumptions of his time, that if he faced the profoundly disturbed soul in front of him with exposure of guilt it might shatter her as well as ruin his career. And it was as if somewhere within what was, in the best of all possible senses, a deep and utterly committed Protestant self, there came a summons as from one of the greatest New Testament exhortations: "And ye shall know the truth and the truth shall make you free."

He confronted the woman with the truth and in two weeks he was able to discharge her. Moreover, even then he did not refer to his unorthodox method and its success to his colleagues. It was the first intimation that in him already the task of healing depended basically on an element in the relationship of healer and sick that was sacred and that whatever success or need for judgement might be implicit in its undertaking, it belonged to life and the mystery of its creation and not the psychiatrist who had been midwife to the occasion. So Jung kept the woman's secret to himself as rigorously as the most dedicated priest kept any knowledge gained from confession. Seeing how much the age believed in judgement and how great its capacity for moral condemnation, he concluded with a compassion, rare as it is moving, that life had already judged and punished the woman enough and that life could only gain by taking her back to atone for an offence against natural law. By living in the world again, as she had been unable to before, she might bear the load of her guilt as if it were a sort of transformer of whatever negative that chance could put in her way.

This story, so charged with universal application for me, was soon to be confirmed by another encounter Jung had, not with a patient but with a woman who came to him out of her own accord. She arrived at his office one morning, refused to give her name, and was to walk out of both the office and Jung's life without revealing it. Knowing Jung, I am certain that if he had thought the name important he would have somehow elicited it from her, but I believe the fact that she was so obviously in desperate need of help was enough for him. She admitted only that she was a doctor and went on to confess that many years ago she had killed her best friend in order to marry her husband. The murder was never discovered and in due course she married the man and had a daughter by him. Consciously she had no moral compunction over what she had done—less even than Raskolnikov, in Dostoevsky's *Crime and Punishment*, because unlike him she had none of the unease of spirit that compelled him unerringly towards atonement.

Such unease as there was appears to have been felt by nature and the atmosphere of murder communicated itself to all around her through the damage it had done to her own inner personality. First, her husband died soon after the marriage. The daughter grew up estranged from her, and ultimately vanished without trace from her life. Her friends one after the other abandoned her and soon even the animals she loved appeared afraid of her. For instance, she loved riding but had to give it up because the horses she had hitherto managed so well became nervous of her and shied; ultimately she was thrown by one of her favourite mounts. She was left only with her dogs and clung to them as the deranged Lear had done as the only "friend to man" left. Then her favourite dog too had to be destroyed and she could bear this exile from life and nature no longer. She came to Jung to confess, and after confession left, and he was to see and hear of her no more.

But the vision of the woman and her total, insupportable alienation from life and nature inflicted on her by the murder stayed with him to the end. He found it important enough to select it from thousands of other encounters to refer to her even in his autobiography, observing there that though one could keep such things secret in oneself, one could not prevent life from knowing it from the consequences of the murder one had done to oneself in the process.

"Sometimes it seems as if even animals and plants 'know' it," he says. And I extract this comment from many others of possibly even greater significance because when he told me of this case in the bitter winter of 1955 at Ascona, I told him how it reminded me of a primitive people I knew in the interior of Africa. They believed that there was no secret so small that nature sooner or later would not extract it. They held in particular that if a person had been guilty of some great natural evil, even the grasses would accuse him of it in the sound they made against his feet as he went walking through them. They had told me a story which everyone among them accepted as an empirical fact, of a man who had murdered a woman unobserved in a dark wood in circumstances incapable of detection. He had buried her deep in the ground and covered the place with leaves and strewn grass. Yet as he walked home a small bird appeared on the branch of a tree in front of him saying, "You are the killer of 'Nshalalla" (the woman's name). He tried again and again to kill the bird, but in vain. It kept him company to the edge of the village, where all could hear him accused of the crime. And I added, perhaps unnecessarily, that for this people, judging by their myths and stories, a bird always represented, as they put it, the thing which they could not have thought of for themselves. I went on to say how impressed I had been ever since the war, during my exploration of bush and desert, by the extent to which one's own most secret intent for being there seemed to make itself known to the nature of insect, beast, bird, and even plant around one. I could, of course, not prove it but it was something I had never thought of before, let alone looked for, and was imposed, as it were, objectively on me and my feelings, however intangible.

I would find, for instance, that when I moved through the bush, to all appearances dressed and equipped in the same manner as for many weeks and always carrying the same gun, the atmosphere and behaviour of all around me changed subtly but considerably on the days when I had to shoot buck or bird for food, and differed totally from the times when I had no need or other motive for killing. I told him that this was not only my experience but also that of many of the most perceptive of the many great hunters, primitive as well as "civilised," I had known. Besides, there were all the many references in Shakespeare's *Macbeth* to what murder did to the murderer and the unknowing ones around him. I remembered the lines:

> Stones have been known to move and trees to speak;
> Augurs and understood relations have
> By maggot-pies and choughs and rooks brought forth
> The secret'st man of blood.

He looked at me and said quietly and rather sadly to himself, "And even so, they go on denying the reality of the collective unconscious!"

Through encounters with disturbed and deranged personalities such as these elaborated here, and others in numbers far too great not just for inclusion in my own experience of his life but greater than even he could record in the profusion of lectures and seminars, books, essays, letters, and other writings that fell from him in the course of his long years like the leaves of a great maple set on fire by some Fall of time, Jung came to the conclusion that every human being had a story, or to put in its most evolved form, a myth of its own. It was as ironic and devastating to him at the beginning of the century as it should today be even more so to us, who persist in the same error, that the word "myth" in common usage was the label applied to what the rationalist in command of the day dismissed as illusion, non-existent, apocryphal, or some other of the proliferating breed of reductive words the cerebral norms of our time produce for dismissing the existence of any invisible and non-conceptual forms of reality. Yet one has only to read Jung's own stories of his encounters with patients in hospital and private consulting room to realise that one is in the presence of a new phenomenon in the life of our time.

I can understand myself in a sense the literal object-obsessed scientist not seeing their obvious significance, although I cannot understand how he continues to ignore their proven therapeutic importance or how the artist in man and the free-ranging spirit of any imaginative individual can go on failing to recognise that these accounts are charged with material of illumination and transfiguration of the highest order. Even in their much abbreviated form in Jung's autobiography, it is clear to me that they are the nearest modern equivalent to the parable used to such everlasting effect in the New Testament and in their Far-Eastern kinsfolk, also so creatively in the stories which are the milestones on the road of Zen and constitute the organic precedents which took the place of dogma, metaphysics, and theology in its development in Japan.

Jung said that he learned from the start how in every disturbance of the personality, even in its most extreme psychotic form of schizophrenia, or dementia praecox as it was then called, one could discern the elements of a personal story. That story was the personality's most precious possession, whether it knew that or not, and the person could only be cured—or healed, as he put it, always preferring to any other modern substitute the word which proclaimed through itself its classical origin and historical continuity—by the psychiatrist getting hold of the story. That was the secret key to unlock the door which barred reality in all its dimensions within and without from entering the personality and transforming it. More, he held that the story not only contained an account of the particular hurt, rejection, or trauma, as other men were hastening to call it, but the potential of wholesome development of the personality. This arrest of the personality in one profound unconscious timeless moment of itself called psychosis, he would tell me, occurred because the development of the person's own story had been interrupted, however varied, individual, and numerous the causes of the interruption. All movement of the spirit and sense of beginning and end had been taken away from it and the story, like the sun in the midst of Joshua's battle against the Amorites, suddenly stood still.

"The hell of the mad," he once told me, "is that not only has time suddenly ceased to exist for them but some memory of what it and its seasons meant to them once remains to remind them of the fact that it is no longer there."

He was rapidly learning even from the nature of some specific hallucination, delusion, psychosis, or neurosis how a personal story was clamouring to be carried on and lived. Even more, he recognised from what his own dreams meant to him how dreams were an essential part of the evolution of the story, if not creator and promoter of it. But none of these things, he stressed, were ever there just for the asking. They could be discovered only by a constantly reiterated, truthful, and face-to-face encounter between patient and psychiatrist. Already he was beginning to see psychiatry in terms of a dialogue at the deepest level between his own outer and inner self and the patient. Without such an interchange, in which both the reality of the psychiatrist and deprivation of reality of the patient faced each other openly as problems to each other, the vital secret remained hidden.

A vital difference of approach to that of Freud was symbolised in its simplest and most direct form. In Jung's consulting room both he and patient sat opposite each other as two human beings joined in mutual consultation over an interdependent problem directed to a resolution important to both, whereas in that of Freud and his followers the patient lay stretched out on a couch and the psychoanalyst sat invisible and behind the patient, listening to what he had to tell, rarely taking part, and in the end delivering judgement according to a preconceived rule on what had been so impersonally revealed.

Moreover, Jung did not regard this story and the secrecy which he had to extract for the purposes of healing as his own. Since it was to him, as must again be stressed, so great a point of departure it was to become, the most precious of the patients' possessions, its extraction was justifiable only because he needed it for the destruction of the inner barrier, whether thrown up by injury or neglect in the world without or self-inflicted from within. Once this provisional demolition task was done, he held, with all the passion for living truth which possessed him, that the sooner the story was returned to the patient for private and personal keeping, the better.

It is, therefore, of the utmost importance to realise the clear limits he set to the uses of what we call understanding. He never confused understanding and knowledge or made it dependent on knowing. It is true that knowledge and observation obviously played a great role in the process, but understanding for him was far more than mere knowing, even more than what we can conceive of understanding itself with all the non-rational elements of awareness we can add to it.

"Nothing worse could happen to one than to be completely understood," he told me once, with a twinkle of mischief in an acute glance and an almost *Mona Lisa* smile of the inspired irony native to living wisdom. "One would be instantly deprived of one's personal *raison d'être* if one were. I'd hate it myself. I learnt very early on at the Burghölzli how hurtful it could be to my patients to give them a feeling that I knew and understood them better than they did themselves."

The only creative and helpful form of knowledge and understanding, he would elaborate, was one that grew naturally out of a process of respectful interchange as of two clouded and mutually searching souls. There was a way of understanding, he discovered, that was not understanding which came out of respect for the mystery of the otherness of the human being. No two persons or cases were alike. It is true that a psychiatrist had to have a method as a kind of compass, but there were as many exceptions to prove its rule as there were cases, and each one had to be treated as different and on its own merits.

Even when he felt convinced he knew the solution to a person's problem it was not for him to proclaim it but to hold back and use it only in so far as it helped to lead the patient to recognise it for himself. Once the patient discovered it, the sooner the transfigurative knowledge was handed over to him the better, and the sooner the psychiatrist forgot it himself even better still.

I wish that I could quote in full here something Jung wrote about understanding the modern way, as far back as 1915 during the First

World War, when he himself was almost overwhelmed by problems of understanding his own secret self. This was a long letter to Hans Schmid, who was himself a psychotherapist, a friend and pupil who had helped Jung a great deal in his work on psychological types. Jung could write to him on the subject as to few others without fear of being misunderstood. Although the letter was written after he left the Burghölzli, its origin and application belong so much to his point of departure there that I recommend its reading in full for the total grasp it reveals of the paradoxical nature of living understanding. Here I can only quote what seems to me relevant and synchronised with the rapidly evolving psychologist at the Burghölzli.

"Understanding is a fearful binding power," he wrote, "at times a veritable murder of the soul as soon as it flattens out vitally important differences. The core of the individual is a mystery of life, which is snuffed out when it is 'grasped.' That is why symbols want to be mysterious; they are not so merely because what is at the bottom of them cannot be clearly apprehended. . . . All understanding in general, which is a conformity with general points of view, has the diabolical element in it and kills. It is a wrenching of another life out of its own course, forcing it into a strange one in which it cannot live. . . . True understanding seems to me to be one which does not understand, yet lives and works. . . . We should bless our blindness for the mysteries of the other; it shields us from devilish deeds of violence. We should be connivers at our own mysteries but veil our eyes chastely before the mystery of the other, so far as, being unable to understand himself, he does not need the 'understanding' of others."

"I was standing in my garden," he says about a dream he had, "and had dug open a rich spring of water that gushed forth. Then I had to dig another deep hole, where I collected all the water and conducted it back into the depths of the earth."

Nowhere else have I encountered as in this dream so rounded a definition of Jung's approach to others and in particular of the essence of what he evolved as an instrument of healing in the Burghölzli. It was as if the scientist, the dreamer, the visionary, the subject of the mighty activity within himself he had in adolescence termed God, and something of the artist in him, had all joined forces, enabling him to receive the secret meaning of the symbol in the personal story of the sick confronting him and once having received it, returning it immediately, like the water in the dream to the earth, to the hidden eternally feminine in the human personality for reconception, protected gestation, and rebirth, where the minds, prejudices, predilections, and preferences of others could not get at it.

I had dropped in at Zürich on my way back to England from Africa, as had become almost a matter of routine since our first meeting. Apart from a longing to see him again, I wanted to ask his permission to dedicate a book to him. In the process I told him that it was about the first people of South Africa, their stories, and the meaning their stories possessed for them as well as myself and could possess, I hoped, also for the world. I remember how keen his attention became when I told him how difficult it had been to get the Bushmen concerned to tell me their stories. I was as always at that moment amazed by his capacity for listening when he himself was constantly almost bursting at the seams with things to say. One had only to put a worthwhile question to him to release a flood, not out of any egotistical source or personalistic urging but purely from the constant fountain inflow of new perceptions and fresh inspiration as well as information and wisdom stored up in him as in a reservoir built against a great drought in the life of man. In this regard he always made me think of Bach, whose *Kunst der Fugue*, the last of his works, was for me a kind of compendium of revelations to all the composer had written before. Perhaps surprisingly for someone accused of indifference to music, Jung had listened and relistened to its twenty fugues and canons with great care and out of a feeling that it could tell him more of the nature of music than perhaps any other composition. I remembered a story of how Bach was approached by a young admirer one day and asked, "But, Papa Bach, how do you manage to think of all these new tunes?"

"My dear fellow," Bach is said to have answered, according to my version. "I have no need to think of them. I have the greatest difficulty not to step on them when I get out of bed in the morning and start moving around my room."

Jung, I believe, could have said the same about the material petitioning and crowding his imagination, as is obvious from the abundance of his work right to the end. Yet in conversation he was the best of listeners and on this occasion interrupted only once with the question, "And those resistances to telling you their stories, what did you do about them?"

I explained how baffled and even hurt I had felt about the refusal of this desert people to tell me their stories, all the more because they had lied to me and had said they did not know what I meant by "stories." They said they were only poor old Bushmen who had never heard of such things. Yet I knew from the history of my own family, who had been in contact with them for some three centuries, that they were perhaps the greatest story-tellers Africa had ever known. I remember how happily Jung laughed when I went on to tell him about an old Bushman grandmother in this regard. I had gone to her one evening because I had heard a young hunter, who was my favourite companion, whisper to his youngest brother to take a tortoise they had just found as a present to his grandmother, saying that she would undoubtedly reward him by telling him a story. Immediately I decided that I would be there to hear it. But when the moment came and the old lady was eating the great delicacy which a tortoise baked in its shell was to them all, with the young children gathered round her, no story was told and only the most trivial of polite exchanges put in its place, until I protested, "But, Grandmother, I thought you were going to tell us all a story tonight."

"Excuse me, please," the old lady replied. "I am utterly deaf."

"It is true what she says." All the others who by now had joined the children loyally came to her support. "She is very deaf and cannot hear what you say."

"You see," the old lady hastened to add, "you must listen to what they say. I am very deaf and cannot hear what you say."

Of course I joined in the laughter and was inexplicably moved because suddenly I thought I saw the motive behind the resistances and how what I called lying was justified, as any lie is justified to prevent a person holding a pistol at one's head from pulling the trigger. I realised that the story was their most precious possession and that they were protecting it as best they could. They knew how dangerous it was to have a foreigner, above all a white foreigner, in on the secret of any of their stories, because he might destroy it either by making fun of it, using it against them, or merely not joining in its progression as they did.

I was aware at the same time of something allegorical in the moment, an illustration of how we Europeans have destroyed primitive societies and even more sophisticated cultures the world over by taking away or rejecting the story which was seed and essence of their history, their present and future. Even with the best of motives, as in the sudden imposition of our version of Christianity on primitive societies, we had been thieves and killers of some aboriginal story and so deprived them of their own particular reason for being what they were—indeed, had at one stroke deprived both their yesterdays and today of meaning and purpose.

I realised there and then, I told him, that without a story of its own no culture, society, or personality could survive and I tried no more to get stories from them. Happily the time came when I had proved somehow that I could be trusted, and of their own accord they told me stories. When they saw how honoured and delighted I was by this, they themselves appeared to find a new meaning and almost ecstasy in delivering their myths and legends to me.

To my amazement Jung thanked me in a manner that was almost overwhelming, even for someone whom I always found most fastidious and circumspect in his treatment of a guest, someone who the French would have said possessed not so much the ceremoniousness that passes for good manners among so many races as real *politesse de coeur*.

These resistances I had mentioned, he said, were so like those he encountered in the society of the sick at the Burghölzli. He had to learn to respect those resistances because they too had a meaning. Either they were a sign that the sick were not yet ready for the exchange, the dialogue that was psychological analysis, or that they should never be disturbed behind these barriers because the cure might be worse than the illness and kill off what was left of them. And how right that the grandmother should have been such a bastion of protection of the story. Only the wise and eternally feminine in life knew how vital secrecy and reticence were in these matters; they knew it out of the experience of creation in the heart of themselves; they knew that it was only in the dark, calm, and silence within the walls of the womb that the vulnerable, defenceless living cell of new being could be conceived and receive its impulse to grow from uninterrupted community there with the living mystery in being already in the body which sheltered it.

All the time he had been listening to me, he had found himself thinking back to one of his earliest cases at the Burghölzli. She was a comparatively young woman, he said, and had been sent to the asylum as insane beyond redemption. He no longer remembered the exact prognosis of the day because he had already seemed to find the prognoses unhelpful except as the vaguest and most generalised descriptions of symptoms. After a considerable effort he got her to tell him one of her dreams. From that moment on the dreaming process in her and the interchange between them accelerated and intensified. She progressed as a result at such a pace, finding a new sense of reality and meaning and the courage to test both again in the city from which she had come, that he was prepared to let her go from the asylum months before he had expected to be able to do so.

On the morning on which she had to go, she came to see him for the last time.

"Are you not feeling nervous about going home today?" he asked her.

"Of course I am. What do you think?" she replied with spirit that surprised him.

"Did you by any chance dream again last night?" he ventured again.

"Yes, I did," she answered, paused, and then added, "And it's no use badgering me, because for once I'm not going to tell you what it was."

"I cannot tell you how moved I was," Jung told me. "I could have wept for joy because you see at last the dream, the story, was her own again. And at once I discharged her."

And as if to emphasise how great a meaning there was in this experience not just for Jung, and through him for myself, but for life as a whole as well, the relevant coincidence to render it, as it were, beyond doubt was inflicted on me a decade after Jung's death.

I had cause to go to the Burghölzli and ask the director if he would allow me to go through the records of Jung's early case histories in the archives. He produced a mass of folders, all dressed in covers the colour of the Swiss military uniform, suitably so, I thought, because they themselves were citations of human conduct in the field of battle for life and meaning. As I read through them I was impressed how Jung, even before his meeting with Freud, was using dream analysis in his own natural comprehensive and unslanted way.

Then suddenly I was made to sit up mentally even straighter than I had been before. I was reading through a case that seemed familiar when I came to the last sentence, concluding the answer to the final question put to the patient, whether she had dreamt the night before: "And for once I'm not going to tell you what it was." I realised I was reading the abbreviated clinical record of the very story Jung had told me at length.

If I had had any doubt, it would have been killed by Jung's own final word at the end of the dossier. His handwriting to the end was strangely youthful, at least for me, who heaven knows is no graphologist. It never appeared to change in character and only seemed to grow larger as his eyesight became less clear. And there, written in the same hand was one word: "Erlassen." Of course the idiomatic translation of the word is "discharged," but the idiom does less than justice to the meaning implicit in the original German, which means "let go." For that was what seems to me to have been the whole purpose of the exercise in healing that had just taken place; that which had been so disastrously held back in the feminine personality had suddenly been set free and "let go." And the manner of the writing of "Erlassen" across the yellowing page seemed in itself excited, flowing and streaming almost like a banner in a wind of morning.

The dream as a result had long before become like a sword in his hand to cut away real from unreal, illusion from reality, and the weapon itself, once the preliminary battle was over, surrendered to the patient for future use. Some of his most spectacular successes were accomplished almost entirely in terms of a dream process both in himself and his patients and one of his most moving recollections was of a woman who came to him listless, depressed, without sense of purpose, and yet left him some two weeks later restored to her own full self and future, almost entirely because he told her of a dream or two he had had about her and had gone on to uncover them with her help.

I could multiply the examples because I have read, deeply moved, other case histories of Jung, now dusty and unthumbed in their blue-grey folders in the archives of the same hospital where he did break the code of derangement, established contact, and brought back to the world men and women who had appeared lost to it forever, and certainly would have been lost a few years before he had begun to work there. But enough is enough and this should show how Jung came to the conclusion which still rang out like a bell announcing the day when he told me of it more than half a century later.

"I learned there," he told me, "that only the physician who feels himself deeply affected by his patients could heal. It works only when the doctor speaks out of the centre of his own psyche so provisionally called 'normal' to the sick psyche before him that he can hope to heal."

He paused, and added that maxim straight from the centre of those ancient places of the mystery where healing was attempted like Epidaurus: "In the end, only the wounded physician heals and even he, in the last analysis, cannot heal beyond the extent to which he has healed himself." He had to accept, however humiliating to his pride in his own "sanity" and "normality," that he could take no one further than he had taken himself. Nothing was more dangerous to the sick than expecting of them qualities the psychiatrist had been incapable of realising in himself. Indeed, that was as much a problem beyond the walls of the Burghölzli as it was inside. A fundamental problem of the life of his day, as it is ever more so in our own, was that individuals as well as their societies were continually expecting others to meet standards they themselves could not attain. The favourite yet lethal game was being high-minded in the lives of others, so that one evaded the necessity for being so in one's own. The pretensions, the confusion, the damage done thereby caused an increasing kind of mass production of fodder for mental asylums.

It was at the Burghölzli too that Jung evolved his own method, the word-association test, and made it an instrument for charting out suppressed and secret areas of injury not only in the mentally disturbed but also in so-called normal men and women. It was an amplification of a psychological test adapted by Francis Galton, a cousin of Darwin, to evaluate degrees of intelligence. Galton would put one of some hundred key words to a person and an observer with a stop-watch in hand noted the seconds taken to produce a reply. But so little of value for testing even just intelligence was obtained from the method that it was abandoned.

Jung, however, reintroduced it with important modifications: when the person took longer than usual to produce the first word that came to his mind, Jung would question him about the hesitation and his associations with the word. Observing also how often certain words quickened an unaccustomed emotion in the person's response, he would note it carefully and explore that area as well in a process of more specific question and answer. There was a day, for instance, when the word "horse" put to someone was followed by a reaction of over a minute's silence. Subsequent discussion revealed a story of great emotion about a horse that had once bolted with the patient and caused an accident, with other dramatic consequences which the patient had completely forgotten. From this and other similar experiments, more and more accurate and embracing, it became obvious to Jung that in human beings there was a repressed area wherein they tended to bury experiences too painful to be remembered or too hurtful and damaging to their pride and the picture they presented to the world. To describe areas of hidden experience and suppressed hurt, whose uncovering is critical for the emancipation and development of the personality, he used the word "complex."

I have mentioned the word-association test here not just for its chronological relevance but because it demonstrates how thoroughly empirical in his approach Jung was from the beginning and how inventive also in the practical and almost mechanical exactions of his work. It is important because he was soon to be branded a "mystic" and the adjective "mystical," which I know from bitter experience is an equivalent of "mistical" in the minds of those who use it most of all, was to follow him to the end of his days and so prevent numbers of modern persons who are by nature born to be at one with what he did from even examining the evidence of his work. I needed no reminding of the abuse of the term in this regard, seeing how I myself had fallen for it before the war.

It was with the "mystical" as it was with the myth. Few if any of us know what mystical experience really is, being incapable of it ourselves. The experience itself in any case occurs relatively rarely in the rarest of spirits. Jung in his own writing never pronounced on that area of himself which lay in the neighbourhood of the mystic. He steadfastly confined himself in print to what had been proved, observed, and established objectively of his immense intuitive self in his own circumspect empiricism and what is revelation in the history of man.

Of course, an intuition as great as Jung's was always in a hurry and made great exactions on his scientific discipline, so that in a sense he was like a rider always needing all he had of skill and power to prevent a high-spirited, swift, and easily provoked race-horse from bolting. He found it essential, therefore, as soon as he had reached a phase in his work which appeared established with relevant objective proof, to put the results and his conclusions into written form and move on.

Moreover, he established as early as 1904 a laboratory for experimental pathology and drew a number of notable American associates to it. By the time he produced his important paper "On the Psychological Diagnosis of Facts" in 1905, he already had a dozen other papers and essays, all of scientific note and full of evidence of originality and impending change in the approach to what he had first encountered under the name of diseases of the personality in Krafft-Ebing. Accordingly, when he came to do battle on Freud's behalf in 1906, he possessed a considerable reputation on his own.

Most important of all, the more experience he had of the pathologically abnormal at the Burghölzli, great as his interest in that area of the work was, he became more and more interested in what was considered a lesser phenomenon, that of neurosis. He was already uncovering in the depths of his most pathologically psychoid patients patterns that seemed to him non-personal and belonging more to the mythological past and history of the mind and spirit of man than to the present. This, joined to what he was learning from neurosis, held to be a "purely imaginary" illness on the part of the neurotic, gave him a conviction that psychology must be freed from identification with the pathological and given a much wider and greater relevance in the wide world without. His conviction was all the stronger in this regard because his experience at the Burghölzli suggested that unless he had a psychological framework that was valid for humanity as a whole, its pathological confinement to mental hospitals would never work for the patients there as it should.

It was as if through the phenomenon of neurosis encountered in normal man he was at last on the track of the original cause of the rift which had exercised his imagination so disturbingly over the years. The world of the so-called normal, he suspected, was perhaps even more in need of healing than the abnormal, because it was in command of the day. He was amazed that a world moved to instant concern and succour of a person with broken limbs could be so blind and indifferent to the suffering manifesting itself as neurosis, which to him seemed far graver, more painful, and considerably more difficult, if at all possible, to heal than any shattered bone.

He knew this much with all the greater certainty because news of his success in treating the mentally ill in the Burghölzli had spread to the outer world. Already his stature had been recognised in a world singularly impervious to recognising the sort of incomparable originator he was, and he was appointed to the medical faculty of the University of Zürich as *Privatdozent* in 1905. But even more significant, people thought normal and afflicted with this "imaginary disturbance" called neurosis came to consult him in increasing numbers. After nine years at the Burghölzli the demands of his private practice were to grow so much and his own inner focus shift so much from the pathological to the so-called normal man that he was to leave the Burghölzli for good.

I say "so-called" normal because by this time normality had become for Jung an unreal abstraction. He had been through the most disturbing encounters with personalities who walked in the world of men with authority, success, and an air of unassailable moral integrity. Some of the most "normal" of people he had ever seen had come to him as patients and so appalled him by the abnormality lying underneath their worldly attitude that he refused to treat them, knowing that any attempt at healing could release vast forces of abnormality already mobilised below appearances and overwhelm them. This kind of latent abnormality in the "normal" he recognised as one of the deepest pitfalls on his road, and he taught himself to respect the precarious balance the "normal" had struck with the "abnormal." If he had the slightest hint from dreams and fantasies that an encounter with their deeper selves would shatter them irrevocably, that the cure would be worse than the disease, he would withdraw from those patients' cases as creatively and as soon as possible.

Much as his belief in an analytical approach had broadened, he realised it was only for those who came to it, as it were, as beggars feeling themselves in the New Testament sense "poor in spirit," and suspected those who wanted to take to it straightaway as a means for healing others. It was not surprising that the statistical abstract called normal for him soon was like the average rainfall, which has always struck me in my own arid part of Africa as the one rain that never falls. In all this, Freud meanwhile had come to play a considerable role and to make in both a positive and a negative sense an immense contribution to Jung's future, a contribution that has not been considered before. Despite its chronological origin in his years at the Burghölzli, it belongs more truly through its consequences to what was about to happen to Jung.

Perhaps only one more fact about his psychiatric years needs evaluation here. Asked once how many of all the people who came to him had been healed, he replied that he had made a rough assessment once. He thought that one-third of the vast number had not been healed, one-third only partially, and one-third entirely. He added that the middle category was most significant and least conclusive because he was constantly amazed how persons included in it saw the meaning of what they had learned in their work with him only years later and so indicated thereby that the number of healed could be far greater than he in his most conservative estimates had calculated.

In any case, he emphasised over and over again, only the most naïve of attitudes assumed that the analytical process was aimed at resolving the problems of life. In essence life was problematical and men derived their purpose from living it as if in answer to the problem it posed. "I myself," he told me once, "have never encountered a difficulty that was not truly the difficulty of myself."

All the psychiatrist could do was to encourage an honest attempt at living in the patients, giving them at most what they had of resources within themselves to do battle with any problems thrown in their way. It was nothing if life did not become also a process of self-analysis and self-synthesis to be continued on the part of the discharged patients to the end of their days.

Asked then which people he had found most difficult of all to heal, he had answered instantly, "Habitual liars and intellectuals." I myself thought this negative association of liars and intellectuals so interesting that I asked him why he had bracketed them together. He implied that the association was not arbitrary. Heaven forbid, he said, that he should be thought to despise the intellect. How could one possibly denigrate what was one of the most important attributes of the human spirit? When he used the word "intellectual" he had in view a person guilty of intellectualism, attributing a kind of final omnipotence to the intellect which the whole history of man and in particular the scorched, disordered scene of day proved it did not possess.

Perhaps he should have called the person he had in mind in that regard an intellectualist rather than an intellectual, but in the sense as amplified to me the intellectualist was also by constant deeds of omission a kind of habitual liar. He was untrue to other equally important and valid aspects of himself. More, he tended to be a coward hiding behind his intellect from the demands of his life. He tended to lead a highly compartmentalised existence, creating concepts to shield him from reality and, as fast as they were challenged, inventing new ones to take their place and shift his ground. With the resulting "ism," like all other "isms," he spoilt by his excess something of value to us all.

Jung explained with some dismay how he observed the success of this intellectualist tendency to identify intellect with spirit, which was so much greater because it included all the feeling values as well as the other non-rational sources of awareness in man.

What had happened to the passion of the spirit, he once asked rhetorically of me, that it should have declined into an arid exercise of intellect alone and what of the effect on consciousness that it should be held as the equivalent only of that which is capable of verbal articulation? Think of that, he said, and I would see how the spirit of the West had been impoverished and become sick in a vital area of itself. To correct all that in his patients was as common a task as it was difficult.

He was appalled by the numbers of persons Western civilisation was casting in the role of mass producers of conceptions as a whole-time occupation. The amount of thinking for sheer thinking's sake, without any hint of the obligations of thought to the rest of the personality, was one of the causes of our profound collectively pathological disassociation from our past and the loss of a sense of the dependence of our future on an honest historical assessment of ourselves and our cultures. And the loss was almost total, he added, of the myth or story which, as I had discovered for myself in the desert of Africa and he had proved over and over again in his work, was vital to the well-being of man. Such a disassociation in the consciousness of men was generally the fateful prelude to their confinement in institutions like the Burghölzli. It was the overture to forms of psychosis most difficult of all to heal. And alas, not only individuals so disassociated went and were made mad; whole societies, cultures, and civilisations, out of the same self-inflicted psychological partialities, likewise became demented. Had we not just been through two world wars to prove how demented our civilisation could be?

It was not surprising, therefore, that one problem connected with the profoundest of disassociations of all pursued him to the end: the dichotomy generally described today as schizophrenia. It was so difficult to heal, I believe, because it was supported by a similar tendency to dichotomy in the spirit of an entire civilisation backed up, as it were, by all that was negative in the twentieth-century *Zeitgeist*, and so was in a sense incapable of cure without healing at the same time the mass of humanity and cultural pressures rallied unconsciously behind it.

Even so, he had his successes after what seemed to him a disproportionate effort, since it demanded from him so great a concentration that he hardly had time or energy left for others, let alone for himself. But there were countless others, lost in a world which seemed increasingly cold, impersonal, and fundamentally mythological, ruled over by unknown powers against which a mere man from without fought in vain. He was to confess that he never clearly understood what caused the severest forms of this particular sickness of spirit. In one of the last of his utterances just before he died, he suggested that there could be pathological forms of psychophrenia that might have a physical origin in some undiscovered mutation in the chromosomes and genes of the individual. This demonstrated conclusively, I would have thought, that dedicated as he was to psychology and the world within he had never been fanatically dedicated, and that he had always remained open to the claims and validity of the physical and the external as well. Yet he stood firm and proved in his practise that many more cases than were imagined, condemned as incurable forms of this disturbance, could be made whole again by applied analytical psychology.

It was in some such fullness of an awareness of phenomena such as these that he turned his back on the Burghölzli and took to work again on his own in the world, to find himself pulled in a direction which even he had not anticipated and which demanded such attention that on April 30, 1914, just before the outbreak of the First World War, he was to resign his post as *Privatdozent* as well.

❧Errant and Adventure

Le chemin longue de la queste et l'aventiure.

Froissart's Knight

I HAVE DELIBERATELY not dealt with Jung's relationship with Freud before because in essence it seemed to me least concerned with Jung's time at the Burghölzli and belonging far more to the wider world of psychiatry as a whole, full of important implications not only for its own sake but for Jung's own personal development. Jung had read Freud's *Interpretation of Dreams* on its publication in 1900, but it does not appear to have made much impression on him then. He reread it nearly three years later and immediately saw how there were links between Freud and what he was trying to do, as, for instance, in his own evolving word-association method, which was revealing areas of hurt in men of which they were unaware. Freud's concept of an unconscious at work in the mind of man, and a source of mental disturbance, therefore, made immediate sense to him. Above all, he was struck and excited by the importance Freud attached to dreams and restored to honour a process which the rationalism of Western Europe had either forgotten or had dismissed as some idle old wives' matter, too ridiculous for serious consideration.

This, of course, was not surprising in one who had his first great dream when he was barely three and had assumed that something imposed upon him so naturally from within had natural meaning and so had continued against the trend of the world and his own education to cherish and go by them accordingly. It was remarkable to me, going through some of his own case histories at the Burghölzli both before and after his encounter with Freud, how from the beginning he was using the dreams of his patients as an instrument of healing and using them, moreover, in a comprehensive sense alien to the slanted method Freud was to develop.

Yet Freud in this particular work of his was so truly on the scent of a new truth, or rather the rediscovery of an ancient one, and so much more advanced on the trail than anyone else that Jung warmed to him instantly. He recognised that a great iron gate shut for centuries in the face of the inquiring spirit of man had been swung open. That for him, I believe, remained Freud's greatest achievement. Jung's debt to Freud in this regard was unqualified. He stated it clearly in *Memories*, saying that Freud, "by evaluating dreams as the most important source of information concerning the unconscious processes, gave back to mankind a tool that had seemed irretrievably lost. He demonstrated empirically the presence of an unconscious psyche which had hitherto existed only as a philosophical postulate."

He wrote to Freud at once to tell him of his appreciation and gratitude. However, in one sense the discovery of Freud was not all *that* welcome to him. He was busy writing a paper as passport to a new academic career. He knew how Freud was reviled and unacceptable in the academic world of his time and how damaging any openly acknowledged support of Freud's theories would be to him. Considering that unaided, through his word-association method, he had already arrived at many of Freud's own conclusions, it would have been only too easy and morally plausible to present his paper without reference to Freud. He refused to do so and I mention it here not so much because it demonstrates how Jung possessed moral courage of the highest order or proves his utter dedication in all honesty to truth, since I believe both are demonstrated beyond doubt by his earlier life, but for the reason that it shows how alive and active his excluded No. 2 personality had remained. It was the first clear indication for years that No. 2, far from being content as a

mere force in being, was preparing to assume a much more forceful
and differentiated role in his future development.

In the midst of this temptation not to mention Freud, his No. 2
spoke up clearly and told him that not to mention Freud would be
cheating and that he could not "base his life on a lie." From that
moment, he became quite openly a supporter of Freud, and though
warned by two eminent German professors of the danger to his
career which his partisanship of Freud constituted, he continued to
defend him.

Even more, despite the fact that from the beginning he had doubts
of his own about some of Freud's assumptions, he did in private what
he could to broaden what appeared too narrow an approach in
Freud. They began to correspond regularly and in 1907 he and his
wife visited Freud in Vienna, where at their first meeting the two
men talked for thirteen hours without a break, and although Jung
emerged from the marathon session with mixed feelings, an
association began which meant more to him, I suspect, than any
other ever did. Up to the day of his death, he never quite completely
made his peace with the pain inflicted on him both by the association
and the parting with Freud, and the matter, therefore, needs closer
examination.

The need Jung and Freud had of each other, I believe, was far
more in a human and psychological dimension than a scientific one. I
think their scientific need of each other could have been met and
perhaps more fruitfully fulfilled by exchange of letters and findings
than in terms of a friendship between two natures so fundamentally
unalike. No one in his right senses could ever regret the association
because of its consequences for psychology as a whole, but these
consequences, I believe, cannot be properly understood unless one
sees the association clearly for what it was and rescues it from the
miserable and humiliating partisan interpretations to which it has
been sacrificed.

To begin with, Freud, although he was already a firmly
established influence in science, was still controversial and assailed to
the most despicable extremes of which even that quarrelsome world
had proved itself capable, seeing that it was so unaccustomed by
deliberate discipline to the emotional realities of life that a young girl
of four as a rule could be held up to it as a model of maturity for
self-correction. He had committed the Promethean sin of recovering

a great, transforming truth and, like Prometheus, was being punished for it night and day by the gods of his world. He had found this gateway of dreams into an unconscious region in the spirit of man, and performed the Odyssean task, as Homer puts it, of "pointing the way to the gates of the sun and to the land of dreams."

By implication of his work and an inner compulsion of his own, all he did was an attack on one of the most neglected and cruelly repressed areas in European man: the attitude to sex. In this he was taking on at least some two thousand years of Christian history and a great deal of Old Testament man as well. Even in this permissive day one stands back amazed how our civilisation, in so far as it is an attempt at Christianity, has never attempted to evolve a truly Christian attitude to the role of sex in man but continues to sweep its natural claims under a carpet of narrow ethical assumptions, raising in its place a lofty, Gothically aspiring concept of the relationship between man and woman, based, as far as one can judge, most inadequately on only a few foundation stones: one solitary utterance of Christ, used out of context of the all-embracing and predominant value of love for which he was crucified, and some of the lesser utterances of Saint Paul.

Saint Paul's attitude to sex and women was, I believe, in a large measure responsible for organised Christianity's lack of recognition of the sexual values of the spirit, and its profound dismissal of the importance both of the woman in life and the feminine in the spirit of man, encouraged as this tendency already was in the Old Testament and its dedication to a masculine patriarchal concept of God. This rejection of the feminine and this apparent suppression of sex reached its most omnipotent height in the Victorian era.

Freud cannot be properly understood if not set against this background and seen as a long-overdue and acute scientifically informed reaction against it. That was both his originality and strength as well as his weakness. He and we all have reached a point where mere reaction to history and events is not enough. Something new was needed, and although the new was implicit in Freud's reaction, it was also imprisoned in it. Men, alas, tend to make either a god or a devil of what they and their society and time lack and need most of all. Freud, after his great initial break through the barriers of millenniums into the underworld in man, installed sex there as a god with some of the most infantile aspects of which human imagination is capable. He did this, moreover, in the context of Austria, particularly of Vienna, where in many regards, particularly that of sex, man was freer than elsewhere.

And there, I believe, we come to the basic difference and point of departure in the character of the two men which was to make it impossible for them to remain friends. Jung, exposed to the same inadequacy of European culture in its far more severe Protestant restriction in Switzerland, was not content just to react to it. Seeing how great the temptation must have been after his first great dream of a phallus enthroned on gold underground to be slanted towards a literal interpretation of the dream event and become sex-obsessed himself, he reacted, I believe, in a way that was totally new in the spirit of modern man.

In fact, he was even as a child never interested in just reacting to circumstances and events but, as if born to it, committed more to their transformation into something that was greater than either their cause or effect. In contemplating not only what had happened to him but also the history of man, Jung did not fail to note, as his beloved Heraclitus centuries before Christ had done, this perennial tendency of men and their societies to swing over into their opposite, this enantiodromia as Heraclitus called it, but he himself by instinct would have no part of it. The great initial calm which one has already observed in him on the occasion when an obtuse master at school accused him of lying over an essay, and punished him unfairly, descended on his spirit and he thought it of prime importance first of all to discover the causes of these violent pendulum swings in time and human personality, before he considered the reconciliation or transcendence of the two already insinuating itself into his treatment of the sick and his view of his work in the future.

For Freud, fantasy always appeared to have an infantile, wishful, and sexual origin, dreams resulted from a highly censored process which disguised man's unconscious promptings from his socially respectable self, and the symbol was merely a metaphoric and almost literal expression of all. He held that it was for the psychiatrist to determine the meaning of the symbol and inform, or perhaps impose it on would be a better term, the disturbed personality.

Jung saw the symbols in the classical and far more meaningful role, issuing unsolicited and sheer like lightning or passing like meteors through the dark of the imagination. Their contents and their importance came for him from as yet uncharted regions of the spirit, however much the person who experienced them could participate in giving them a specific form. They were for him beyond any total intellectual grasp and sources of great transfigurative new meaning. Among the dynamic forces in the spirit of man he was to explore, they were to remain for him forever among the greatest. The decline and fall of meaning in the world around him, he was certain, was due in no small measure to modern man's increasing inability to guide his life by the symbol. In any case, the significance of the symbol in the life of the person who experienced it could not be imposed from without but had to be assessed in his own associations with it. As for dreams, they in particular were the inviolate, inalienable, and most precious possession of the dreamer in that they were vital to the progression of his story or myth.

They had to be accepted without reservation by the psychiatrist as such and in Jung's view anyone who extended a hand, however well intentioned but uncalled for, to grasp another's dreams after his own fashion was violating the first principle of healing. Even misinterpreting dreams submitted for interpretation by the dreamer he had found crippling to the task of healing if the error were not discovered, honestly confessed, and atoned for by the healer. On the whole he preferred to leave the dreamer to his own dreaming self and whatever it was that dreamt through him. If only he could get the dreamer to honour the forgotten language of himself and life within himself, he thought, half the battle was won.

With such surprising differences it was remarkable not that Freud and Jung should part company but that they should have succeeded in being friends for so long.

First of all Freud, in spite of the fact that adherents to his cause were increasing daily, never had anyone of his own stature to stand beside him. Even Adler, who was to differ violently with him and strike out on his own with a psychological view based on an urge for power in man and who stood head and shoulders above the rest of Freud's supporters, was not half the man to Freud that Jung was. Adler, as Jung himself said in a letter to R. H. Loeb, was always a sidelight, however important. Freud by contrast was the exponent of a real view.

Sensitive, imaginative, and exposed as Freud was to scorn and misinterpretation, Jung came to his support at a moment when he needed it most and gave him a feeling of confirmation and confidence he had not had before. Profoundly concerned as he was in the future of psychological science, he was in a symbolical sense badly in need of an heir and successor to carry on his work. It was one of the indicators of Freud's stature that he was as concerned for the future as he was for the past and present. Jung soon seemed to him born to be his successor, and before long he was talked of by Freud as his "son" and by others as "crown prince."

Although embarrassed by these appellations, Jung, I believe, at first was not altogether displeased by them. I have tried to show already how Jung had suffered from the lack of a father in the world. The place in the human spirit reserved so significantly for the father in the here and now was still vacant in Jung, and the need for its occupation in the world of psychiatry, where he was outwardly and inwardly alienated and alone, greater than ever. Freud, I believe, whatever Jung's protestations, moved in, occupied that place, and was made welcome there during a number of vitally formative years. Out of this great need of each other, they completely overlooked their essential differences not only of character but in their respective approaches to psychology.

What was it in Freud, one wonders, that made him overlook Jung's reiteration with increasing urgency of "man's need for the eternal truth of myth"? And seeing that Freud's authority had already become so questionable a year before in America over the matter of Freud's dream, what of Jung's description of himself to Freud that he was "sitting precariously on the fence between the Dionysian and Apollonian" and could not "muster a grain of courage to promote ethics in public, let alone from the psychoanalytical standpoint"? What of his emphasis that "two thousand years of Christianity can only be replaced by something equivalent" and the addition of a great poetic statement of a fundamental element in Jung's spirit: "An ethical fraternity, with its mythical Nothing, . . . is a pure vacuum and can never evoke in man the slightest trace of that age-old animal power which drives the migrating bird across the sea."

Here and in far too many other instances for quotation was unmistakable evidence of a spirit which saw his science as only a part of an infinitely greater whole and not an end in itself. Yet

Freud, who was doing his utmost to explain everything in terms of a science where method and theory were one, ignored it for years, as Jung suppressed his reservations about Freud and his reductive attitude of "nothing but"—a term derived from William James's statement in his *Pragmatism*: "What is higher is explained by what is lower and treated forever as a case of 'nothing but'—nothing but something else of an inferior sort."

So great was Jung's psychological need of Freud's authority, as it were, that where he ventured to challenge him, as he did over Freud's dogmatic declamation of "the omnipotence of the idea," he instantly back-tracked when Freud objected and apologised as if he had been guilty of some heinous offence instead of merely having delivered himself of an honest expression of opinion. Similarly, their profound differences over the meaning of symbols and complexes, particularly the Oedipus complex, so basic to Freud's teaching, were held back until the moment almost of the parting of their ways.

Jung, of course, was convinced that the Oedipus symbolism and its role in the imagination could not be taken literally as Freud did. He was certain it was not there to protect man actually against some sexual incest. For him it was there as a protection, a portentous warning to prevent "psychological incest" between parents and children. It expressed how vital it was for man's increase that children and parents should respect scrupulously their differences of personality and need, be free from spiritual bondage, and live their own lives. Though neither Freud nor Jung stressed it to my knowledge, I feel certain that perhaps the most important aspect of the Oedipus legend overlooked even now was the fact that the incest took place without mother and son knowing their true relationship. In other words, as always fate struck through lack of self-awareness, for that is what the "not knowing" in mother and son in the myth symbolises. And this element reinforced Jung's symbolic interpretation, that the myth was directed at a psychological emancipation of the son from the mother and a rebirth of himself into his own individual role in life. More, he saw the myth in its ultimate resolution as a union of the individual with his highest meaning and so of an essentially religious sign-post.

He had only to look round him and reconsider all that he had observed at the Burghölzli and in his own consulting room to realise that in spite of this profound inbuilt system of warning symbolised in the Oedipus story, the extent of psychological incest in the life of his time was as great as it remains today. So that despite Oedipus, Teiresias, Freud, and Jung, the world is still full of parents who attempt to live their own lives through their children, daughters who take their fathers' unlived self on themselves, to the extreme even of assuming his unfulfilled sexual self as their own, and sons who do the same with their mothers.

In a very real sense Freud protested so much about sex and Oedipus because it was his own problem projected onto the life of his time. He himself had an archaic concept of the relationship of man and woman, parents and children, reaffirmed by the extent to which he became a mere opposite of what had gone before. And it is indeed strange that he never seemed to ask himself why he took so obsessive an interest in sex and attributed almost divine elements to it.

His interest in the father-son relationship and insistence on the fact that the son wished the father dead are striking evidence of this. He wanted a "son" himself who would carry on his, the father's, work even to the extent of sacrificing a life of his own, a modern version of Abraham's Old Testament urge to sacrifice his son Isaac to his God. Freud had already fainted twice, physically, when Jung had dared to imply a difference of stand in regard to a "death wish" the son was supposed to have towards the father in this regard. Both the facts and details are on record and beyond dispute and in no need of amplification. What is important is something completely overlooked.

Taken literally, of course, this death wish is sheer nonsense, and was particularly so in Jung's regard. But taken symbolically it is full of meaning since it is the image of the son's legitimate striving to be psychologically free of the father. And when Freud suspected Jung of such a secret wish to the extent of passing out twice, he revealed both how much Jung had come to mean to him and that on an archaic level he was experiencing already an intuition that Jung longed to be rid of his symbolic father aspect and abolish his psychological hold over him, in order to defeat the tidal urge to make Jung live his future for him.

There came a moment even when Jung, who did not spare himself in this regard, confessed that he lied to Freud because he still needed him. This occurred in the course of the interpretation of a dream Jung had just put to Freud. I believe this interpretation of each other's dreams was one of the main bonds between the two men at the time and one which will be almost inconceivable to a world wherein psychiatrists will soon be as indispensable on every street corner as newsagents and tobacconists once were. All psychiatrists today have been trained by others and have trusted colleagues to guide them and help them out when they get themselves in a tangle with themselves and their patients.

Both these men, however, had come into the world of an as yet untested unconscious without guides and on their own. They had only each other for confession of their dreams and their interpretations. Jung already through this means had relieved Freud of a painful neurotic affliction and on the rare occasions when they were together they continued to submit their dreams to each other. The detail of this particular dream which produced the lie is irrelevant. All that matters is that Jung could see the way Freud, whom he had come to know well, would be pleased only by an answer which revealed a "latent death wish" of some kind. So he produced one and said the death wish was directed at his wife and sister-in-law. He did this because it was the most devastatingly absurd and unreal illustration he could imagine.

But even to this day I find it a harsh revelation of how crippling and unreal his relationship with Freud had become that he could use—one is tempted to say "betray in words"—however momentarily, for an ulterior purpose someone he loved as much as his wife. One can measure the number of cock-crows in one's recollection of the past by this terrible device—by one's own failures in other more frequent and probably less excusable ways.

The two men happened to be on their visit to America at the time and this dream possessed a particular importance also of a totally different kind. The dream was set in what Jung insisted always, wherever he discussed it, was "my house," a large house of many compartments, two stories high and with a deep cellar underneath. It foreshadowed Jung's uncovering of several layers of the unconscious in man, with the rediscovery of perhaps the greatest of universal contemporary truths, the world of the collective unconscious beneath and beyond all others. This was "his" house—no one else's, not even Freud's; hence always the highly emotive reiteration of the "my."

Combined with the uncharacteristic lie which Freud's spell over him compelled him to utter, the dream, I feel, showed unerringly how doomed their association already was, and in what a totally diverging direction Jung's spirit was moving. He told me how from then on all his doubts about Freud's increasingly doctrinaire concept of "psychoanalysis," his emphasis on sex, raised to the metaphysical heights of psychosexuality, came to the boil in America and the long-concealed differences between them emerged into the open. As often in these things the immediate cause in itself was slight. It came about over a single incident in a long dream that Freud had brought to him.

"I told him," Jung explained to me, speaking like a person for whom the pain inflicted, however far back, was still real and sought relief in being discussed, "that there was an aspect of his dream about which I needed more information. In particular I had to have his associations with the dream if I were to be of any help to him. To my amazement he told me he couldn't possibly do so, and when I asked him why not, Freud answered, 'It would be bad for my authority.' And in that moment something snapped in me. I knew that if a man cared more for his authority than for the truth I could no longer go down the same road with him. And an irrevocable break between us from there on was just a matter of time. But in reality it had started in doubts I had had many years before, but had suppressed out of respect for the many great services Freud had rendered me in particular and psychology in general."

I asked him then, "Could you possibly tell me what that aspect of the dream was which Freud would not reveal to you?"

Jung looked at me with a severity like that of my first sergeant-major putting me as a raw recruit through my first drill, and said curtly, "That is a professional secret."

Asked on television many years later to disclose the nature of the dreams Freud brought to him for interpretation, Jung refused even more resolutely, declaring firmly that "there were after all such things as professional confidences." When told that this reservation really should no longer be allowed to hold since Freud had been dead these many years, Jung answered with great warmth and dignity of feeling, "Yes! But these regards last longer than a lifetime."

Complex, long, and painful as this growth of differences was, in their contribution to modern psychology they can be simply stated, without oversimplification. Freud had discovered a comparatively narrow and special area of the unconscious of man which one could call the "personal unconscious." Jung went deeper, wider, and further to uncover below that what one might call a racial and cultural unconscious, leading finally to the greatest area of all, which he called the "collective unconscious."

"I found," he told me in a voice resonant with awe, "that the more I looked into my own spirit and the spirit of my patients, I saw stretched out before me an infinite objective mystery within as great and wonderful as a sky full of stars stretched out above us on a clear and moonless winter's night."

This, it cannot be stressed enough, was neither a merely subjective world nor one just of suppressed instincts, infantile urgings too painful and inconvenient for human beings to allow them admission into conscious and well-behaved grown-up selves. It was this "inscape" of Hopkins empirically rediscovered, this immense world of utmost objective reality within, charged with the experience of all the life that has ever been—all the possibilities of all that life is and can ever be, arranged in patterns of energy and complete with an infinite sense of direction, a kind of inbuilt radar and homing device peculiarly its own.

Yet more than three years were to go by before the final break was to occur, not because of the pull of the mutual need I have mentioned earlier on, for this had long since been satisfied, but because, I think, of the respect and affection that the two men, despite all, had come to feel for each other and which constituted the material of the tragedy of their ultimate separation.

Their letters to each other at this period, particularly Freud's, make touching and often moving reading in his effort to understand a nature so different from his own and to erase differences by summing up all he had of Old Testament patriarchal benevolence in himself for someone considered a son. The patronage implicit could not have helped, and in a sense was incidental. Jung himself had already accepted the inevitability of the break.

He was writing his first major work, *Psychology of the Uncon- scious,** which was to reveal an attitude to symbols, dreams, myths,

* *Wandlungen und Symbole der Libido.* Retitled in the revised edition, 1956, *Symbols of Transformation.*

and the unconscious so at odds with Freud's own that he knew nothing would stop Freud from disowning him the moment he became aware of it. His wife tried in vain to comfort him, assuring him that Freud would understand in the end, and he himself made a major effort to avert the break as late as 1912 by writing Freud a very carefully worded, placating letter on their differences over the incest theory, trying desperately to make himself not just humanly but scientifically understood. Yet even the overstretched words reveal a presence underneath their ostensible use of an underlying certainty of impending separation. So tormented was Jung by the prospect that for two months he could not go on writing the fatal book.

He may not have succeeded in doing so had it not been for a dream. As always in the past, when he had reached an apparently insoluble crisis in his life, the appropriate dreams came to his aid. He who looks outwardly dreams, he was fond of saying, but he who looks within awakes. Because his attention was directed outwardly towards Freud, he dreamt, and through the dreaming was compelled to look within and to awake to his own self and a greatly extended view of his role and life.

One-half of the dream showed clearly, in a manner so obvious as to need no interpretation, how Freud's role in his life in the form it had assumed in the past was indeed as spent and outdated as his experience in America in 1909 had shown. All that is important for understanding the future course of events is that the image which represented Freud in this dream was an Austrian customs authority, old-fashioned and out of date, trying to control, as it were, the exports and imports of the spirit. And this image possessed a certain poetic justice, however ironic, seeing how much importance Freud attached to a mechanism of censorship of dream material congenital in the dream and how one of the main differences between him and Jung was that the dream for Jung was no façade behind which the meaning of the dream is not merely hidden but withheld.

The other pointed to the way he had to go in the future and merits further attention in a detail and in a manner, I believe, Jung himself did not consciously give it. But before one does so it is important to realise that by this time Jung, out of his need of a father, out of his need of authority and uncertainty in his capacity to walk alone in this new field of science, had done great violence to himself. Of all wounds, self-inflicted ones go deepest, are most difficult to heal, hardest to forgive, and their scars impossible to conceal. This self-inflicted wound hurt Jung to the end of his days, hurt all the more because he would have given everything he possessed except his integrity to have real male companionship of the quality of Freud with him on the lonely, stormy road he was to take. He was perhaps most of all hurt because apart from respect for what Freud had done, he had become also devoted to him.

I think, however, that hurt as he was by isolation and the sustained attack on him by Freud's followers, and therefore driven naturally to hit back hard himself, he behaved with the greatest dignity. The recollection of the respect and love of Freud flared up wherever the long years of controversy gave him the calm to allow it the appropriate opportunity to re-emerge in his life. I know it from the way he spoke to me about Freud and the fact that even after the last war, with the help of his most distinguished male collaborator, Dr. C. A. Meier, he tried hard but in vain to establish an institute in Zürich where all genuine modern investigation into psychology would be studied and taught, including, of course, Freud.

All his friends were aware of the paradox of the experience with Freud in him and influenced by his own positive attitude towards it. I believe Freud realised it to an extent that must have brought comfort finally also to his sorely tried, battered, pioneering, and finally cruelly exiled self. I find confirmation in the fact that when the Nazi explosion threatened Freud's life in Vienna, it was to one of Jung's close friends, also a friend of mine, that Freud's family turned for help and not, significantly, to his Freudian disciples in London. Dr. E. A. (Eddy) Bennet, a close friend of Jung and his family and a distinguished pioneer of analytical psychology himself, helped to organise his escape, found a home, and prepared a welcome for him in Hampstead in London.

On the day Freud arrived in London, Jung and Bennet were attending a conference on psychology in Oxford. In the course of the morning session the news of his safe arrival came by telegram. Bennett and Jung immediately decided to send him the warmest of telegrams of welcome. The secretary of the conference found this so strange a procedure in regard to someone held to be Jung's greatest opponent that he was uncertain and hesitated.

When Jung heard at lunchtime that the telegram had not yet gone, he was, Eddy Bennet told me, angrier than he had ever seen him and ordered the immediate dispatch of the telegram. So perhaps for both men, however much the pain endured somewhere in the deeps of themselves, error was absolved and tragedy redeemed at the end. Yet unless one understands the extent and complexity of the injury done, the consequences that followed separation cannot be fully comprehended.

Jung never ceased to impress on all who came to him in search of psychological teaching that no one should ever attempt psychiatry unless he himself had gone through an analysis in terms of what he now called analytical psychology—a term one regrets perhaps because it expresses only part of what his life's task was to be and that part only the applied aspect of it. He insisted on this as a fundamental for many reasons. For instance, he knew for certain now that psychiatry worked only if the psychiatrist himself too was affected by the plight of the patient. He knew how in various of the subtlest of ways, most of them summed up in the self-evident terms of the "transference" and "counter-transference," which express how the psychiatrist could become overidentified with his patient and need help almost as much as the person he was trying to cure. Above all, Jung knew how "contact" with the unconscious forces that disturbed the patient confronting him could call into violent being unknown elements in himself.

The psychiatrist's only armour against all this was getting to know his unknown self as far as possible and going down into the depths wherein the patient had fallen as some natural game into a pit dug on his instinctive path for that very purpose. So he not only insisted on thorough analysis as an indispensable overture for the would-be psychiatrist, but was immediately suspect of persons who came to him with a request to equip them straightaway for the psychological healing of others. We all tend to see in others first what we need and lack most ourselves, and in the first instance either reject it with moral condemnation of the person concerned or respond more positively by a wish to help them. Faced with the second of the two responses, Jung insisted more firmly than ever on analysis as a prerequisite. In addition, he warned even the most experienced of psychiatrists to have a "father confessor," or better still "mother confessor," to help them out of the subjective entanglement with the problems of their patients which he knew so well from experience was bound to occur.

One recognises not only the practical import but overwhelming wisdom and the disconcerting psychological implications of all this for himself. He was the first in his own field and had none of these complex prerequisites to help him on his way. I believe it is one of the more unmistakable marks of his and Freud's genius that they reached this vital stage in their work where it could be surrendered to practise by others without any example or any other men to help them.

To me it is miraculous that Jung could have got so far and retained not just his sanity but maintained his appetite for pressing on more deeply. For some twelve years he had the unconscious material of thousands flung at him. Besides, had he not since the age of three been bombarded enough with strange, inexplicable, and horrific material from within, without having it multiplied in this demonic fashion?

The burden was so great even in a physical sense that he told me he would have been incapable of enduring it had he not been born with so robust a constitution, seeing how history was full of examples of personalities who had been shattered by such encounters. Yet he would not have succeeded in this had it not been for the dreaming process, all it evoked of symbol and fantasy in himself, and his great natural trust in what had been so naturally imposed on him and certainty that there was great meaning in it all. So one is not surprised that in perhaps the greatest crisis of many in a career so full of hidden, internal peril, the dreaming remained an archangelic constant in him and when necessary came on wings stretched wide to land white with light on the dark earth so native to him to protect him. The second half of the dream which showed how harmful his self-subjection to Freud and to Freud's theories had become was typical of another such archangelic landing and intrusion, compelling a reassessment and reappraisal of all that had gone before, leading to a definite point of reference on the map of his past for a fresh compass bearing, to redirect his going.

This half of the dream, therefore, needs particular examination. It was set in Italy and reminded him of the Basel which was history to him, thereby indicating that it was his own kind of Italy which was the setting of his dream. And what precisely was this Italy? It was pre-eminently that of the Dante and his Beatrice he loved so well, of Petrarch and his Laura, and the scene altogether of the Renaissance, the great rebirth of the Western spirit, as he knew it from

Burckhardt's remarkable study of the event. The dream indeed made it clear from the outset that it had to do with rebirth and renewal. The sun was at its zenith and it was the zenith too of the season which we call summer. The noonday sun was blazing and the light fierce and sharp on the city. The shops were closing, the crowds of people streaming towards their homes. Clearly the business of the spirit was over for the moment, not only for him but also for the seasons.

It was the hour the primitive people in my part of the world call dead, when men, animals, and trees lose their shadows, become unreal and only ghosts, the ghosts who do not portray the uneasy dead but prefigure life as yet to come. It was the moment in which the Chinese say that for all the light about, midnight is being born. There is no doubt that not only is this a dream about rebirth but about renewal made desperately urgent, because a new fall of night in the spirit of man is on its way.

What, I have often asked myself, could have described the state of spirit of the Western world more fully and accurately only some two years before the First World War than this symbolic dream representation? At this moment of climax inevitably too the relevant natural compensation of spirit was called into life. A knight appeared in full armour of chain mail. How significant an element is also this detail, seeing that the armour to come was to be evolved, as it were, by the human spirit in chains out of its links of chain with the living spirit of the past seeking liberating truth for itself. Over the armour fell a white tunic on which was woven front and back—that is, in the future as in the past—a large red cross which delineates the four quarters of the circle cardinal to the rounding or totality of life. Apparently the dreamer in Jung gathered that the knight had appeared regularly thus for centuries in the land of rebirth at the precise hour when midnight was being conceived as its counter and yet no one of the great crowd present had ever taken notice of him.

Unlike the customs official who had done proxy for Freud in the dream mentioned, which foretold the end of his hold on Jung but did not describe it in detail, this knight was no peevish, debilitated person, exercising an outmoded control on the frontiers of awareness, but was full of life and reality to such an extent that the image obsessed Jung for a long time and he was never to forget it. He knew the moment he awoke that the knight belonged to the twelfth century, the age wherein alchemy was to begin an important role in European imagination and above all the hour which witnessed the emergence of the dynamic transfigurative theme of the quest of the Holy Grail.

As a boy Jung had read Froissart, Malory, and their Germanic and Wagnerian equivalents on the Holy Grail, and they had had an profound impact on him. Wagner's *Parsifal* was one of his favourite pieces of music, and the world of the knights of the Grail, ever since he had been fifteen, had been *his* world in the deepest sense, unconnected with that of Freud. He took this dream as a sign that his whole being was seeking something still unknown and far beyond Freud, which might bring back meaning to the increasing meaninglessness of the life of his time. All that obviously was true for Jung on a personal level, but I think it had also a deeper, universal significance, not sufficiently brought out in his *Memories*. It not only describes in the imagery of a universal symbolism exactly the nature of Jung's future role in life, accurate even to the extent to which the world would fail to recognise both it and himself, but shows already how his work would be a turning point in history and time, achieved in the context of our lean and hungry day, to provide us with the means of defeating a new invasion of darkness which was already beginning to attack the human spirit, despite the apparent light and warmth of our day. Jung's was essentially an heraldic and knightly spirit in the most modern of idioms and appears charged in this dream with the quest of finding something that could contain and make at one the divided, imperilled spirit of modern man, with what success we shall see in the course of the adventure ahead.

I remembered, when we discussed this, my own agony as a child at the moment in Malory when the dying Arthur compelled a reluctant Sir Belvedere to return to the waters wherein its image had been born the great Excalibur, the sword which itself in its extraction from stone, the stone the medieval heart had become, had represented so evocatively the awareness of man in action on his quest for wholeness symbolised by the Holy Grail. I was haunted for years by the dismay that the great order of the Round Table had been dispersed and no longer had a Royal Centre around which it could reassemble. It was as if this dispersal and defeat and death of Arthur reflected the defeat and dispersal of what was best in the

Western spirit and the arrest of its essential quest, story, or myth, whatever name served the imagination best of he who reconsidered it, and explained the fragmented and splintered mass formations that had ever since tried to usurp its place. And it was for me, when I encountered this dream of Jung and considered how he proceeded from there, as if the ancient call had gone out loud and clear again and Merlin, who had preceded and tutored Arthur, and all the magic of life which had been buried deep with him in his mound for so long had been unsealed, so that through Jung the order of a reassembly of all we had of awareness left of this most authentic, specific, and urgent quest of Western man was there once more for all to hear and help in the making of a new Round Table for the nourishment of a truly modern spirit. That for me to this day is the real symbolic content of this dream. It is confirmed by the fact that Jung told me the only reason which stopped him from going on to work on the theme of the Holy Grail with the same psychological detail as he was to on other historical parallels—as, for instance, that of alchemy, and as would have appeared the logical issue of such a dream and his associations with it—was that his wife Emma was making it her own special study.

Somewhere in Emma Jung's remote ancestral background there was a family legend of a knight of her own kin who had failed the Quest and she felt called upon to set the failure right even in so late a day. The moment her special duties as mother to five children were discharged she began a vast, imaginative research in the origin and meaning of the legend and Jung felt he had to respect her sense of responsibility and not intrude upon a theme of unique meaning to her.

Jung had been impressed by the fact that invariably, among the hundreds who swarmed towards him as patients, he found at the core of their neuroses a sense of insecurity and unease that came from a loss of faith, a loss of the quintessential requisites of personal religious experience. He found that he never succeeded in what for want of a better word is called a cure, without enabling the patients to recover their lost capacity for religious experience. From this moment on a purely psychiatric approach to the problems of life could no longer have satisfied him, even if it had not been limited in its days in advance by a compulsive grasp of the vitally interdependent roles of science and religion.

The interest of psychiatry itself compelled him to know that it was not enough to reassemble the fragments of the shattered spirit among the men and women of his day and put them together in some sort of working order again, unless he restored to them at the same time a sense of overall direction, a feeling of somewhere meaningful to go. The process of reassembly, the reintegration itself indeed, was impossible without bringing back to his patients a feeling that they were instruments of meaning, however remote.

Healing the sick without a requickening of religion, as he put it to me, was "just not on." He was back at the moment far back in time when the word "heal" formed itself first on the lips of living men, and to heal meant to "make whole," and wholly and holy were both derived from "heal" to describe an indivisible concept of life, so that in the beginning, as in this hour so much later than we think, the condition of wholeness and that of holiness are synonymous. This was the condition symbolised by the finding of the Holy Grail, the transcendental vessel—"graille" was an old Provençal word for a vessel—wherein the spirit in all its apparent self-contradictions could be poured and contained as at one and whole.

This approach made him an inspired healer in the ancient, classical sense, and inevitably compelled him to reach out in his work more and more towards grasping what greater end healing itself served. Even more urgent than the work of trying to heal became the search for what constituted the wholeness that was the condition of holiness. It was almost as if from the moment of his first glimpse of this vast unconscious objective within, he saw the mentally deranged, even the least disturbed of his patients, afflicted with the sickness of an entire age and culture, saw them all, as it were, as guinea-pigs in a vast laboratory of time, and knew that the only valid answers could be guinea-pig answers extracted under the knife of the great vivisectionist of meaning. He had left the Burghölzli for good in some such realisation as this.

He no longer looked for the answer vicariously through the neuroses and mental sufferings of others but more and more in his own deeply wounded self and in the impact of all history upon his own life and mind and imagination. We are all compelled to be "mirrors" to one another of unknown, unacknowledged aspects in ourselves. The mote in our neighbour's eye is invariably a reflection of the beam in our own and the abnormalities we look out on from our own normality in the asylums and clinics of our time a magnification of something similar in ourselves. The suffering there, something expressed on behalf of us all, pleads for recognition as a reflection of inadequacies and possibilities of new meaning in our own lives and the life of our time. It was a nuance of Jung's greatness that he did not hesitate to use his experience as a psychologist as a mirror for himself and set the task of knowing the averted face of his own nature reflected in this mirror before anything else. No physician accordingly has ever taken more seriously than he did the task of healing himself in order to heal others. At his most vulnerable he was being challenged in a way in which he could not avoid thinking and experiencing unthinkables more formidable than in the vision of the shattered cathedral. He was bombarded by symbols and images demanding, like powerful emissaries and plenipotentiaries of an irresistible foreign power who would not take no for an answer, that he should return with them from whatever fathomless depths they had come. Not only were his nights troubled with the strangest dreams but his days were made terrible with visions that shattered his calm at the most unlikely moments. He could not tell when and where and how a normal hour would not suddenly be deprived of light and lose its enchantment because of what he came to call an invasion or intrusion from this other unconscious, where Freud's examples and even his own past work were no help.

He found himself turning to the child in himself as if instinct too were exhorting him to become like the child again which the New Testament exhortation makes imperative, to emerge from darkness into the light of which the Kingdom of Heaven is the supreme image. He went back, as it were, to his eleventh year, when he had had a passion for playing with blocks and making out of them villages, houses, and even fortresses after the manner of Vauban.

It seemed absurd, ridiculously nonsensical at his age and in a man already so distinguished in worldly terms, however controversial, but he accepted the instinct implicitly and began to gather stones on the lake shore by his house at Küsnacht and build miniature villages with them. He became a most impressive example of how the human capacity for achieving new meaning depends on our readiness to let life in a sense make fools of us.

I remember how impressed he was, in what I told him of a Stone

Age mythology in the desert of my native Africa, by the fact that their god-hero was always being made to look foolish in terms of his future self. Foolishness, simplicity, naïveté almost to the point of Dostoevsky's concept of idiocy, he stressed, was a divinely inspired state and had to be served as such. Through some such sort of God-given foolishness too he was led to a rediscovery and a visual continuation in stone of the dialogue started with stone long ago in a vicarage garden on the banks of the Rhine. Despite the eyebrows that must have been raised at so mature and big a man playing childish games with such concentration and zeal, he regained in the process an inner certainty that he was on his own way again—the way he had always wanted to go to discover his own story, his own myth and, through a myth of his own, the relevant myth of his time. From the moment of the completion of his first model village in lakeside stone, the houses huddled at last, as Anatole France had observed of a French hamlet, like chicks around a hen, and the church itself after great inner resistances dedicated around an altar of a special lakeside reddish stone carved into the required shape by wind and water and time, Jung found himself in the right dimension for errant and adventure.

Even so, in order not to lose all identity he had to remind himself over and over again of such realities as that his name was Carl Gustav Jung and that he was a doctor of medicine, a psychiatrist of growing reputation, a man of standing in the everyday world, and that he lived at 228 Seestrasse, Küsnacht-Zürich, in a house where a saying which Erasmus had borrowed from the Greeks was carved in the stone above the entrance, as if it were not only an exposition of the motivic theme of his life but also a sacred exorcism of darkness and evil: "Called or not called, God shall be there."

He would remind himself of all that and go on reiterating that he was married to a woman he loved called Emma Rauschenbach, and had five children by her, and so on and on, so as not to be swept away from his reality in the here and now, out and down into the cataclysmic depths of his mind. Even these numbered footholds on everyday reality were soon significantly reduced by resignation of his professorship in 1913. His mind so under attack had no space or energy left for academic teaching. Indeed, for some years it had not the space even for scientific literature and once his *Psychology of the Unconscious* was safely published, he had no heart or mind for writing. All, all was needed for this earthquake and eruption of spirit within himself.

He told me how he would suddenly see in trains visions of a great tide of blood coming up over Europe from the north and rising higher and higher until it lapped at the rim of the Alps like floodwaters at the top of a dam, and this vast swollen tide of blood transformed into a kind of porridge of mangled corpses and torn-off limbs and bones until he could almost cry out aloud at the horror of it. This particular vision, with even more enigmatic variations in dreams, was inflicted on him many times without making any sense to him at all.

"So unaware was I of those things at that moment," he told me, "that I did not seem even to have noticed that this vision invariably came to me when I was travelling by train in the direction of my wife's home near Schaffhausen, which is on the German frontier, and therefore overlooked one key to its significance as an image of a warning not only of private and universal peril but also a foreshadowing of its macrocosmic manifestation in the First World War."

By the end of 1913 the pressures of this and other calls not to ignore the element summoning him from this great new objective within were so many and so great that he could no longer ignore them. Although he recognised, in the dreams and fantasies, psychological material and patterns he had encountered only in the most schizoid and psychotic of his patients, he felt he had to accept them also as part of himself. How could he pretend to cure others when he failed to recognise similar things in himself and deal with them accordingly? He felt he owed it even more to his patients than himself not to shirk such fantastic issues. No one could possibly know better than he the dangers of succumbing to such dark forces—he had seen defeat of this kind too often; yet the feeling that he would be doing it for others as much as for himself sustained him in his choice.

So on the afternoon of December 12 of that year, sitting in his chair at his desk, he took one of his bravest decisions, subordinating reason to apparent unreason, even at the risk of sacrificing sanity to insanity. He committed himself absolutely to this equinoctial urge from within. He had always wanted to know how the human spirit would behave if deprived of all preconditioning and left entirely to itself. He had an intuition that no real beginning would be possible unless he had some experience of what mind and imagination did if allowed to act naturally and completely on their own. And he was about to find out, and in a way a world which does not recognise the reality of "these mountains of the mind and their cliffs of fall, frightful, sheer, no-man-fathomed" of which Gerard Manley Hopkins had spoken cannot measure. His whole spirit must have reeled with an inverted vertigo and horror of what he was about to do.

As he put it to me, without hint of laughter, "I said to myself, 'Well, Jung, here you go,' and it was as if the ground literally gave way under me and I let myself drop."

That was the greatest of his many moments of truth and so far did he fall, and so unfamiliar and frightening was the material he found as a result, that there were many moments when indeed it looked as if insanity might have overcome sanity. He told me how, for instance, just before the outbreak of the 1914–18 war he was summoned to address a meeting of British scientists in Scotland and for long debated anxiously with himself whether he should go.

"I had to face seriously the chances of being mad," he told me. "I argued with myself day after day whether it would be right to go, and whether by going I would not merely spread among a world audience what could be a mental contagion in myself. But I went despite my doubts, delivered my paper, and on the way back, in Holland, heard that the war had broken out. Tragic as it was, I felt immensely relieved in the sense that it came as some sort of outward explanation of the terrible visions of a tide of blood that had been inflicted on me, and confirmed a feeling that nothing had happened to me which was not in a sense also happening to the life of my time, and that more than ever I was to investigate the link between the two levels of experience."

New as this confrontation was in the terms of the life of his and even our own day, there were parallels in world history, art, and literature that help our own understanding of what happened. One thinks, of course, of Dante, who "midway through life found himself in a dark wood." Jung himself at that moment was approaching the halfway mark of his own life and in a season of himself to which Dante's metaphor was just as applicable.

Dante too had to go down into a netherworld right to its uttermost depths. Only Dante's task was easier because he was, in a sense, supported by one of the most highly organised systems of religion the world has ever seen. The vast establishment of the Holy Church maintained a belief that the terrible world of the *Divine Comedy* did exist, and accepted such events as Dante described as facts of life. Without detracting for a moment from the quality of a poet of genius for whom I have a particular love and to whom I feel immeasurably indebted, Dante's imagination was following a way not only comprehensible to his peers but in keeping with the religious tradition of his day. Yet this journey down of Jung's too was essentially a Dante-esque journey, although the vehicle was not poetry and the object scientific, however religious the intent. Dante, moreover, had as an overall guide and protector his love of a woman whose face, once seen when he was a boy in the streets of Florence, changed the course of his whole life. All that this woman and this face evoked in him grew into a love that was total, universal, and outside space and time, however limited its ration of reality in the here and now. It became a power in his spirit that made Dante feel always firmly directed and safe.

One finds, for instance, at moments when even Virgil, who was his immediate guide on the descent into Hell, was full of fear, Dante could declare without a tremour of doubt, "I have no fear because there is a noble lady in Heaven who takes care of me."

All these, of course, are quintessential elements in the classical pattern of confrontation of so cosmic an order. Men in other idioms and contexts of civilisation and culture have been compelled to confront unknown aspects of themselves and their societies and go down into their own deeps in order to rescue life from arrested aspects of itself which would lead only to disaster and death. And always by dispensation of life, some feminine spirit from within the nature of themselves has been prescribed, some messenger of love beyond the boundaries of appearances and knowledge summoned to act as guide, like Ariadne, who provided Theseus with the golden thread which brought him out of the labyrinth in Crete after he had killed the beast which was devouring the youth and beauty of Athens and so depriving the gleaming city state of the renewal and greater future self of which its youth and beauty were the image.

And up to now, with rare exceptions as that of Dante, the male spirit, once the feminine soul which had guided him so well had served its purpose, tended to abandon it and leave it forgotten, isolated on a rocklike aspect of itself in a sea of unknowing, as Ariadne was left in an Aegean of her own tears over her betrayal. One was to see the same basic theme reiterated when all the rediscovered feminine values of Greece at its noblest, which had joined the masculine of the Roman in the European spirit to bring about that immense flowering of spirit the Renaissance, were rejected in the Reformation that followed. For instance, Leonardo da Vinci, so obsessed himself by the importance of the feminine in man that even his sexual instincts were transformed accordingly, expressed the Ariadne pattern of redemption and abandonment by the masculine spirit in that heart-rending painting *The Virgin of the Rocks*, so prophetic of what was to come.

"You see," Jung was to say to me many years later of this painting, "there is the eternally feminine soul of man where it belongs in the dark feminine earth and see how tenderly and confidently she holds in her arms the child—our greater future self. But make no mistake, Leonardo saw her there not only in her Christian role but also joined to her pagan aboriginal version. That is why the painting is so meaningful. She is not just Mary the Mother of Jesus but the feminine soul of man, the everlasting Ariadne, her immediate uses fulfilled, forgotten and abandoned on the rocks. Rediscovered as she was briefly in the Renaissance, Leonardo's prophetic self foresaw already that she was about to be abandoned again, and the wonder, the really new element about her is that, unlike Ariadne, she is not in tears. She is content, confident, and unresentful because she is also the love that endureth and beareth all things and beyond faith and hope knows that in the end the child will grow and all will be well."

Because the law of life in these matters is as timeless as it is impartial, Jung also was guided in this going down as he had been up to the edge of the abyss by a spirit that was essentially feminine. But it was shattering proof of his originality and measure of his greatness that he came to this feminine spirit, this guide within, unlike any man before him. It is easy enough, after all, for the imagination of a man to follow a beautiful feminine face and form. But the feminine spirits that led Jung on his first essays were not beautiful at all. We have seen one representative already described by Freud as a "phenomenally ugly female" and she was by no means the only one. There was long before that his own mother, whose influence on him, as we have seen, outweighed that of his father. She was a formidable and by no means cosy or particularly seductive feminine spirit. As Blake said of Milton and his *Paradise Lost*, she was "of the devil's party without knowing it." It was her unconscious interest, her sympathy almost for the aspects of reality symbolised by the devil, that not only made her give the boy Goethe's story of Faust and the pact he made with the devil to read, with much benefit to himself, but enabled him to enlarge its meaning now into this deeper journey into himself.

Even as a student his eyes were first turned in the direction of what wandered, luckless and unappreciated, beyond the boundaries of the intellectual interests of his day, in the shape of that young woman who in ordinary life was of so modest a station but in mediumistic moments had shown herself capable of trancelike pronouncements wherein she figured as a grand lady of the world with a power of dominion of her own. Then in his work at the asylum and in his private practice women held his interest in a way that no man ever did. It is no accident that in looking back just before his death, almost all the cases he discusses in his autobiography as of a special interest and importance for his development were women. Nothing could make it clearer that the rejected feminine concerned him even more than the rejected masculine and evoked his powers of mind and imagination most powerfully.

It is not surprising therefore that his gigantic Dante-esque journey had begun by a pursuit of the fantasies of an American lady with the totally unmythical name of Miss Miller, whose own conscious self was ultimately lost in the floodwaters of an invasion from her own unconscious. Yet, following the apparently dubious trail of this Miss Miller into an underworld of her own, he entered a labyrinth of mythology and history and came to write that very book, *Psychology of the Unconscious*, which had caused Freud and his followers finally to break with him.

That such a frail, fanciful feminine spirit could combine with a host of others of her sex similarly afflicted to lead any rational man to any meaningful intent, of course, made no sense to anyone else at the time, and made Jung more suspect than ever. In a sense it was as understandable as it was inevitable because there was no exact parallel to confirm the validity of this sort of approach in history or even in the mythologies, legends, and modern literature of the world. There were only hints and intimations of the worth of what he was attempting in the despised and long-neglected dream world and fairy tales considered fit only as scraps of food to keep the hungry imagination of children quiet.

There are, for instance, stories like that of Cinderella. Fairy-tale ground is parable earth. Like the parables of the New Testament, they are charged with the seeds of new being and they are told to children out of an instinct that no imagination can take them in without shifting course somewhat in the direction implicit in the story. The psalm which spoke of the stone that the builders refused becoming the head-stone in the corner, which as one has already pointed out could serve as text for the main theme of Jung's life and work, is rooted in the same earth as this story of Cinderella. Jung's imagination was obsessed with Cinderella aspects of the mind and spirit. His nature predetermined that his truest seeking would follow the greatest rejecting of all in life, which is that of the feminine and makes Cinderella so moving a composition of imagery of the processes of its rejection. For there the beauty that serves as a symbol of the highest feminine values, disfigured by the ashes of the burnt-out fires of the world of her suppressors, wears the rags and tatters that are the uniform of rejection as the lowest of the low, working unrecognised and despised in some sordid kitchen of life.

Already in the course of his work in his asylum and even more in his vast private practice, Jung had rescued many a Cinderella spirit from some ignominious and dishonoured state of itself and transformed it into a personality once more capable of walking, enlarged and reintegrated, in a way of its own. But even in this recognition there is a foreshadowing of a gift of perception, amounting to a power of divination almost, not present in any of the prescriptions we have inherited in this regard. Jung clearly had the capacity both to see and to act as a catalyst of transubstantiation and transformation, which are the magic the godmother possesses in the parable of Cinderella. Like the godmother, he could recognise beauty in its rag-and-tatter state long before it became obvious at the ball. This was his own special genius and sets him apart and ahead of any others who have ventured into this enigmatic region.

It is easy enough to recognise the beauty of Cinderella transformed at the ball. It is easy enough, with the benefit of hindsight, to denounce the iniquity of her rejection. But only Jung in our day possessed the extraordinary capacity to see in advance beyond the dirt, the triviality, and even the banality of appearance and make it his most immediate and urgent task to reveal the vast potential of beauty suppressed and hidden underneath.

The achievement was all the more remarkable because this pattern of rejection has almost too much history to it. It seems to have been part of the mechanism of the spirit of man since the beginning of time. One searches in vain for a culture in which both the masculine and feminine values, both the man and the woman, have been honoured in their full proportions and each allowed an unimpeded role in life. The history of civilisation appears to be a sorry, one-sided history of domination by man. One can, of course, point to brief moments of matriarchy in which an archaic, suffocating femininity producing another disastrous imbalance of spirit has presided over our destinies. But almost invariably the basic cultural pattern has been the work of man. Whole areas of history are darkened by the ignorance of men of the truth that they can create only through the feminine in their own natures just as they procreate in the world without through woman alone.

Significantly, the most creative moments in history have come about when the imagination of man was alive to the reality of the warm, loving, caring values of his feminine self as the spirit of Dante glowed in all that was evoked in him by the face of Beatrice. The height to which his spirit ascended—and the height was Heaven—corresponded exactly to the depths of Hell and Purgatory through which the thread of his own feminine nature led him as safely as the golden thread of Ariadne had led Theseus through the labyrinthine maze of Crete.

This truth in the dimension of the civilisation wherein the European spirit has its roots, however uprooted its appearance today, is illustrated perhaps in its most striking manner by the difference between Greek and Roman cultures. Both have their origin in one and the same story or myth, which joined to the Hebraic theme as set out in the Bible was to provide the greatest formative values of the complex of the Western spirit. Both had a common point of departure in the Trojan War, which represents in an extroverted form the struggle to establish what role the feminine is to play in the life of man. The Helen about whom the war was fought is perhaps the first non-biological stage beyond the Eve, the woman at the beginning, and introduces the evaluation of a fundamental image reflecting man's profound inner dependence on the feminine and his need to give it a value uniquely its own in the law and order of his being. But it is essentially a war fought in the world without about the feminine in her external role. Helen is fundamentally a masculine reflection of the feminine and the war is only between men about the role it is to be allowed in their lives. The feminine is never consulted and utterly taken for granted with such unawareness that tragedy, not surprisingly, overtakes almost everyone involved in the war, victors as well as vanquished.

Greece, not Rome, was the natural earth of Jung's mind and it is significant that with all that immense interest of his in antiquity, and Rome, as it were, almost next door, he never went to it although he was to come close to it, twice by visiting Ravenna and once on a visit to Pompeii. Once even, I believe, when a kind of inner sense of uncompleted historical duty made him feel he ought to visit Rome, he went so far as to go to a travel agency to buy a ticket, but he was overcome by an attack of fainting at the ticket counter and never went at all. It was, I suspect, too partial or slanted a place for him to endure, although he obviously had other reasons as well for not going, which he had expressed at length in print. He felt it all the more deeply because he knew even then, as we should know more clearly now, how we are caught up in another Roman moment of decline and fall in the spirit of man, where worship of the material and subservience to the value of power have driven from life the feminine and its accompaniment of love.

As Jung "let go" and fell, he came to an area of his spirit so dark and so deep that he stood where the source of all life gushed out as a fountain of blood, vivid, dazzling, red as the fire with which he was compelled later to paint it. Aspects of the Western spirit he and the world had long assumed dead were rediscovered alive and in a personified form there, including that of his own primitive aboriginal self, alive and full of meaning in a reassumption of a feeling of belonging to an endless process of birth, death, and rebirth proclaimed in a diversified imagery of dawn, day, sunset, night, and dawn again in one of his greatest dreams. But of most immediate personal relevance, he rediscovered the personification of his cultural heroic self in the great Siegfried of German mythology, whom to his horror he had to kill. Once he was awake and capable of analysing the dream, it was plain how symbolic the dream-killing was. The death inflicted on Siegfried was to enable him to be reborn another way. Siegfried had represented too archaic a concept of the heroic in man and not at all the illuminated modern one Jung's imagination was after. He represented the German hubris whose maxim was, "Where there is a will there is a way." He was the central figure in a drama of willful, rationalistic man trying to impose himself, as the Germans were, on the worldly scene and all the rest of life and spirit.

Above all, Jung had the clarity and honesty of spirit to recognise that Siegfried's hubris had been his own too in regard to all this strange new material coming at him. In a sense he had been wilful towards it and his own attitude had to become more humble and accepting before it than he had allowed it to be. As a result, he came not in a dream of sleep but most significantly, as in that initial vision of God and the cathedral of Basel, to a revelation in his own daylight imagination.

Jung had painfully taught himself to give freedom to his imagination to go wherever it felt it had to go on this December descent into his own netherworld. One day he went deeper than he had ever been, so deep that he might have been in the land of the dead, until he discovered on a steep slope of rock two figures: an old man with a white beard and a beautiful young girl. He went nearer and saw that they also had with them a black serpent, which immediately took a great liking to Jung.

According to Jung, the old man called himself Elijah and was, I believe, another personification of the wise old man in the human spirit; the girl, who called herself Salome and turned out to be blind, was a visualisation of the feminine element in man he was to term "anima" in his delineation still to come of the patterns in this objective world of the collective unconscious within himself; to these he was to give the name of "archetypes." The snake, since it appeared in many an heroic myth as counterpart of the hero, was a symbolic confirmation of the fact that the dream was concerned with an heroic mythological content, although Jung hastens to add that such explanations would be excessively intellectual, and that it would be more meaningful to let those profound personifications be what they were for him at the time—namely, events and experiences.

Salome was no less a mythological character than Siegfried and in a way a more meaningful one since she was not Germanic but an emanation of the whole Greek, Hebraic, Roman, and Near-Eastern complex of culture that was Western and above all a feminine figure, of whom there had been a notable scarcity in Jung's dreams and fantasies up to now.

It is true that there was earlier on, as a portent of what was to come, the dream figure of a young girl and a dove, messenger of the Holy Spirit, in an Italian Renaissance setting as well, where the girl was not only clear-sighted but had embraced Jung tenderly, as if to say, "Whatever happens, I shall be there at the end, for I, child that I am, am mother of your future self." But that apart, there was no visualisation of the feminine until this profound encounter within himself.

Jung had repeatedly warned that to have such encounters and not to draw from them the necessary lesson for one's own life is as dangerous as it is unethical. But here for once, because of some undisclosed reason, however good, he is uncharacteristically curt and reticent. I feel compelled, therefore, to ask myself what the encounter meant to him personally and as he does not provide the answer, give one as best I can.

The ancient called Elijah is the reappearance of his long-suppressed No. 2 personality in a much more mature and dynamic form than ever before. Indeed, I feel this is proved by the fact that Jung's imagination seized instantly on Elijah and evolved another and even greater ancient out of it, from the pattern of the long mythological years of ancient Egypt. This Egyptian experience stressed that the ancient in the Old Testament form still had a tendency to fly off the earth, as Elijah had done, in a fiery chariot, and was attempting to by-pass the agonising renewal through death which is indispensable to our transformation by going straight up to heaven. Jung referred later in his letters, not without a certain dismissive irony, to the "curious flight" of Elijah and the even stranger disappearances of Enoch from the worldly biblical scene. But the Egyptian experience, a far earthier one possessing a *gravitas* the Elijah aspect lacked, was necessary to give it the "greater personification" Jung called Philemon. In fact, Philemon imposed himself on Jung with so charged a vision as an old man with kingfisher-blue wings, the horns of a bull, and four keys in hand, that he was compelled to paint and repaint him.

Henceforth, Philemon accompanied him as a kind of archangelic guide throughout his journey, as Virgil had been for Dante. He represented superior insight to Jung and we shall find him in due course honoured, calm, and authoritatively installed in that tower and fortress of the being of himself he was to build in his house of stone at Bollingen on the upper shores of Lake Zürich. From him, Jung says, he was to learn real psychic objectivity. It was he who taught Jung how there was a dream, as it were, dreaming him, and that what he had regarded as his own thoughts were no more his own than tables and chairs encountered in a strange room. Just as Jung would not think of claiming that he had manufactured such pieces of furniture, Philemon would tell him, he could not claim that he had made, unaided and alone out of his own conscious self, the thoughts that were in his mind. They too were objective events within him; they were thoughts thought through him and his conscious self. He was not their creator but observer and at most guardian and pilot in the world without.

The serpent proved that he had re-established contact with his deepest instinctual self, because that is the image the much persecuted and reviled snake has been compelled to bear and in consequence was to be cruelly, ruthlessly punished for it in the spirit of man as well as in the world at most times and places. Yet if considered with all the positive and compensatory associations attached to snakes, Jung stood there in the presence of the vital elements that would assist in healing the rift within himself and his time. All these latter associations explain why a snake to this day is curled as a badge of healing around the Hippocratic staff of medicine.

But what of Salome? Jung confesses he considered her in all her biblical and other aspects but does not say what they were. He only hints at the fact that she is an image of the Eros, the principle of love and feeling values of life, before abandoning her undeveloped. The next time there is any reference to the feminine in himself it comes much later in the dubious image of a sophisticated lady patient of his, highly endowed but pathological, who tries to persuade him that this encounter with the unconscious is an artistic engagement and that he is not really a scientist so much as an artist. The leap and gap between Salome and this other insidious feminine sophisticate is too wide and deep even for so great a spirit as Jung to straddle just like that, and the need for there to have been a bridge between these two stages only too self-evident, as I believe its provision was foreseen and real.

I believe that it is no accident that Salome was so young, beautiful, and blind and no idle chance that called her Salome. It is true, as Jung says, that such relationships appear frequently in the history of sages in their old age, like the dancing girl in the life of Lao-tzu. Salome, as we know, was a dancing girl too and the story and the legends surrounding her so familiar to Jung that he could not have failed to see the obvious personal associations involved. For him to say that Salome was blind, because the anima is incapable of seeing the meaning of things, is really another way of confessing that he himself could not see the meaning of Salome. For the anima, this feminine in man, as he himself has shown us so many times, is full of a potential womanly vision uniquely her own since she personifies all the experience of the feminine in the life of man.

One is compelled to remember that it was Jung's great original gift of genius that up to now he had allowed the rejected, despised, deprived, and persecuted feminine in life to be his guide. It had done its work accurately and so well that it had brought him as far as it could without fatally wounding him as itself had been hurt. It is as if in that vision of Salome all that had guided his yesterdays is saying to him, "Look at that girl. That is what life has done to us. It has denied us our own feminine vision and so deprived us of meaning. That is what is wrong with your so-called civilisation; that is the wrong so great that even you who had allowed us to guide you hither have been maimed likewise. We can do no more now. You know now what the trouble is and knowing it, you ignore it at your peril."

It is the moment of the greatest danger in Jung's encounter with his unconscious, the danger which accompanies all opportunities of renewal to such an extent that it explains why ancient Chinese uses the same symbolic ideogram for "crisis" and "opportunity." So there, then, is this urgent warning implicit in the blindness of Salome indicating that unless she is made to see in time, Jung's own venture is doomed, despite the healing presence of the snake and the protective wisdom of Philemon. Jung, I believe, unaided and alone as he had been in this protracted self-analysis of his, something which he had stressed was too dangerous to be permitted in the career of anyone who wanted to practise psychiatry, clearly had come to a point where not only could he go no further without help from someone else from without but was in danger of failing the task he had set himself. The deranged feminine had done its work; a guide of a positive and integrated feminine self, with eyes wide open and alerted, was needed through what had to follow. This conclusion, of course, is purely my own reading of the situation.

Jung had always stressed how all his friends and colleagues, except Riklin and Maeder, abandoned him after Freud disowned him. He meant by that, of course, that all the men he valued forsook him except those two. He does not say that, in fact, all the women around him stood fast and not a single one of them of any consequence abandoned him on the march or even fell out of step. They were the nucleus of what was to become one of the most remarkable groups of remarkably gifted women ever assembled round a single man, however great. I was to meet and become friends with a number of them and was profoundly impressed by their quality as well as the importance of their unwavering support to Jung, and will return again to the subject at the right time and place.

But at this blind Salome moment in Jung there were two who stood out far and above the rest. There was, of course, his own beautiful and extraordinarily gifted wife Emma. Engaged as she was at this moment not only with the bringing up of a family of five, but wife also to a great man involved in the battle of a lifetime with himself, she hardly had the space of time and mind to give Jung the kind of help he needed at this point. And even if she had possessed the time at that specific moment, she did not as yet possess the necessary qualifications. She had never been a patient of his nor did she ever need to be of him or any other man.

Happily, however, there was another woman who was a close friend and possessed all the necessary qualifications; that was the Toni Wolff to whom I referred earlier and with whom my wife studied and worked in Zürich. She is not mentioned in Jung's *Memories* and one understands the omission in a measure because the book is a record of quintessence only. Jung's own personal relationships are deliberately not part of it. His gift inflicted a special form of loneliness on him that was part of an overwhelming compulsion to serve a cause of universal meaning. The cause always had to come before men and women. I have known numbers afflicted likewise: soldiers, statesmen, writers, and artists who have had to set cause or work before human relationships. They appeared incapable of ordinary friendships, because their most urgent loyalties were not to men but to their causes. At times they seemed ungrateful and ruthless to a point of cruelty in ignoring the claims of family and friends.

Yet from what I myself know of such people both in my own life and history, I find it remarkable that being so heavily burdened with historic occasion and responsibility before life and time, Jung still gave so freely, warmly, compassionately, and generously of himself to family, friends, and fellow sufferers. He himself was keenly aware of the sacrifice demanded of him in terms of human relationships. He once compared himself poignantly in conversation with me to a man committed to fight on a desperate battlefield. Friends and companions were shot down all round. Yet he was not allowed to pause or stay to nurse their wounds and comfort them, as he longed to do, but had to move on and deeper into the battle if it were ever to be won.

In his autobiography, concerned with the cause and the battle, there is no pretence that it is also a full account of his life. It is, as the title says, memories, dreams, and reflections, a session of an old soldier remembering the battles he had fought. His own wife is barely mentioned and his feelings over her death, of which I have a moving record in a long letter he wrote me, are not admitted. But there is not even the barest of references to the woman of flesh and blood who went with him all the way on this stage of his journey. With so many other associations of great distinction not referred to, one should not be surprised, perhaps, by this omission. Yet I for one am, and feel compelled to mention her in enough detail to explain the significance of her role to Jung at this critical moment. It is all the more necessary because, however much I understand and sympathise with it, there is still what I find a reprehensible silence about her among the persons who are alive and knew her and who behave as if she did not render the particular service that she did to Jung, and therefore to psychology.

I hasten to add that one of the most notable among the exceptions has been Dr. C. A. Meier, who has seen to it that Toni Wolff's written contributions to psychology are preserved, collected, properly edited, and published, so that her distinguished record in this regard at least is secure, and her own psychological achievement is there to be studied and used.

But of the woman herself little that is authoritative and authentic is said and less still is known to those who have come to carry on the work of Jung, and almost all the rest left to gossip and imagination, which as always tends to be negative in these regards and does less than justice to a noble story. The situation is made more obscure by the fact that Jung burnt all his letters to Toni Wolff and her letters to him, so that history shall forever lack its own witness to how they, the immediate trinity of Emma, Jung himself, and Toni Wolff, conducted with such honesty, courage, and dignity what at any time must be the most difficult of relationships, but at that Victorian-Edwardian hour almost unendurably so. One knows, of course, all the excuses for the silence because those who knew Jung at this period were only too painfully aware of how he was constantly under attack from the outside world up to his end. They would have seen in any open discussion of Toni Wolff's role a kind of delivery of just another weapon of attack into the hands of Jung's enemies. But Jung is dead and that time is long since over, and no full account of him is possible without inclusion of Toni Wolff and a proper and decent assessment of her role. I would go further and say that I believe all that is true in Jung in so inspired a measure (and I deliberately use the historical present because I am certain the truth of the man is so great that it will stand), despite the withholding of his consent implied by burning of letters that must have been an agonising reminder of suffering, confusion, and near defeat, would demand that it is done.

I think I have an inkling of why the letters were burnt, not for any unworthy motive but out of the most understandable of human reasons: he could not bear the thought of strange, impersonal eyes of future generations prying into what had been of such intimate, immediate, desperate, and secret concern to him. I believe the clue to understanding is in the word "secret." All that happened took place in an area of the personality where the secret of the growth of the future self in the presence of the *numinous* must be kept forever, since no one except the self committed utterly to it can know the reality of the experience without destroying it—a principle we have already seen so obediently observed in Jung's own childhood and adolescence and initiation into manhood. He has kept it thus, I believe, so that we can understand it according to our several capacities, not only with the kind of "not understanding" he mentioned before but also understanding through our own need of a secret that is sacred and vital to the growth of our own self.

I believe this to be true all the more because of something he wrote on love to Mary Mellon, who had been a patient of his and to whom he was especially devoted. The letter seems to me to gain in point because it was written during the dark night of the Western spirit we call the Second World War. "You should come up to the level of such understanding whose vehicle is love and not the mind. This love is not transference [a psychological state of projection frequent between patient and psychiatrist and which Jung always guarded against] and it is no ordinary friendship or sympathy. It is more primitive, more primeval and more spiritual, than anything we can describe. . . . That upper floor is no more you or I, it means many, including yourself and anybody whose heart you touch. There is no distance, but immediate presence. It is an eternal secret—how shall I ever explain it?" And the key words are "eternal secret" and confession of his inability to explain. Yet though one cannot explain the eternal secret, one can understand and explain the inability, and indeed is forced to if one's evaluation of him is not to be maimed. I assert the right of freedom to follow the meaning which the omission has for each of us with greater confidence because he told me he emerged from the long years of his encounter with the collective unconscious convinced that it had enriched him so that his life was no longer his own or his family's but belonged henceforth to the generality of man. All that battle and suffering and shaping of unknown forces ultimately had meaning for him because it was a specific of experience that was capable of transformation in a great universal.

As for Toni Wolff the woman, who was to be his companion, she was a great and rare spirit, one of the few patricians and certainly the truest in Jung's immediate company of collaborators. She had a courage and vision of conduct perhaps alien to the *haute* Swiss and international bourgeoisie who surrounded Jung. She brought with her what was perhaps best in the spirit of her native Bern. In this country of city states Bern too was unique. Basel might have had more of intellect and sense of history, Zürich more of the life of commerce and exchange with the material world, Lucerne more of the evolution of a Swissness from the foremost aboriginal Swiss stock, and Geneva might see its role as the fortress of conscience and culture of the uniquely French contribution to Switzerland; but in Bern, where the Latin and Germanic in the Swiss character met and were united as a double-edged one, there grew in time a truly classical, aristocratic approach to life. The Bernese too thought themselves a cut above the rest—a cut, however, not of the qualities of which the others boasted but of superior "breeding," which imposed responsibilities that made them almost the most serious of citizens in a naturally serious country.

Toni Wolff had in full measure all that is best in these Bernese attributes, perhaps oversimplified as they are here. She was an aristocrat of mind and spirit and ready and capable for a role in Jung's life outside the realm of the eminently respectable, so conceivable and natural was it to her, as anyone who has read her essay on the psychology of types in women will instantly recognise. In that she added to Jung's definition of the four functions a concept of woman born into four types: the woman as Mother and Wife; as Hetaera, companion and friend of man; as Amazon, the woman with a calling of her own, self-contained and independent of man; and finally woman as Medium, at home on the frontiers of the unconscious and conscious in the human spirit, as unegotistical in her seeking as the Amazon tends to be the egoistic if not egotistical. She herself seems to me clearly to have been born an inspired Hetaera and one cannot read what she has written on this type without experiencing it as flame and flicker of her inmost self. In this essay and others she was to make her own contribution to analytical psychology and she could enlarge Jung's concepts of the masculine in woman and the nature of feminine psychology, which were obviously hidden even to such a man, precisely because out of an inherited sense of a special right of breeding she placed herself outside the restrictions of the conventional.

Even her clothes proclaimed the manner of the person she was. In an unworldly society such as that of the women who surrounded Jung, no one paid undue regard to style and indulgence in dress. Toni Wolff was always for me a notable exception of the best and most fastidiously dressed woman of all. She carried herself with natural elegance, had a formidable intelligence and generally a great air of something select and special about her. Even the bone beneath the skin of a fine, distinctively modelled face seemed to be of an unusual precision and delicacy, utterly without excess of structure. But I myself remember above all those wide-open dark eyes of hers. When I first met her I remember thinking, in the primitive way natural to me, that they were eyes capable of seeing in the dark. I always thought of her instinctively—and I had some knowledge to confirm the instinct—as the human equivalent of the porcupine who in the mythology of my native desert was the daughter-in-law of the god-hero, a Stone Age Ariadne married to a son who was for Stone Age man the rainbow element in the sky, always an image of a conscious discriminating element in the human spirit, for them as in the Bible and Goethe. This porcupine had large sensitive eyes that could see through the dark and were held to be so precious that when she retired to her bed at dawn in some burrow in the sand, two bats came to hang upside down over the entrance, to protect her eyes from the light of the fierce desert day.

Indeed, this feminine porcupine was not only a creation wise in the ways of the night but with its highly developed sense of smell an embodiment of the intuitive, of that which tells us of what lies hidden and to come in the life and spirit of man. Moreover, it is she who in the god-hero's fateful encounter with the "all-devourer" sees to it that the dark, destructive power is killed and the god-hero rescued from its stomach and restored to greater life and meaning than before.

Jung loved this story of the Stone Age god-hero's encounter with an "all-devourer" above all others I brought him from Africa and I had to tell it to him several times. In his own descent into what was the "all-devourer" in himself and his culture, Toni Wolff was both porcupine and Ariadne to him. Great as her services were in the conscious orchestration of his psychological theme, therefore, I do not think they can compare with the service she rendered Jung in this way and I for one believe the world owes her on this account a gratitude which no one yet has attempted to assess, let alone openly express.

She was so singularly qualified a spirit for this purpose because she had come to Jung originally as a patient. One is not allowed, I believe, even now, because of those regards which Jung himself said last more than a lifetime, to say what was his diagnosis of her condition. All one can say is that it must have been affliction of stresses proportionate to the meaning that came out of it. That presupposes something considerable. As a result, on that day when Jung decided to let himself drop, she was the only one capable of understanding out of her own experience and transfiguration what Jung was taking upon himself. This world of the unconscious which he was entering as a man she had already inhabited and endured as a woman and, thanks to Jung's guidance, had re-emerged an enlarged and reintegrated personality.

In 1911 she was a co-delegate to a famous conference with Freud and his followers, the Third International Psychoanalytic Congress in Weimar. In the official photograph taken of the occasion she is conspicuous among the other participants, staring wide-eyed with a wondering, unpreconceived glance at the camera.

As a person whose thinking and intuitive functions were superior attributes, she appears the one in the group almost overwhelmed by a sense of the importance of the breakthrough into a new level of human awareness to which the occasion testifies, and as yet so innocent of the exacting role which was to be imposed on her later that one is strangely moved and troubled on her account. I say exacting, but can hardly avoid adding adjectives like "harsh" and even "cruel" because I believe that of all those closest to Jung she suffered most. She was by nature too proud to complain and in any case found more than reward enough in the meaning she gained in being Jung's most intimate companion and guide during those long, protracted years of his critical and at times, psychologically speaking, most dangerous moments of his encounter with the blind Salome forces of his own collective unconscious. But the dignity and willingness with which she accepted this role and the apparent ease with which she ignored the envy of a world jealous of her special relationship with Jung should not be allowed to disguise the staggering burdens it all imposed on her.

I have known men and women who were hosts to Jung and Toni Wolff when they travelled on psychological missions outside Switzerland and these people have spoken of their dismay when in the intimacy of their homes they observed Toni Wolff repeatedly in the grip of great distress. I doubt whether any man is capable of fully comprehending what she was called on to endure, let alone of measuring her achievement. I have a feeling that it needs a woman aware of the burden of projection of man's own blind and demanding feminine self which her sex has had to carry throughout the ages to do her justice in this regard. Yet even a man can guess at the scale of both stress and achievement by the difficulties he himself endures in carrying the projection of other natures onto his own. This ruthless mechanism of projection of what is rejected in a personality onto some other suitable and convenient human being demanded in the first instance, in a nature so profoundly introverted as that of Jung, an externalised form that would not give under its weight. Indeed, it demanded externalisation or, perhaps better, a living personification in the world without, sufficiently lasting and authoritative in its own right not to surrender to the forces that invested it or to disintegrate under doubt of the other being who could so use it.

Throughout these long years Toni Wolff stood fast and in the process not only sustained the full weight of Jung's undiscovered feminine self, enabling him thereby to live it out through her into maturity, but inevitably became also the vulnerable intermediary between himself and his embattled shadow. Both these burdens, of course, were proportionate to the man and the greatness of his seeking; years later when the projection could be withdrawn and received back with honour by its first cause in Jung's spirit, and the heavy problem of the shadow was firmly positioned between his own immeasurably broadened shoulders, it must have been as if somewhere on the margin of the universe, trumpets were sounded for them.

And yet one wonders if at that moment of what appears to an outsider a great victory for the human spirit, Toni Wolff did not feel herself to be declared redundant, to use one of the most sinister euphemisms of our day, and condemned to unemployment for the rest of her life. She certainly would have been less than human had she not been tempted to see it so but if so, the temptation did not triumph, even if, as I suspected, it never gave up and was to go on trying in vain again and again. Whatever the problem left, she accepted it as her own and the material with which she should look for work. Indeed, with the insight gained into her own nature and that of men through this close alliance in battle with Jung, she became self-employed with an effect even greater than it is acknowledged to have been, as will soon be evident when her last collected works and papers are published.

What she meant to Jung on that perilous journey can perhaps be summed up best in something he told me towards the end of his life. He was carving in stone, which had become his favourite visual medium, some sort of memorial of what Emma Jung and Toni Wolff had brought to his life. On the stone for his wife he was cutting the Chinese symbols meaning "She was the foundation of my house." On the stone intended for Toni Wolff, who had died first, he wanted to inscribe another Chinese character to the effect that she was the fragrance of the house. The imagery of meaning of which this ancient Chinese ideogram is a direct visual expression is clearly saying thereby that she was the "scent," which represents the faculty of intuition I have mentioned.

And finally and most conclusive of all, there is the testimony of Emma Jung herself, great spirit that she was. Just before she died she told a friend of mine close to both herself and her husband, "I shall always be grateful to Toni for doing for my husband what I or anyone else could not have done for him at a most critical time."

This gap, this silence, then is the guiding and the bridging that was Toni Wolff in Jung's hour of trial and peril, the most significant outside aid that brought him to total emancipation from the negations personified by a blind Salome. He was ready, armed and prepared now for his discovery of the profoundest level of all of the rejections of the feminine of which man had been capable. This was the rejection in the depth of the spirit of woman of what she had of a creative masculine element, which though it may be personified in the imagination as a "man," is as sexless in its intent as the "feminine" is in man.

However honoured woman has been in history as mistress, wife, and mother, they discovered together on this journey, there is no sustained period in which she is acknowledged in this other aspect of herself that is beyond all those recognised states of her being and when, with all her exacting biological and social duties to life honestly done, she goes on at long last to create in her own right as man has always done in his. History remains unilluminated by any realisation that just as man has a feminine self through which he creates, woman has this masculine self, not to be confused with the man without, through whom she longs to make a contribution to life, no longer as wife or mother or in some vicarious role but in her own unique right.

What there is in history is ominous evidence enough of a hidden instinctive resentment in woman over the failure of man to recognise and honour this aspect of her spirit and a backlash of vengeance and revenge over this ignorance that produces her slanted and one-sided association with man. There was the phenomenon of the Amazons in the myths and legends of Greece, and the fact that they were one of the forces with whom Jason had to come to terms before he could successfully accomplish his mission to retrieve the Golden Fleece, an image of life transformed and made whole. The Amazons were one of the earliest manifestations in the Western spirit of the phenomenon we know today as Women's Lib. And, of course, there was the Virgin Goddess, the huntress Diana, to provide a portentous image, serving notice on our imaginations of this urge in women to give birth also to a meaning peculiarly their own. But the hints were not taken up and the warning notices ignored.

All our yesterdays contrived to determine that when Jung set out on this journey, it was in a context of life where what woman personifies was twice rejected, first in the shape of the feminine in man and then in her own masculine creative self. One of the most significant facts that Jung brought back from this journey was that man and woman are not merely a biological twosome joined through sex, to carry as best they can the burdens and mysteries of life. They are a foursome, the man and this feminine self personified by the Beatrices, Ariadnes, and ultimately Sophias of history and legend, the woman and a masculine self not yet so accessible to understanding because, due to the heavy duties imposed on her by her own biological nature and her exploitation by man, she has not up to now been allowed, except vicariously, to articulate it for herself. She indeed became so much part of the machinery of her own rejection that she was unaware of it and, when not aiding and abetting it, could only hint at it to herself and others in imagery that came unbidden to her spirit.

The havoc caused by the long denial of this element in human relationships between men and their women, mothers and sons, fathers and daughters, as well as the disorder and disaster in societies and their cultures, has been immense and cries out for historical recognition and definition if history is ever to achieve its full contemporary meaning.

Anticipating one set of the main conclusions Jung drew from this journey into the unconscious, one is compelled to say, therefore, that for the first time it is now possible for man and woman to join together and stand, as it were, four-square in the battle for new and greater being. The prospect of enrichment and enlargement of life is immeasurably increased. A greater relationship between man and woman, a complete renewal of their attitudes to one another, promises, whatever the confusion and agony of the present moment, a richer partnership of the human spirit than any life has ever seen.

But none of this, of course, was to be foreseen at the start of Jung's journey wherein the only form of guidance was discredited in advance as mentally deranged and sick. Even apart from the doubts induced thereby, he had troubles of another kind. From the day on which he said, "Well, Jung, here you go," and fell, he had nothing in the experience of man to help him in his evaluations. He did not know how to deal with all the other aspects of that strange material gushing up out of this underworld like the lava of a volcanic eruption, except by taking seriously the promptings of a long-neglected instinctive self, however trivial, absurd, or improbable. He had already had to learn, as I have tried to show, like a child of the spirit learning to walk, to take everything, no matter how formidable or chaotic, with the utmost seriousness and to give each trifle such expression and form of which he was capable. In addition to his toy modelling, despite all he had of help in the world without, he found it necessary now also to write down meticulously his dreams and put into words the erupting visionary material. Where words and his considerable powers of articulation failed him, he took to drawing and painting. He read deeper than ever into history and mythology and whenever he found a parallel followed it in an endeavour to recover the continuity which he appeared for the moment to have lost.

His first record was kept in a black book. That in itself I find most meaningful. I feel it is awesome evidence of how in this world of the unconscious there is nothing that does not matter and is not there for a purpose, however enigmatic and infinitesimal its manifestation. An imperative of underground logic seems to have demanded that Jung should begin with something black if he were to proceed on his journey accurately. He had no choice in the matter. A law of the symbolism through which this great unknown of the human spirit speaks to us presupposed a black book, because always with all acts of creation there is darkness at the beginning. The light that the spirit is allowed in the first instance is a dark light streaming out of a night dreaming of transformation into the light of day. Just as meaningful, therefore, is the fact that some relief came to him from the pressures of his journey by their transformation into the world of his black book, because the Word as we know, was synonymous with light at the beginning.

He steadily became more confident of the worth of the material so recorded and this relief and confidence impelled him to transfer the record to a greater book known today as the Red Book. There was the same progression of unconscious logic in that too. It is the badge of work of a life-giving intent. It is almost as if this Red Book were both pledge and armour for a questing spirit, a parallel of the imagery of the quest for the Grail of a Parsifal, who wears red mail too, so vulnerable is he in utmost simplicity of spirit, typical of the state of blessed ignorance and impressionability which precedes the greatest of human ventures, and which Jung too showed in this phase of his journey.

It is no accident that round about this time, in this netherworld of his imagination, Jung should have a vision of a fountain of blood rising up and spurting high and wide through the earth. For blood too is red and both fire and furnace, where new meaning is forged in the smithy of ourselves. This fountain of a fire of blood is an image of a requickening of the spirit and a drive upward of long-buried meaning hastening to bring new light against the darkness which presses so blue against the little glass of our day.

One longs for the Red Book to be published in facsimile. It is Jung's first and most immediate testament, and infinitely evocative. When I first saw it, my eyes were stung by its beauty. I thought there was something numinous about it. A kind of Merlinesque gift seemed to have determined the deep colour and grave proportions. My first reaction had been not to open it, as if it would be prying. I was not tempted, however, by any ordinary curiosity. Had not Jung himself discussed it openly with me and others, referred to it in several books, and without hesitation used visual material from it whenever necessary for illustrating his meaning, I would never have wanted to see it. Also, I knew that nothing Jung ever did ultimately was private or personal in any egotistical or formal collective sense.

All that he did in this regard was on behalf of a gift which demanded that he should be one of the foremost servants of meaning in the life of his time.

Everything in the Red Book was ultimately intended to help the cause to which his life was dedicated, and was important to every human being with a problem of his own. This instant impact of beauty was, I believe, a consequence of the movement from black to red and so an annunciation of transfiguration. The transfiguration is in the writing. The ancient illuminated script glows with the light as of a dream and shows something old and forgotten, remembered and made new. The parchment is of a thick, medieval texture and the painting which illustrates the text is of royal authority.

All in the Black Book is dark, and such light as there is dwells in the words. But in the Red Book all is light and colour and in the smouldering beauty the glow of new meaning caught and made visible. For perhaps the greatest of all forms of beauty of which our senses are capable is inspired by a meaning that has been denied life. It is the dress of welcome to aspects of the spirit returning from a dark night of exile into the company of its peers. It is the Cinderella in man arriving at last at the ball. It is, if one were to use the language of theology now dishonoured and rejected, an expression of joy over evil redeemed, the outward sign that what was base as lead has been transformed and transfigured in some alchemy of ourselves, into gold. It is chaos made free and accessible in form and proportion.

For all these reasons and more, the imagination is compelled to salute arrival at a new stage of the spirit at some remote frontier hospice of meaning with an assertion of beauty in whatever material is most fitting and nearest at hand. It does not matter whether the material was stone, which Jung was to use again later, the word, colour, or even more mysteriously some movement or sound not seen or heard before, combining to produce an effect that rings out like some kind of trumpet call of Reveille to sleeping senses. It is the final imperative of a demand of life which cannot be evaded without mortal injury to itself and insists that all should be lived in the grace of the beauty, since what men have long labelled with the drab and now unfashionable word "morality" is obedience to a law of a life demanding to be lived with the harmony called beauty. Ethics, in so far as they are real, also have their own aesthetic of behaviour.

Jung, of course, had never thought of himself as a painter and any voice within himself suggesting that he should become an artist was regarded as the voice of temptation from which he devoutly sought to be delivered. Yet the painting of dreams and visions in the Red Book are not unworthy of comparison with William Blake. For me Blake's work, for all its authority and power, has a cold, graveyard monumentalism about it. Jung's, I find, even where the hand is less experienced and certain than Blake's, is warm and rich, his touch so near that one feels one has only to stretch out one's own hand to meet it. The paintings are all the more moving because they are proof how in every human spirit, however unschooled, there is provision for doing whatever is basically necessary for its survival, if it has the humility to accept the unfamiliar forms in which the means, the unlikely opportunity, and time to do so reveal themselves.

Nothing to my mind shows as this Red Book does how in the confrontation of Jung with the great unknown in himself and the life of his time, the strangest of material yielded progressively to more and more significant form. Though as abstract at times as any pattern inflicted on Euclid, the vision is nonetheless given a definite and almost measurable shape, until suddenly the abstraction becomes capable of personification. The material is suddenly orchestrated in recognisable forms of life.

It is as if the word at this strange beginning in this chaos of himself suddenly becomes flesh and blood. Some of the paintings are from a Hieronymus Bosch stage of himself, others like those of Blake magnetic with shapes of man. There are illustrations as of some Ulysses on his journey home and black ships returning from war on some great Trojan plain within. One of the first is of a world under a sun with a red Crusader's cross inscribed on it, the cross that is the sign of all four seasons and four quarters in man, and so a compass of a life to be encircled and made complete.

Last of all there is a painting of a castle, four-square, as in a green-gold haze of space and time. It is of a design Jung was later to recognise from the Chinese material brought to him from the lonely Wilhelm as another imprint of the abiding theme of their yellow castle. One glance shows that this is the end of a great beginning, a Prospero moment in Jung's life when figuratively the book and all its magic is about to be buried, as the *Tempest*'s was, "deeper than did ever any plummet sound."

It is for me in all its austerity the most moving of all the paintings because it confirms Jung's safe arrival at an impregnable destination. It makes the moment of which the unfashionable Kipling wrote in a poem which draws keenly on the language of the fairy-tale world of his childhood, "Let down the drawbridge for the dreamer, the dreamer whose dream has come true."

The last page of the Red Book is finally turned and Jung, fortified, returns to the world of recorded history and time, to put his journey in the context of his own increasingly desperate day and produce facts and evaluations of his achievement in an idiom contemporary man can understand.

How long the confrontation had lasted and in what protracted detail it had been fought, recorded, and all the psychological spoil specified and classified, emerges from the single statistical fact that the year wherein he painted the castle which announced the last battle won and the campaign ended was the year 1928. The immediate practical message of all these years for Jung was clear. All the great intangible, imponderable, ineffable, and yet objective demonic images, dreams, fantasies, and things with which he had been concerned were not just to do with himself but with modern man as a whole. He had not only ceased to belong to himself in the process but had lost the right to do so. He had always held the belief that it was immoral to know just for knowing's sake while remaining without a moral commitment to the knowledge and trying to live according to the ethics of total commitment to the cause of life. This commitment had been now, as it were, empirically established for him.

The long *queste* and *aventiure* might be over but, home to himself in a way he had never been home before, he accepted that he would have to take all the treasure of new meaning for all to share in the world from which his deepest self had for so long been withdrawn; take it, moreover, in the only way he knew it could understand and accept, the hard empirical and scientific way wherein he had been trained. He knew he could only do so without deviation by a rededication of his total self to the psyche, to the search of modern man for a soul which was in its seeking as masculine as it was feminine, and all so devout in love.

He was as always confirmed in this step by the dreaming of a new dream—perhaps the most moving and beautiful of the many rich dreams he dreamt in his long life. It was set in Liverpool. Why

Liverpool? Because the "liver" in antiquity, in anatomical symbolism, was the source of life; "pool" was the water, which was the most evocative of images of unconscious creative elements. The city therefore was not the drab, dingy, sprawling harbour city of England but a place of singular meaning in the imagination. The harbour aspect of it was important, of course, because it suggests an image of the area of his imagination where voyages began and ended, where outward- and inward-bound traffic met and the cargo of his own spirit went out for vital exchange and gathering of meaning from beyond the seas of himself home in its place.

The streets of this place still were dark and the real inhabited part of the city on cliffs high above him, but he could not fail to notice that all was arranged radially as if presupposing a circular perimeter of the township with a square at the centre. Why circular and why square? Both were images of totality and wholeness, as Jung was to amplify and demonstrate empirically with circumspection. They were images of collective wholeness and the company of six other Swiss with him, suggesting human collectivity in the dream, not only failed to be interested in any of this but just complained endlessly, he told me, how awful the weather was, as it is indeed only too often in the Liverpools of the world. He in the dream hardly noticed them because he was utterly absorbed, senses, spirit, and all, in another kind of vision. In the centre of the square, despite the fog, rain, and smoke, was a round pool and in the centre of the pool, blazing in sunlight, a small island. In the middle of the island stood a splendid magnolia exploding into flower with reddish flames which added a light of their own to that of the sun. His companions could not see the tree and spoke only of another Swiss who lived there. Only Jung, enchanted, saw it and knew why that strange other Swiss lived there in such a city: because that was his new and as yet strange self, coming home at last to his island totality.

It is because of this that I find the dream almost unbearably moving. It confirms all that we have suspected of meaning in the mythological groping of our confused, muddled, and bloody yesterdays; we have all an island self with a tree of life in flower. The tree might be winter-bare on the first day of sailing, but if the voyage is continued to its true Odyssean end the tree is in flower and in the sun on the day of return.

Here Jung is about to complete the golden chain of the authentic spirit of man, however lost, over the horizon of history, and is at one with Odysseus and his return to Ithaca, as he is with us who are still seeking similar self-realisation, reunited with the impoverished boy who walked down at heel in cheap and patched clothes along the Rhine to school, and fashioned a sextant, and experienced a foretaste of his island self manifested in this dream through the creation in fantasy in midstream of the urgent mythological river—a fortified island kingdom of his own.

ಿ Point of Total Return

> You yourself are even another little world and have
> within you the sun and the moon and also the stars.
>
> Origen, *Liviticum Homiliae*

THE DEEPEST OF ALL the patterns in the human spirit is one of
departure and return and the journey implicit in between. Perhaps
one of the most concise and dynamic definitions of this pattern of
departure, journey, and return and its meaning is to be found in the
New Testament parable of the prodigal son. Taken at a manifest
level the parable is a story of a great injustice. The son who takes his
inheritance in advance from a rich father, spends it, and is reduced
to such a state of poverty that he lives with swine, is welcomed back
by the father as if he had done more than was expected of him and
had fulfilled his youthful promise to an extent not achieved by the
brother who had stayed at home and had done all that duty to father,
family, and society demanded of him. No wonder the brother feels
himself unjustly treated, but this injustice is condoned in religious
convention by the fact that it enables the father to demonstrate his
capacity for forgiveness. For this is the one lesson derived by
theologians from the parable and preached from Christian pulpits all
over the world to this day.

But there is another and I believe far more significant symbolic

level to the parable, designed to sow quite a different seed of being
and new sort of truth in us, totally apart from the perfunctory
concept of our obligation to forgive one another—important as that
so obviously is. This truth is that the parable dramatises legitimately
the imperative of the need of man when young to separate himself
from the father and live a life of his own. The money he receives
from the father is an image of the talents he has been given by life
and the story tells him that far from hoarding these talents, which
the New Testament has already warned no one must bury, far from
being thrifty about them as the brother left at home is, it is the duty
of the young to spend them utterly—in other words, to use his
talents until they consciously seem worn out and he is enabled to see
at last how impoverished his collective self is, how inadequate and
provisional the world and the social realisations demanded by it.

And yet even so, considered in both these meaningful dimensions,
the parable is still strangely incomplete. Why is there no mention of
the prodigal's mother? Surely she must have rejoiced too at the
return of a long-lost son as much as the father, out of the natural love
of which the feminine in man is the keeper. Was she dead? The
parable does not say, but if so it means that even in the New
Testament and its profession of divine love, there was lacking the
feminine element necessary to complete it. Or was she alive and not
considered worth mentioning? If so, worse still, because though
there for the asking, the feminine in life has been wilfully oppressed.
The parable for me as expression of this profound father in man
would only have been totally fulfilled if both father and mother had
been present to welcome in equal measure the prodigal sailor in man
home from the sea.

Jung's too was a prodigal return but to both the masculine and
feminine in man, strengthened by trial as few have been tried. To
put it in its classical Odyssean imagery, he had returned despite
numerous shipwrecks, storms, and encounters with one-eyed Titans
like the gigantic scientific establishment of his day, whose inadequacy of vision had been prophetically summed up as "one-eyed" by
Blake in the famous accusation hurled at Newton nearly two
centuries before. One-eyed too in its vision from the spires of the
vast edifice of organised religion had been the formidable enmity
incurred from eminent divines and theologians. There had been also
temptations of siren song like that of the lady posing as anima who

tried to lure Jung from science into art. He had also suffered and survived abandonment, Odysseus-like, after his crew, his colleagues and friends, forsook him when Freud excommunicated him for the heresy of denying a dogma and doctrine of psychosexuality, id, ego, and super-ego. He had to endure more shipwreck again in his voyage within until he must have felt in his final encounter with the collective unconscious, as Odysseus did in the storm to end all storms hurled by Zeus against him, that the gods were resolved never to let him see again the smoke of evening falling over the housetops of his island home. Yet in the face of all this and more, he had endured to come at last to the true feminine in himself and walked out of the deep sea onto firm land in the here and now, as Odysseus had done, to be welcomed by his own inner version of Nausicaa, and now could be made ready for final return to the harbour city by the island water of life hastening to his relief in a dream as of some Liverpool.

What was even more surprising is that in the midst of so much, he had made time to fashion the one instrument essential for communicating his discovery to the world without danger of being misunderstood by anyone willing to hear and examine the evidence. He knew that one never had armour adequate for turning back the assaults of those who just would not want to hear and look objectively at the evidence. They would, of course, be the vast multitude, but what he could do was to make certain that he should not be misunderstood by men and women of good will and good faith. He told me how often he thought in this regard of the example of Christ, whom he saw as the Western world's total revelation of the eternal pattern of the Anthropos, the self, in the spirit of man, which was the supreme value brought back from his journey.

He would remind himself again and again how Christ appeared to have addressed himself only once to the masses of his time and that was in the Sermon on the Mount. Thereafter Christ had behaved as if he too cherished at heart the truth of the ancient Chinese saying, "The Master speaks but once." He henceforth confined himself to those who sought and asked for him in their hearts and concentrated on his twelve disciples as if to imply that if he could transform only those twelve he would have accomplished what he had been born to do.

When I said that I had often thought Christ's remark of where two or three were gathered together in His name was His definition of a maximum and not a minimum, Jung did not smile, as I had perhaps hoped he who was so quick to warm to irony might have done. Instead he said gravely that he often did not even have the comfort of two or three in his far less exalted role on the journey behind him but had to find his solace from the saying referred to in the Apocryphal New Testament, "And where there is one alone, I say I am with him."

So he had concentrated what there was of him to spare on making certain that there was a new psychological form of communication, a common code for deciphering all the many psychological ciphers of communication present in life, confusing their form with the content of this meaning, so that those who searched and asked the sort of questions he was asking could not get at cross-purposes with him or themselves and would have a fair chance of understanding as they wished themselves to be understood.

This new psychological language was set out in a long book published in 1921 when the campaign, though far from over, was beginning to release a feeling of ultimate victory through the atmosphere within. It was called *Psychological Types*, or *The Psychology of Individuation*. (The subtitle appeared only in the English translation published two years later and may have been the contribution of H. G. Baynes, the translator.) Typically Jung had turned his mind to the task which seemed nearest at the time. He had realised instantly that the unconscious in man could be observed only through what was conscious in man and that unless this phenomenon, so subjective and diversified in its quality and extent in every human being, was itself most carefully investigated and its working understood, no common evaluation of its role and consequences would be possible. The book was therefore the first serious empirical examination in our history of the phenomenon of consciousness.

Its immediate motivation was rooted in Freud's traumatic quarrel with him. After the first shock—the deepest personal shock, I believe, associated with any other male relationship experienced in his life—Jung rediscovered that significant calm which first came over him the day he was falsely accused of plagiarism over the brilliant essay he had written at school in Basel. He discovered that far more interesting and important than the personal pain inflicted on him was the motive of Freud's break with him. They were both persons of good faith, dedicated to the service of truth; he never doubted Freud in this regard or questioned his greatness. And yet they had fallen out with each other. Why? He knew all the rationalisations of their differences, all the plausible excuses and justifications for Freud's decision to exile him and go his own way, but none of them satisfied the sense of truth in him. He was convinced that there was more to it than that and wanted at first to probe into the deeper causes he suspected of the quarrel in Freud as in himself. But he felt incapable of doing so impartially at that time. He was too closely and painfully involved in personal history and consequences with Freud. So he turned instead to ground where he could explore similar material more objectively. Freud and another of his earlier adherents, Adler, had also quarrelled and it was out of an examination of the underground of this epoch-making dispute that the larger work commenced.

I remember one cold winter afternoon walking with Jung by the black Maggiore water, the snow pink in the evening sun on what are for me the most sinister of hills in the Alps. He was unusually depressed and had upon him one of those moments of self-denigration which came to him from time to time. He complained with heart-rending conviction that he had done nothing, absolutely nothing, of his essential task in life and with each "nothing" he would hit a rut of snow beside him with that stout English country walking-stick of his. I protested vigorously and said, "If you had done nothing else but given us that great instrument of understanding one another in your book of psychological types, and made us capable of speaking at last a common psychological language, you would have done more than enough."

I said that because it is a cardinal belief of mine. This difficult and much neglected book of Jung is a turning point in the art of human communications about which we hear so much and do so little these days. It is a discovery, as it were, of a fool-proof technology of mind for making communication intelligible between all men, no matter what their differences. I told him how in itself it was, I felt convinced, the greatest and most courageous of achievements that in the middle of his life-and-death confrontation with the forces of the unconscious, he had had the space of mind and time to devote himself to finding the answer to why it was that persons so absolutely dedicated and honourable as Freud, Adler, and himself should disagree. And, I added, what a real breakthrough for us all it was when he came to the conclusion that it was in the first instance a problem of inborn type.

He had demonstrated in this book that all human beings were born what he called either extroverted or introverted. Freud was an extrovert, Adler an introvert. They represented two extremes of psychology that cut right the way through life and made a great divide in the history of the human spirit. Here was the origin, for instance, of classical and romantic urges in art, the Apollonian and Dionysian in the mind, the Greek and Trojan in legend and history, French and German, and so on up to the vitalists and mechanists in the sciences of our own day.

It was characteristic of the objectivity and respect of truth in him that he could say, "I have often had patients for whom a Freudian approach or an Adlerian approach worked better than mine and did not hesitate to use either, because my own did not exclude what was valid in theirs."

So historically the extrovert had tried to achieve meaning by form shaped to contain, the introvert by change and moving outward and on. One sought his meaning mainly within, the other without; the one, as it were, by breathing in, the other by breathing out, but neither making the whole being of man. What life demanded was a state of man whose spirit breathed both in and out.

His book supported this with detailed evidence from the progression of philosophy, religion, art, and science and then went even further. He found that within these two great divisions there were other differences as well. Each human being had four "functions." Two of these, called feeling and thinking, were rational functions. ("Feeling" here is not to be confused with "emotion." Owing to the limitations of English in this regard it has to stand for the function in man which evaluated.) "Thinking," in an age which it has so singularly arrogated to itself, needs no defining.

The other two functions were irrational, or perhaps better, non-rational. These were intuition and sensation—not to be confused with the sensation on which "sensationalism" is based, but the function through which man has his sense of the here and now.

These definitions are, of course, simplifications of an extremely complex concept and Jung always stressed how they were not complete and, as it were, signposts on the road to understanding. But what it is important to realise is that his empiric evidence shows that man is born with *one* function consciously in command and another working in close support of it, and the other two pushed down towards the unconscious. One of the supreme tasks of becoming whole himself, therefore, was to eliminate not only the warfare in the spirit of man between the superior and suppressed functions but the warfare that was caused by this great divide of the extrovert and introvert.

The human spirit, once seen in this way, is utterly deprived of any justifications for the state of civil war in which it has existed since the beginning of time. I think of Anatole France's saying that had travelled the battlefields of Europe, Africa, and the Far East with me: "Human beings are forever killing one another over words, whereas if they had only understood what the words were trying to say, they would have embraced one another."

After Jung's *Psychological Types*, I am convinced, we no longer have any valid excuse for not realising that we are all ultimately trying to say the same things and express the same longings in terms of our own unique natures. We have no excuse any more for destroying others just because their own psychology demands a different idiom of utterance, for the message is always the same.

The consequences of providing mankind with a common code for the first time in life are formidable. The achievement is a preliminary for attaining this brotherhood of man which I shall try to show is already waiting prepared and fully armed in Jung's hypothesis of the collective unconscious. I told him so plainly during those walks at Ascona. But he was not in a mood to be comforted, and remained uncomforted for a long time. Soon after my return to England I had a letter from him in which he concluded, "I am an increasingly lonely old man writing for other lonely men."

In all this he did not fail to call himself to account and I shall deal later with the psychological type to which he believed himself to belong. What mattered, despite the deprecation by himself that day of a book written nearly forty years before, was that it proved that no one could succeed ever in freeing himself of profound bias and prejudice and acquire a full-ranging taste and evaluation of life, science, and art unless he had some idea of the kind of type he himself represented. Without it we certainly could not set to work on our inferior and less conscious functions, as Jung proved was essential for a greater awareness and realisation of ourselves.

In this regard an example not from our own controversial time but from history is perhaps more helpful. Goethe, for instance, plainly was not only an extrovert but an intuitive, feeling type with thinking and sensation in the shadow of himself. *Faust* is only partially understood if it is not seen also as an expression of Goethe's inferior aspects, thinking and sensation. That is why Goethe was of so great an importance to the German spirit; he was a compensation to the Faustian will and predominant thinking and sensation functions of his culture and the whole drama of *Faust* achieves its universality because through it Goethe brings into light what is dark, dangerous, archaic, and angry in himself and the spirit of his time. And I chose Goethe also because of his significance in this regard to Jung, and in particular for his orchestration of this drama of what Jung was to call the "shadow" in the human spirit. Jung took the task of Goethe in this regard symbolically upon himself and tried to correct through his own example what he thought inadequate in Faust. Faust's murder of Philemon and Baucis, the masculine and feminine who had been worldly hosts to the gods, he regarded as a singular sin. For in his pact with the devil, the power of darkness, Faust committed the classical hubris of swinging over from one opposite into the other, setting up another form of tyrannical partiality as a whole, thereby eliminating man from his instinctive experience of the mighty other activity Jung called God.

One of Jung's main tasks, therefore, was to enable modern man to allow these two elements of Philemon and Baucis to be reborn and grow in his spirit and once more open himself and all others to the experience of the ultimate urge and resurge of life. He laboured in vain as far as Germany was concerned but need not have laboured in vain as far as we and our future are involved in the same dilemma. It is for this reason that his No. 2 was called Philemon, as we have seen, so that calm and at his ease and always acquiring new insight from him, Jung installed him, some two years after publishing his difficult book on types, in the tower he built at Bollingen, calling part of the tower "Shrine of Philemon: Repentance of Faust." As token of the antiquity and validity of this process of atonement and redemption, he carved the phrase in Latin firmly in yellow stone.

How deeply he had taken this problem to heart and how much he had worked on it to the immense benefit of his own awareness is illustrated, for example, by the difference in attitude displayed to the first and second world wars. The first, judging by his correspondence and conversation, did not strike nearly so deep as the second. There was little outside mention of it, partly, one suspects, because of his own desperate battle started within and the fact that the war seemed to him then mainly a great portent of confirmation in the external world of the importance and validity of the war raging in a similar pattern within himself. But the march of Europe and the world towards the war of 1939 was a totally different matter.

There was a brief moment at the beginning when this stirring of unconscious forces he saw in Germany seemed to him capable of a positive potential. This may seem surprising in someone who had already been aware of the perilous and rapidly widening dichotomy in the German spirit from so early an age—first through Goethe's *Faust*, then the fate of Nietzsche's tragic genius soaring with a demonic zeal towards an ideal of a superman, as if he were a modern equivalent of Icarus, before plunging to annihilation on the earth whose claims he had scorned; through Burckhardt and his grim, precise intuitive foreboding of the consequences of this uncorrected slant in modern German history; and finally his own experience in trying to deal with this dichotomy in himself and others, to such an extent that as early as 1918 he addressed a sombre warning to all who would listen against the possibility of a breaking out of a "blond beast from an underworld prison" of the German spirit with disastrous consequences. Yet it is only too understandable if one remembers that in the infant years of the Nazi upsurge in Germany he himself was still under the spell of how much his own encounter with the collective unconscious had enriched him and inclined to assess any activation of it in others positively rather than negatively. But within two years he had changed his mind. His warnings against events in Germany became more frequent, urgent, and unqualified, ending in such outright condemnation that when the war broke out his own books were banned in Germany and he himself was placed on the Nazi blacklist for liquidation at the first opportunity.

No one who knew him and has studied the facts and read his work can honestly doubt that if he had foreseen in the first instance the catastrophic potential of evil in the first Nazi stirring in

Germany, he would not have given it in his own mind even the slight, short-lived chance that he did.

Had this been his only error, the matter might have been overlooked, but unfortunately he did two other things which were to become more debatable. At a moment when the Nazis were beginning to accuse the Jews of defects of spirit and cultural attributes which deprived them of all right to common human consideration, and used this patently spurious and amply discredited approach to justify their persecution of the Jews in Germany, Jung himself spoke of the differences between the culture, psychology, and character of the Jews and others. Not only were his remarks misunderstood and taken out of context to be used by the Germans as additional justification for stepping up their inhuman campaign against German and Austrian Jews but they also gave grave offence to the Jews and opponents of Hitler everywhere in Europe. Jung was totally taken aback by the storm he had gathered about himself. His remarks were truly innocent of any derogatory or malicious political intent. Utterly bewildered, he asked why it was in order for him to discuss differences in French and English psychology or Western and Chinese psychology without reprisal but could not do so about the Jews. He ignored the timing of it all, of course, as one might judge that he perhaps should not have done if one does not take into consideration how profoundly he was engaged in a totally different dimension of reality. He was even more dumbfounded when the Jews resented what they regarded in his reference to the Chinese as his comparison of them with "Mongolian hordes."

I say dumbfounded because at that moment he was working hard on the China of the *I Ching* of Richard Wilhelm and *The Secret of the Golden Flower*. Deeply impressed as he was by it all, he meant the comparison as a compliment. His letters to his Jewish colleagues at the time, like those to James Kirsch, himself a most distinguished German scholar, show how baffled he was by the accusations of anti-Semitism hurled at him.

However much anyone might deplore the timing of Jung's remarks on the Jewish cultural character, one would be relieved forever of suspecting Jung of anti-Semitism by the reading of the letters he wrote in defence of Neumann, who had escaped from Germany and settled in Tel-Aviv. In these letters he shows such a profound understanding of the plight of the Jews in history, such compassion for all they have suffered from Christian projection of the Christian shadow onto them, such appreciation of their unique and indispensable contribution to the spirit of man, that one would shed the last traces of suspecting him as anti-Semitic and not even need recourse to the host of established facts which in any case refute the disgraceful charge beyond all dispute.

Best of all, one should read Aniela Jaffé's analysis of the whole affair as set out in her masterly essay "Der Nationalsozialismus," which she wrote largely at my sustained pleading over several years, because I was so dismayed by the way this unwarranted charge continued to be raised against Jung. As a Jew herself, a refugee from Nazi Germany, a pupil and collaborator of Jung, she has, I believe, said with final authority all that there is to be said about the matter. She deals admirably too with the second reason for Jung's pro-Nazi, anti-Semitic labelling, his acceptance of the chairmanship of the International Society for Psycho-Therapy in those dubious Nazi years, which meant that for a while he had to work with the head of the German branch, a Göring who was a cousin of the notorious Hermann. That one of his main considerations in all this was to protect his Jewish colleagues in Germany and to provide them with some international status if expelled from Germany is by now well known. Nonetheless, his participation in this form was abused by Göring and others sufficiently to provide his accusers with more ammunition to use against him. Yet he did so much for his Jewish colleagues and even after his resignation continued to help them with such immense courage, ingenuity, and generosity that the persistence of the anti-Semitic, pro-Nazi charge in the face of it all must have some other motivation.

Like Aniela Jaffé, I believe it has a mythological, although a clouded mythological origin. I believe it all goes back to the traumatic break with Freud. Never in the history of the world had two such great personalities in so charged a dimension been so conspicuously placed in the centre of the stage where a new drama of time was being enacted. Immediately both in their various ways personified the projections and aspirations in the unconscious of an entire age. Unfortunately, in the way of all collective projections, the personifications were oversimplified out of all human verisimilitude until Freud represented the great benevolent, wise, generous Jewish father, the patriarchal dominant of so much of Hebraic seeking, and Jung the "adopted" non-Jewish son, the Gentile, who betrayed the great father, reducing the relationship to which we owe so much and which hurt Jung perhaps even more than Freud, though none of his accusers ever seem to think of that, to an ignominious contest between Jew and non-Jew. It is true that Freud himself did think of his psychology as sufficiently a Jewish phenomenon to regard Jung's support of him as a welcome connection and enrichment of his cause. But Jung never thought of it in any similar terms. His psychological approach was on so profound and universal a level that its racial implications were the least of all to him. Nonetheless, a vulgar mythological use of the personal story of Freud and Jung themselves continues and it is in the mythological abuse of the story of their relationship, I believe, that lies the real explanation of this continuation of the campaign against Jung for having been pro-Nazi and anti-Semitic.

One of the final ironies of this false situation is the contribution made to it indirectly by Freud himself. Until the thirties Freud had been the only distinguished Jew whom Jung had known intimately. What he knew of Jewish psychology and culture was in large measure picked up from Freud, and Freud unhappily was shockingly ill informed about his own people and their post–Old Testament evolution, as were so many German and Austrian Jews to such a tragic extent. Even what Freud knew about the Jews was restricted in the narrow confines of his own scientific approach. He rejected the Jews' greatest contribution to the history of man, their national genius for religious experience and revelation, as "occult-ism," "archaic psychosexuality," and similar reductive labels. He knew nothing, for instance, about Jewish mysticism, the eventful evolution, despite millennia of persecution in a way recorded history has not seen, of Jewish religious awareness through the mystique of the Kabbalah and the Chassidic phenomenon in central Europe. It was not until the Nazi horror brought Jung into wider contact with Jews that this side of Jewish culture became available to him and his response to it was almost as immediate and procreative as that to the China of Wilhelm had been.

Evidence of his admiration for the inspired concern of the Jews for all things of the spirit is to be found in the fact that of the three literary trustees appointed by him, two are Jews; the other one, his beloved daughter Marianne Niehus-Jung, alas, is dead. As conclusive for me is the fact that the gallant Rabbi Leo Baeck, when he heard Jung's side of the story at a meeting they had in Zürich immediately after the war, became completely reconciled to him and announced the fact publicly.

I can add perhaps one anecdote to illustrate where Jung the man stood in these desperate years of the thirties. He told me that at one of the last conferences of the international society in Germany he heard the goose-stepping Nazi hordes going by from the hall where he was speaking, and paused to say to someone on the platform beside him, "There goes the march of an age into the night."

The same day he was summoned to see Goebbels. Reluctantly but with studied correctitude he went, in the midst of a city that was reverberating night and day with the tramp of vast armies of fanatical men transported with what Jung had already described, as Caesar had once done, as *furor teutonicus.*

"I am told you have something of importance you wish to say to me," Goebbels demanded in his most aggressive and commanding manner.

"On the contrary, I was told you had something to say to me. I have nothing to say to you," Jung declared.

For a while reiteration and counterreiteration continued between the two men until Goebbels in a rage banged his desk with his fists.

Whereupon Jung stood up, totally uncompromising, and walked out, as he had already walked out in early 1933 of any idea of giving the Nazi phenomenon any more of a chance.

When war finally broke out, he was deeply committed in spirit to its meaning and consequences. He made no secret of the side to which he had committed himself. "Three cheers for Old England!" he would write to H. G. Baynes. Or again he wrote to Mary Mellon, "The devastation of London hurt me as if it were my own country."

He called the war by many names but always with the Germanic adjective of possession as in terms of "the German evil," "the German disease," "the German poison," and so on. He had no patience with Germans who after the war could emerge prepared to behave as if nothing had happened to them in the process and they themselves had not been responsible. It is true, he thought it important that we should realise how the whole trend of spirit of our time had contributed to the catastrophe so that we too were not without blame in a strategic, spiritual sense, but he made it absolutely clear that the immediate responsibility was a German one. The most scathing of letters I think he ever wrote was one of rebuke to a German notable who seemed to feel that business as usual of interchange of spirit with the rest of the world could be carried on without admission of responsibility and plea for forgiveness.

"It was most remarkable," he told me once, "how as the war became more desperate and widespread, I found myself dreaming more and more of Churchill. It was almost as if there were a kind of dream telepathy and state of dream participation between us. I would wake up in the morning having dreamt of him and read, for instance, that he had just been on another long and dangerous journey by plane. That happened not once but lots of times."

Long before 1939 he had left his work on psychological types far behind him. It was never meant to be an absolute aid to navigation of oneself but a relative one, and an exhortation to all men to realise how important it was to work all one's life on raising what was dark and inferior in oneself to the same honourable estate as what was light and superior without any sacrifice of the illuminated values.

His first immediate concern thereafter as a result was to establish with an empiricism beyond honest doubt the validity of the objectivity of the collective unconscious and all the material uncovered in his encounter with it. This material went far beyond the personal which the normal psychiatrist uncovered in his patients. Indeed Jung, even during his earliest psychiatric years, had discovered in his most profoundly disturbed patients elements of meaning, patterns of fantasy, and symbols which seemed to him of a disturbing relevance to the great objective universals of the history of civilisation. He had established, he was certain, with all the immense dedication to empiricism and his faith in science as his discipline, that there were similar objective forces of indescribable power active in himself. Empirical as his approach even to himself had been, he knew that the hypothesis which the facts were massing to impose on him, and which ultimately he was compelled to accept most reluctantly, since he hated theorising, would not be acceptable to others unless it was supported by outside evidence as well.

He embarked, therefore, on an immense historical enterprise in search of evidence beyond doubt in the story consciously recorded of all that we call civilisation or culture in man. That the instinctive objectivity of this new world was an established fact he could prove from his clinical work and analytical sessions with the patients who came to him by the hundreds every year, prove its validity above all by the fact that when uncovered, taken seriously, and restored to a role in the lives of his patients, they were healed. The problem, of course, the apparent causes of the neurosis and its symptoms, did not disappear, but suddenly the energy necessary for dealing with them re-emerged in the stricken personality and neurosis itself vanished.

"Why," he was driven to exclaim again and again, "cannot men who call themselves psychiatrists and doctors see that acceptance of the reality of this discovery and its activities works, and that it heals people whose sickness orthodox medicine could not help?"

And yet there is no need to examine in detail the way he accomplished the historical aspects of his task. It is best followed in his own words and the several books devoted to it. Compared with the book on psychological types, they are easier to read, clearly and forcefully setting forth how it was done with elaborate and convincing detail in a manner no educated, interested reader can fail to understand. *Roots of the Unconscious, Archetypes and the Collective Unconscious, Psychology and Religion,* and *Modern Man in Search of a Soul,* to select only a few of his major works and leaving out the great stream of relevant colloquial seminars in between, through the titles alone convey the range of his achievement.

For the purposes of this account of my own experience, I can vouch only for the importance this all had for me because Jung made his point of departure what is primordial and primeval in life. His work established also that there was a primitive self even, or perhaps above all, in civilised European man which had increasingly been denied a legitimate participation in his life. Because of this denial and the rejection of natural feeling values which inevitably followed, civilised man had become less and less civilised in the classical sense and more and more of an "intellectual barbarian" or "technological savage," as Jung called him to me.

His voyage to Africa in 1925–26, which among others was to confirm his re-emergence into the world, provided the final proof hardly needed of what is first and primitive in even the most modern of spirits. He discovered an embarrassing wealth of illustration and proof in the story of civilisations as remote as that of Babylon, Assyria, Persia, Egypt, and, somewhat nearer to us, those of Greece and Rome. But between them and the emergence of the medieval church and himself there were wide and disturbingly inclusive gaps, an apparent disassociation and lack of continuity which could not have been there if his hypothesis of the collective unconscious possessed the universal objectivity he knew now it did in so unqualified a measure. There were, it is true, tantalising hints that the theme had not altogether vanished as, for instance, in astrology, which for him had nothing to do with the stars as such and their direct involvement in the fate of man, but was a projected form of psychology, an attempt of antiquity by way of the instinctive attitude of seeking for a new truth in its reflection in the mirror of the world about us. But this aspect of it can perhaps be best reconsidered in his ultimate investigation into the role of time in the life of man.

There was another intimation of the continuity he sought in the history of the Christian Gnostics so ruthlessly repressed and persecuted by the early Church. He recognised a kinship in Gnosticism with his own experience but its representation in history, almost entirely by Church Fathers ranged against it, was too partial and uncertain for him to take up the thread with confidence until much later, when the discovery of the Dead Sea Scrolls and new Coptic papyrus scripts from Egypt gave additional scope to this line of investigation. He was to find the ultimate realisation of continuity in the hitherto obscure and much-despised story of alchemy. He would not, perhaps, have been able to do even this had not the external world at the appropriate moment provided him with the right key to a door so firmly shut.

The dream of the magnolia tree, the flower of East and West, aflame in blossom, was proved to be prophetic, because soon after this Jung received from Richard Wilhelm the translation of an old Chinese alchemical text called, believe it or not, *The Secret of the Golden Flower*. Through this alchemical text—the year in which he received it was already 1928—added later to Wilhelm's translation of the even older *I Ching*, he found the door to European alchemy wide open and the validity established beyond any further possible doubt of the universality of his hypothesis of the collective unconscious in man and its revelations in distinct, diversified patterns of energy active in incalculable numbers in the spirit of man.

He was no Chinese scholar, had made no special study of Chinese history or culture. He had read with great profit the Upanishads of Hindu India, which was geographically near China but in reality as remote from its spirit as its European kinsmen. There was obviously no connection or possibility of influence from China in the conclusions he had reached, but now through Wilhelm he was introduced to a progression of culture older than our own wherein all he had learned from psychology in Europe was made manifest and worked on as established fact. He needed to go no further than to give the Chinese material its exact European parallel in the dreams and fantasies of his patients as well as in the purpose of all Christian seeking—above all, in its living revelation of a transcendental self, the Anthropos, the "golden flower" or "diamond body" as his great spiritual unbeknown forebears, the ancient Chinese sages and alchemists, had called it while endeavouring with an integrity and passion not seen in Europe for centuries to arrive at the lasting translation of their ephemeral selves into continuous and endlessly continuing truth beyond the here and the now, beyond our prescribed cycle of birth, life, and death.

The Pauline "not I but Christ in me" had always been for him an arrival at a self-realisation far beyond any egotistical aspiration of man, an achievement of an everlasting state of truth where at last the man in living bondage to a value greater than himself was freer than he had ever been. And this conviction now was confirmed as a clear parallel by the overriding Chinese alchemical seeking of the creation through a union of two great opposites of spirit symbolised in dark and light, the yin and yang in themselves, ringed with fire as in their visual image of Tao itself, a golden flower of light in the "diamond body" which was the same incorruptible greater self Paul discovered through the pattern of Christ within himself.

"In the Pauline Christ symbol," he wrote, "the supreme religious experiences of West and East confront one another: Christ, the sorrow-laden hero, and the Golden Flower that blooms in the purple hall of the city of jade. What a contrast, what an unfathomable difference, what an abyss of history!" Yet he was to show that although they started poles apart in the transcendental symbol of their final seeking they were one, as the spirit of East and West should work at one.

From that moment, Jung felt no further need for proof of the hypothesis of the collective unconscious; his brief contact with

Indians in America, and above all the Elgonyi in Africa, had demonstrated how it held good for the primitive as well as the "civilised"; his contact with Wilhelm proved in a much more complex and evolved manner how another great civilisation like China, without any tangible connection with his own, had come to the same conclusion. The Upanishads had already established the same pattern in the sophisticated culture of Hindu India and a brief visit to the subcontinent itself was to demonstrate how the Lord Buddha too, after high Himalayan fashion, was another realisation of the pattern of a greater self in man. He found himself immeasurably enriched thereby but in an honourable and dignified way of the spirit, as that of a pupil learning humbly from the ground up at the foot of new masters in this field. And characteristically, as a result he addressed an urgent warning to his own culture, a warning even more urgent and relevant today than it was when he was alive. The warning had its earth in his basic conviction that science is the finest instrument of the Western mind, even though not the end it is often presumed to be, and that it had on no account to be abandoned in his approach to all this wealth of empirical material from the East.

More doors could be opened with science than with bare European hands. Picking the pockets of wisdom of his Chinese pioneers was just not on as a serious task. Ancient China, for instance, could help Europe to another wider and more profound as well as higher understanding through life, but it was of no use to us in the indulgence we see all around as though it were a mere shadowy sentiment, to be disposed of as "Eastern wisdom" and pushed into the obscurities of archaic faith and superstition. For him this Oriental material, far from consisting of sentimental exaggerated mystical intuitions, bordering on the pathological and emanating from ascetic recluses and archaic cranks (significantly, on his visit to India he asked devoutly to be preserved from professional "holy" Hindu men), was wisdom based on practical knowledge, hard spiritual empiricism, and a totally original exercise of intelligence of the finest kind. He could not bear to see it undervalued and abused as magical formulas and spiritual amulets for correcting our own European disorientation. Above all he warned against blind imitation of Indian and Chinese practices, as he had warned and been warned himself against adapting primitivity the African way. Western imitation of China and India was doubly tragic in that it arose from a psychological understanding as sterile as "current escapades in New Mexico, the blissful South Sea Islands, and central Africa, where primitivity is staged in all seriousness in order that Western man may conveniently slip out of his menacing duties, his *Hic Rhodus, hic salta!*"—the admonition lifted from Aesop's fable of the overarrogant frog boastful of his powers of jumping, "Here is Rhodes, now jump."

It is not for us to imitate what is organically foreign, he urged, or worse still to send out missionaries to foreign peoples. It is our task to build up our Western culture, which sickens of a thousand ills. This had to be done on the spot, on our own doorstep. "Into the work must be drawn the European as he is in his Western common places, with his marriage problems, his neuroses, his social and political illusions, and his whole philosophical disorientation."

In fact, Jung had nothing but pity for the spiritually impoverished European who went, as it were, to beg for spirit in the East. One did not do one's best by beggars, he would say in their regard, in giving them all they ask for as alms. One does it ultimately only by helping not to abet their effort to escape working for themselves but by freeing them from the necessity to beg by relearning the value of work. So we could justify what we took from the East not as beggars, thieves, or pirates of their practices, coming home with shiploads of spiritual spoil from Asia, but by translating the meaning of Chinese wisdom into our own humdrum European lives and living the meaning out together with our own in the same devout measure of integrity and honesty as those who in an age full of troubles as horrific as our own, had lived their lives in their own context and at their own peril before they could acquire so great a wealth of wisdom. Yet even so, despite the warning, the road to Katmandu is still crowded with young European beggars of spirit and pirates after this fashion, despite their possession of a key of their own to all they seek in Jung. The roads to Tibet and Peking would be as crowded, I am sure, had they not been closed to such traffic by the totalitarian Manchu domination of classical China, the Manchu who were part of the barbarian horde against whom the Great Wall was built, and the Chinese equivalent of the Prussian in the history of Germany. But how close Chinese and European parallels were, was evident even in a common negation; in both there was the same formidable denial of the feminine. Both were essential manifestations of the masculine domination of the evolution of the spirit.

Not the least of Jung's services to his time was his demonstration of how the dreaming process in man, far from being archaic and redundant, was more relevant than ever. This symbol moving between his dream and daylight self, however, was crucial at this moment. For years Jung had observed a sort of circular movement of awareness, dreams, visions, and new inner material round an as yet undefined centre like planets and moons around a sun. It was a strange rediscovery of what had once been called the "magic circle."

Christian use of this symbolism of the circle was common in the medieval age, usually in paintings of Christ at their centre and the four Apostles arranged at the cardinal points of the compass around him. But no one had ever seen the symbolism implied in the pattern. Some of Jung's women patients who could not describe it in words or paintings would even dance the magic circle for him. And, as I was able to tell him also, the Stone Age man of Africa to this day does as well. Jung found this circular pattern such a compulsive, one is inclined to say transcendental, constant in himself and others that he started to paint it and to derive such comfort and meaning from it that for years he hardly drew anything else. He called the process and the movement of spirit the maṇdala, taking the Sanskrit word for "circle," because by this time he had seen drawings by his patients that were almost exact copies of drawings used in religious instruction in Tibet. When I told him how I had discovered that "mandala" was used in African Arabic also for spectacles, signifying thereby an enlargement and two-way traffic of spirit, he was visibly moved.

He instantly told me how important a piece of evidence the discovery of the famous "sun-wheel" in Rhodesia had been to him, since it was perhaps the oldest visual representation of this pattern. I was able to tell him of other possibly older abstracts of similar and related patterns in an immense expanse of stone which had once been the bed of a river in southern Africa. This primitive confirmation as of the first primordial human witness to the truth of his own conclusions helped him greatly. Indeed, his own confrontation with the unconscious had ended with some superb paintings of mandalas. One called *Window on Eternity*, though painted long before his meeting with Wilhelm, is included in the "examples of European mandalas" accompanying *The Secret of the Golden Flower*, of which the dream magnolia was obviously an example. It shows a flower, a diamond with light in the centre, the stars in their courses about it and surrounded by walls with eight gates, the whole conceived as a transparent window, constituting as complete a visualisation as imagination is capable of rendering of the whole of life and its meaning.

It was followed later, however, by another, the last of all the paintings in the Red Book, of the yellow castle. He always thought of it, as did I and those with me seeing it for the first time, as oddly Chinese. Hence the name yellow, not only because it is the colour associated with the Chinese but also because it is the colour of resolution of the gold of *being* which both Chinese and European alchemists sought. So without sacrifice of special meaning in terms of his own life and time, he returned to alchemy more zealously than ever before.

Yet this return, despite the Chinese precept, was as difficult a task as any he attempted before. He bought all the modern books on the subject available and when these failed him went about the market-places to buy the work of long-forgotten alchemists in their original Latin, which he still read as easily as we do English. He came to possess what I believe was the largest library of original alchemical books in Europe. But they all seemed at first obscure and meaningless, until he decided to treat them as some intelligence officer in a great war engaged in breaking the cipher, wherein the most immediate messages of the enemy were encoded in fragments of intercepted messages. He wrote down carefully all the patterns of phraseology recurring most often and then he got it. Like the Chinese, the alchemists were his true authentic, however remote, forebears. When the medieval church began to fail the questing spirit of Europe, as it did more and more from the first Christian millennium onwards, and such thread as it had with the living historical past appeared irrevocably cut, the alchemists had increasingly taken over the original quest.

Their persecutors, who accused them of being vulgar materialists in search of the wealth that was gold, could not have been more wrong. Much of what they had done was inevitably achieved in secrecy and expressed with great obscurity for reasons of security as well as the originality and intractability of the material which confronted them. But Jung, the code broken, soon saw the gold they were after was no common gold; the philosophers' stone they sought was no ordinary stone. They were trying to achieve through the external world with their alchemistry what he sought through his psychology. As always, the authentic process of arriving at new meaning began by seeing its reflection and symbolism mirrored in the world without.

They were seeking to create a new sort of man, a greater awareness of reality and increase of meaning. It was obvious to Jung now that their work was full of living symbolism of the most transformative kind. There was not one of any distinction among them from Hermes Trismegistus to Paracelsus who did not lay down as the first and most important laws of his science those of purity of heart, honesty of mind, love of God, and the patience of that love which endured and bore all things to the true end. From as far back as that unremembered African hand which inscribed a rock in Africa with its version of what the Tibetans call the "wheel of life," on through the story of Babylon, Egypt, Russia, Palestine, Greece, Rome, and so on up to the present day, the continuity of the essential theme of life was empirically established as having remained unbroken and intact.

The detail of all this is in Jung's *Psychology and Alchemy* and there is no need to follow it further here, except to add that though this book appears formidable to the eye of the reader and, with all its necessary and laborious footnotes, fit only for scholars, it is one of the most rewarding books of history I know, easily read and in the end leaving one humble, grateful, and infinitely reassured. Far from difficult, it is a great Homeric epic of the Western spirit and, although obviously not written in heroic couplets, a resounding poetic statement. One starry utterance after another comes out of the alchemical dark at one such as:

> I sleep and my soul awakens.
> Imagination is the star in man.
> Thus there is in man a firmament as in Heaven but not of one piece; there are two. For the hand that divided light from darkness and the hand that made Heaven and earth has done likewise in the microcosm below, having taken from above and enclosed within man everything that Heaven contains.
> As the great Heaven stands, so it is implanted at birth.

D. H. Lawrence in one of his most inspired moments wrote that in the dust where we have buried the silent races and their abominations we have buried so much of the delicate magic of life. Through his reinterpretation of Chinese and European alchemy, Jung uncovers much of this "delicate magic of life" and shows that it is not dead but relevant and alive in the symbolism of our imagination and continues to be of great concern to our well-being in the present.

Until this moment of Jung's return, it would not be unfair generalisation to say that in so far as the existence of an unconscious in man was accepted at all, it was in a negative way. This in a sense was not surprising. Both Jung and Freud had come to it initially in their search for the causes of neurosis and derangement in the human personality. Both had traced the source of neurosis and derangement to an unconscious area in the mind of man. There was a moment even when this unconscious appeared as a comparatively shallow area, existing not so much in its own right as created out of a conscious and wilful suppression of instincts and experience too painful for the comfort of man. In so far as it was thought of as existing on its own, it seemed to be in active opposition and a state of cloak-and-dagger warfare with what was conscious in man. Both Jung and Freud themselves established significant patterns of conflict between conscious and unconscious in men, but Jung's view of it was a vastly different affair. Its negative aspect dwindled into insignificance beside his revelation of its positive objective nature and its own vital involvement in the enlargement of consciousness in man.

The conflict between conscious and unconscious forces which filled mental asylums, crowded the consulting rooms of Freud, Jung, and their collaborators, and emptied the churches of the day, were nothing compared to the problem of enrichment and increase in the conscious life of man Jung found concealed in it. This was no dark, disordered world, basically antipathetic and committed to war on consciousness. Where it was dark, it had its own form of starlight and moonlight for the probing spirit to steer by, and laws of order and determination as precise as those that kept the stars in their courses in the universe without. The negations came only when man's conscious self ignored his dependence on this world of the collective unconscious which had so mysteriously brought it forth and tried to establish some kind of independent tyranny over what ultimately only sought to nourish and increase their partnership.

The trouble started only when the part of the human personality which was conscious behaved as if it were the whole of the man. There was nothing this unconscious world abhorred more than one-sidedness. When one extreme of spirit attempted a monopoly for itself another extreme sooner or later rose titanic in the unconscious to overthrow it. That is why the history of man was so much a swing from one opposite of spirit into another as Heraclitus had observed millenniums before.

This new and revolutionary view of an unconscious was set out by Jung with an immense wealth of empirical detail, drawn not only from his work in the mental asylums and in his practice but from history, art, literature, and the mythologies and religions of the world. The labour and scale of imagination and concentration he put into this work, for anyone who has taken the trouble to glance at it, make complete nonsense of the charge, which I myself had once so naïvely accepted, that he was another loose and vague kind of mystic. He established through a way no scientist can deny that this collective unconscious within man was objective, that the visions and dreams and imagery in which it communicated with man's conscious self were utterly objective facts, however subjectively they are experienced. He showed clearly how conscious man ignored such facts at his peril, and moreover taught himself and men how to read the language of dreams as if they were the forgotten language of the gods themselves.

He revealed how in this collective unconscious of the individual man were infinite resources of energy, organised in definite recognisable patterns. Each of these patterns had at its disposal its own form of energy and somewhere located, as it were, in the centre, between the unconscious and conscious, there was a master pattern to which all other patterns subscribed and all their other energies could be joined in one transcendental orbit. He called these patterns, first of all, "primordial images," a phrase borrowed from Burckhardt as indicated before, but later changed to "archetypes," an idea rediscovered from Saint Augustine, and before him from Hermes Trismegistus, who exclaims in the *Poimandres,* "You have seen in your mind the archetypal image!" In this one detail again one sees the selfless, unegotistical Jung, determined not to set himself apart and above history but wherever possible to contain all he did in the context of his own culture. He showed an awareness that became a fixed article of work and faith, of the importance of never throwing away his own cultural inheritance but of accepting it, however imperfect, as the basic material of his work, and the only aboriginal stock on which his own contemporary spirit could flower.

His capacity for deriving new meanings from all civilisations was unbounded. He drew on the experience of such different extremes as the Chinese and Red Indian, Hindu India, and primitive Africa, not as substitution but enrichment of his own cultural inheritance. He scorned the growing numbers in Europe who exchanged their own culture for another as an evasion of the difficult task of truly being themselves and once described such a dubious "traffic" to me as obscene.

Meanwhile, he found that these archetypes, a word that is so much in use these days that it is in danger of losing its value, were so highly organised and vivid in the unconscious, impinging so sharply on conscious imagination, that they could be personified or at the very least given abstract expression, as in that final drawing in his own Red Book of a castle that was yellow.

An example of how vivid and complex this world of archetypes was, could be found in its instinctive and intuitive representation in Greek mythology. This system of spirit is the most highly differentiated, accurate, and detailed model of the forces of the collective unconscious the world has perhaps ever known. It is precisely because of this exceptional instinctive awareness of the collective unconscious, demonstrated in their myths and legends and all that flowed from them, that the Greeks were able to make so formidable a contribution to the evolution of the human spirit.

Jung himself in his Red Book, in the mural paintings he did so magnetically on the walls of his tower at Bollingen, and in his carvings on stone, gave visual expression to his own personifications and abstractions of some of these greatest archetypal images and powers. He himself indeed had been familiar with one in personified form when still a boy. He had visualised and with great benefit to himself had had a dialogue almost as far back as he could remember, as we have seen, with one of the greatest of all archetypes, that of the wise old man, the inner master or guru, the *sensei* of Japan, which life has formed of all its experience and intimations of where and how it wants to take itself further, implanting it in the imagination of every human being, so that did he but know it he was not born utterly naked, ignorant and unarmed in the jungle of the world but had great guidance and protection within.

As he looked back from this high, assured new vantage point of himself, on a life lengthening so fast behind him but closing in on him so swiftly from ahead, I find nothing more moving than this vision of Jung as a young boy, when a father he had loved had failed him, putting a trusting hand instead in that of this wise old figure who came to him unsolicited in the stillness of his own imagination and let it lead him on safely to his meeting with the destiny to which he was committed at birth. We have seen how in all his moments of greatest abandonment, when he had no male company of any kind, this archetype stayed firmly with him. Embattled as he was, Jung was moved to go on painting and repainting his portrait at Bollingen in a manner which is so decisive and electric that no imagination can look at the painting and doubt his validity. One could hardly sleep in one's bed there at night, so alive and urgent was his presence in the murals around the room. And perhaps strangest and most significant of all, the relevant coincidence, in high Chinese fashion, had come to confirm the authenticity of the vision the first time he tried to paint it. The vision came to him in kingfisher-blue wings. Jung painted it with an electric-blue immediacy that to this day is quite startling. Some hours afterwards, walking in his garden by the lake, he found a dead kingfisher lying there. The bird in any case was rare and he had never seen one there before nor was he to see one again. Since the bird always and everywhere from Stone Age man to Stravinsky has been the image of the inspiration, the unthinkable thought which enters our selves like a bird unsolicited out of the blue, it was for Jung, as a Zen priest once put it to me, one of the signs of confirmation from nature that sustain the spirit in its search for enlightenment and emancipation from the floating world of appearances.

Unfortunately, the archetypal patterns of Jung's evolution are far too many to be enumerated specifically even in so simplified a manner, and there may be more even than either the assembly the Greeks recorded in their mythology and legends or those Jung discovered. But two deserve special mention because of their unique importance to our own time. These are, of course, the great twosome: the feminine in man and the masculine in woman. Jung called the latter "animus" and the first, as mentioned in his encounter with Salome, "anima," thereby using again a term borrowed from the forgotten language of Christian religion when it was still alive and fresh with its message of love in the power-drunk world of the Romans.

It was precisely because of this denial of the archetypal aspect and its supreme value of love that the history of the world, as Jung saw it, was such a cataclysmic waste-land. It was this denial that made modern man increasingly sick in mind and spirit and caused him not to know where to turn, so great was the loss of sense of direction which resulted from this rejection. It was the equivalent of what my African countrymen, as Jung instantly appreciated when he lived among them, to this day call the "loss of soul," which they fear and abhor as the greatest disaster that can befall any human being. And this loss of soul, Jung's encounter with the collective unconscious joined to what he had experienced as a psychiatrist convinced him, was the main cause of man's private and collective derangement.

The soul of man, after all, as one of the earliest fathers of religion had said, was naturally religious and now was proved to be so scientifically. Clearly it gave man a hunger greater than any physical hunger. And if this hunger were not nourished, men and their societies either withered away or perished in some disaster unconsciously brought down on themselves. Wherever Jung looked he saw a world sickening more and more because of a loss of soul, and because of a loss of soul deprived of meaning. Meaninglessness was the greatest disease of his day, as it is of our own. We all, without exception, to a greater or lesser degree, knowingly or unknowingly, are Pirandello characters in search of our author.

From that moment on, Jung's concern became more and more a religious concern, however scientific and empiric the instruments chosen for the service. The unconscious was no longer a source of conflict and derangement but a world in which health and sanity and salvation had to be sought. Important as it had been to discover and explore the unconscious in the interests of the abnormal, it was now recognised as an affair of life and death for so-called normal man.

Derangement and neurosis were regarded more as a measure of man's estrangement from his full unconscious self, an affliction sent to redirect him and set him on his true course, so that in every neurosis there were the seeds of something positive, of new growth and new meaning. The moment Jung could direct his patients to see a meaning in their own suffering, the suffering, even if it did not go, became endurable. More and more he found in the suffering of the individual a mirror of what was culpably inadequate in the full terms of the collective unconscious in the life of a whole time. No recovery of a sense of meaning seemed possible without a recovery of personal religious experience.

Jung was back with that concern he had always felt from the moment of the first great dream experienced at the age of three. But never before had he realised so clearly how the future of mankind depended on a rediscovery of his capacity for religious experience accessible in a twentieth-century idiom and not in the archaic, dogmatic, doctrinal, conceptualised way in which it had been imposed on him for centuries. It is remarkable how always those who in the end could gain most from his work misunderstood and attacked what he was trying to do, like the churches and institutions of science. He knew, he protested over and over again, that only religion could replace religion.

He had not abandoned his own Christian inheritance because he acknowledged the validity of the religious experience of other races and cultures. He was concerned only in making religion real again for modern man. Exhortation, dogmatic utterance, and conventional religious ritual and symbolism, he recognised, still worked for a dwindling number. He acknowledged that there had been a moment when the creed and dogma of the Christian church had achieved as complete and accurate a definition as possible of the aspirations of the Western spirit. That was why not only the spiritual aspirations of men but all he possessed of art, science, music, and grace had been put to its service as well. But that moment had long passed.

Jung's task was to make religion once more credible to unbelieving men and women for whom belief and exhortation were useless if not insulting. He had to do it in an empirical and scientific way in the first instance, and then, through the objective eventfulness of their dreams, fantasy, and imagination, bring them to an area of the spirit where the mystery, the awful mystery, he stressed, of the Divine was more likely than not to happen again.

The mystery of what happened there was not mystification. It was the mystery in a sense of regrowth. As Dr. C. A. Meier, his colleague, speaking for Jung, put it in his book on ancient Greek healing, it was like the bringing together, as it were, of two ends of broken bone. There was no doubt that as a rule the bones would join and grow as one again, but how they did it was a mystery they shared between themselves and the mystery of creation around them. No one, no scientist could yet show or say what this growth was. It was a great mystery, yet it was real and it worked.

The role of the dreaming process was crucial. Writing to a friend later, Jung was to say something to the effect, and I quote from memory, "You tell me you have had many dreams lately but have been too busy with your writing to pay attention to them. You have got it the wrong way round. Your writing can wait but your dreams cannot because they come unsolicited from within and point urgently to the way you must go."

He also wrote:

> The dream is a little hidden door in the innermost and most secret recesses of the soul, opening into that cosmic night which was psyche long before there was any ego consciousness, and which will remain psyche no matter how far our ego consciousness extends. . . . All consciousness separates; but in dreams we put on the likeness of that more universal, truer, more eternal man dwelling in the darkness of primordial night. There he is still the whole, and the whole is in him, indistinguishable from nature and bare of all egohood. It is from these all-uniting depths that the dream arises, be it never so childish, grotesque, and immoral.

Of the psyche, the soul which invokes the means of all the love of the feminine in man and which is at one with the source of the dream and as such must be defined with it, he wrote even more evocatively:

> If the human soul is anything, it must be of unimaginable complexity and diversity, so that it cannot possibly be approached through a mere psychology of instinct. I can only gaze with wonder and awe at the depths and heights of our psychic nature. Its non-spatial universe conceals an untold abundance of images which have accumulated over

> millions of years of living development and become fixed in the organism. My consciousness is like an eye that penetrates to the most distant spaces, yet it is the psychic non-ego that fills them with non-spatial images. And these images are not pale shadows, but tremendously powerful psychic factors. . . . Beside this picture I would like to place the spectacle of the starry heavens at night, for the only equivalent of the universe within is the universe without; and just as I reach this world through the medium of the body, so I reach that world through the medium of the psyche.

Yet even in dogma, pre-eminently a theological field, he did what he could to preserve its symbolic validity. His correspondence with numbers of clergymen, priests, and philosophers testifies to his efforts despite scepticism and prejudice. He wrote profound essays on the meaning of the Trinity, the Mass, and other basic aspects and articles of Christian faith, making them contemporary and accessible to ordinary educated men and women in a way their rational preconditioning could not deny. Most important of all, he established that no matter what the race or creed or colour or culture, the need for a living religious experience was equal and vital, and that in this collective unconscious the same patterns never varied but were all of one and the same measure.

There, already, all men and all races and colours are kin and enjoy one and the same parentage. It is the great religious ocean into which all the religious streams of the world flow. For the first time in the history of man, religious imperialisms are outmoded—in fact, irreligious; religious colonisation is at an end; even sectarianism or the equivalents of caste and class systems in religion are out of date and man can unite in the service of a common religious search derived from the same experience in one uniquely contemporary idiom. We are only at the beginning of the consequences for man of this aspect of the discovery of the collective unconscious. The societies of man and his political systems alone can ultimately never be the same because of it.

Ignorance in English law is no excuse for breaches of the law. In the collective unconscious, ignorance, unawareness, is not only inexcusable but the greatest offence with the most dire consequences. That is why in Greek myth, legend, and art the villain is always the ignorance that serves as an image of unawareness; it is always the "not knowing," the non-recognition of man's own inner eventfulness, which is the real crime. Always it is man's unawareness that evokes the vengeance of fate, and man's lack of knowledge of himself and his motives that calls up disaster. How much greater, therefore, the culpability of a consciousness like our own that knows and will not face up to the responsibility of what it knows! For no one since Freud, and above all since Jung, can any longer plead ignorance of where our failure starts.

Theologians always firmly held that all men were equal in dignity before God. This pattern in the collective unconscious is precisely of so great a potentiality for the human spirit, because all men are equal in dignity before it, in the sense that they are all raised and equipped there with equal impartiality.

Jung put all this forward not as argument but as experience. Experience is before and beyond argument. One of the gravest indictments of the intellectualism of his and our age is a strange determination to deny human beings the validity and dignity of their own experience and to subject it to some external, preconceptualised devaluation. Jung held on to this experience of all these patterns in the collective unconscious as vital points of departure so that when asked in public if he believed in God he said, "I do not believe . . ." and then paused.

I who heard him at the time remember the sense of darkness that came in at the windows at the pause, and how it dissolved swiftly into light when he added, after what seemed an age, "I know."

He knew because he had experienced what was once called the living God. He had experienced as no other man in our time has done, through confrontation with the collective unconscious, what it means to apprehend God as the ultimate and greatest of meaning of which life is capable and in whose direction all our searching is turned. God revealed himself, as it were, immediately through this master pattern in the collective unconscious in a manner that no man could have endured had he not possessed an intermediary, an intercessor, between himself and this fearful reality. The intercessor, of course, is the only partially apprehended, and as yet inadequately explored, pattern of the feminine.

"I cannot define for you what God is," Jung wrote to me just before he died. "I can only say that my work has proved empirically that the pattern of God exists in every man, and that this pattern has at its disposal the greatest of all his energies for transformation and transfiguration of his natural being. Not only the meaning of his life but his renewal and his institutions depend on his conscious relationship with this pattern in his collective unconscious."

So in the final analysis Jung's life was of a profoundly religious person, religiously lived to a truly religious end, however scientific the manner. His last years were spent almost entirely in exploring this relationship between individual man and the pattern of God in the human spirit. He was convinced that our spent selves and worn-out societies could not renew themselves without renewing their concept of God and so their whole relationship with it.

He had in this journey into his own unconscious self discovered another archetypal pattern of the utmost significance in this regard. He called it the "shadow"—a pattern that had at its disposal all the energies of what man had consciously despised, rejected, or ignored in himself. One sees immediately how aptly the term was chosen, because it is an image of what happens when the human being stands between himself and his own light. Whether this shadow should be properly regarded as archetypal in itself, or whether it is another shadow of archetypes themselves, is almost academic. The dark, rejected forces massing in the shadow of the unconscious, as it were, knife in hand, demanding revenge for all that man and his cultures have consciously sacrificed of them in the specialised conscious tasks he has set himself, are real and active enough to keep us too busy for academics and scholasticisms. They show how all our history is a progression on two levels: a conscious and unconscious, a manifest and latent level. Here is another overwhelming example of how he helped my own tentative groping in this direction and how he helped to banish the sense of isolation spoken of in the beginning.

The manifest level provides all the plausible rational justifications and excuses for the wars, revolutions, and disasters inflicted on men in their collective and private lives, but in reality it is on this other latent level where, unrecognised, the real instigators and conspirators against too narrow and rigid a conscious rule above are to be found. There, proud, angry, and undefeated, they move men and women on the manifest level about as puppets in predetermined patterns of their own revengeful seeking, or like a magnet conditioning a field of iron filings on a table above.

That is why all men tend to become what they oppose, why the

New Testament exhorted us not to resist evil because what follows logically is that ultimately the dark, dishonoured self triumphs and emerges on the scorched level of the manifest to form another tyranny as narrow, producing another swing of the opposites of which Heraclitus spoke. The answer, as Jung saw it, was to abolish tyranny, to enthrone, as it were, two opposites side by side in the service of the master pattern, not opposing or resisting evil but transforming and redeeming it. These two opposites in the negations of our time could be turned into tragic enemies. But truly seen psychologically and again defined best perhaps in the non-emotive terms of physics, they were like the negative and positive inductions of energy observed in the dynamics of electricity; the two parallel and opposite streams without which the flash of lightning, for me always the symbol of awareness made imperative, was impossible.

Containing those two opposites, putting the light of the superior functions at the service of the dark, bearing all the tensions induced thereby, the individual could grow into a resolution of the two into a greater realisation of himself. One says greater because the self realised thereby is more than the sum of the opposites, because in the process of their resolution the capacity of the individual to join in the universal and continuing act of creation wherein his own life participates enables him to add something which was not there before.

So this role of the shadow in the life of the individual, the life of civilisation, and the reality of religion, not surprisingly, was one of Jung's closest concerns. He demonstrated in a way that cannot be denied how this mechanism of the shadow was at the back of the phenomenon of the persecution of the Jews in history, how Christians for centuries blamed their own rejection of the real meaning of Christ on the Jews who had crucified him, ignoring how they were recrucifying him daily in their own lives. It is an elemental part of the mythological dominants of history, as I called them to myself in the beginning, and gave me a clearer, deeper, and more precise understanding of their working. The mechanism of the shadow, for instance, was the explanation of Hitler and his own persecution of the Jews, and also of all racial, colour, and personal prejudice. Before I knew Jung I had written the essay mentioned in the beginning on how some such explanation could apply even to colour prejudice in my native South Africa.

Jung revealed in great detail how the individual imposed his quarrel with his own shadow onto his neighbour, in the process outlining scientifically why men inevitably saw the mote in the eye of their neighbour. It was not just out of ignorance of the beam in their own but unconsciously to avoid recognising it as reflection of their own. He defined for the first time in a contemporary idiom a primordial mechanism in the spirit of man which he called "projection," a mechanism which compels us to blame on our neighbour what we unconsciously dislike most in ourselves.

All at once it was clear that man could only be well and sane when the quarrel between him and his shadow, between the primitive and the civilised, between the Jacob and the Esau in himself, was dissolved and the two reconciled and together enter the presence of the master pattern as Jung's imagination had already done. Only there and then did he become something Jung called whole. Wholeness was the ultimate of man's conscious and unconscious seeking; indeed, consciousness was so important because it was the chosen instrument of the unconscious seeking the abolition of partialities in a harmony of differences that is wholeness. This wholeness was only possible through a life lived religiously. To heal, or make whole, once more was demonstrated to be a Pentecostal task of the utmost holiness.

The messages to the churches and temples of the day was clear; they were emptying fast because they had defaulted on their mission of enabling men to become new and whole, and would empty altogether and crumble unless they returned to healing in a contemporary way leading to an achievement or wholeness in a twentieth-century context. And none of this healing was possible except by facing honestly and with the utmost courage the problem of the shadow cast not only by man in himself but by God on life.

This last at least should not be too difficult to grasp because its impact on the human imagination has been so great and is of such long standing that it is amply personified in religions, mythologies, art, and literature of the world. One is speaking of something that goes by many names. Generically it is the evil spirit, the devil, but more particularly in the European tradition it is known as Mephistopheles, Lucifer, or the proud Apollyon of *Pilgrim's Progress*, who preferred ruling in Hell to serving in Heaven, and so on.

It was typical of Jung that he did not make any attempt to establish the shadow as a great universal, projected outwards from the collective unconscious, before he had sorted it all out scientifically within his own nature and in the individual problems of his own patients. He had faced up to the problem of his own shadow on this long Odyssey of his, so squarely indeed that one of the most significant paintings in the Red Book is a portrait of his shadow personified. There, in what looks like a room in some basement covered with black and white tiles, the colours of the two opposites, Jung portrays it as some cloak-and-dagger figure cowering against the far corner of the walls. The position seems deliberately chosen to indicate that he had this aspect of himself "cornered" at last, appropriately below the surface level of himself.

I myself have often been taken to task for not speaking more about Jung's shadow. But I cannot speak of what I did not experience. I knew him only in the closing years of his life when he was much more resolved and the shadow less evident than when young. Of course, great as he was, he must also have had a great shadow. No one could be real and not throw a shadow. I had learned this as a boy from my own black friends in Africa who, if they wanted to pay a sincere compliment said, "But you do throw a shadow." One would look at his own shadow, Quixotically lean and long at sunset, and say of it, "You see that man there? When I die he goes up into the sky to join the sun, but I go down into the earth where he now lies."

The important thing to me is not what Jung's shadow was but that he never ceased to work on it and never was unaware of it. Coming to terms with the shadow, the problem of reconciling the opposites in a whole greater than their parts, was an ultimate of his seeking. And for him it was also the most urgent practical necessity of our time if we were not to destroy ourselves. Working at it, he found himself in conflict not only with himself but with the churches. He never wavered in his acceptance of Christ as the West's greatest symbol of the self but could not accept that the coming of Christ or blind imitation of his being had abolished the reality of the shadow, whether in man or God.

As far as the shadow of the All-Highest was concerned, it had bothered Jung all his conscious life. The significance of it for both God and man, as opposed to the sequence of man, the devil, and only then God as its progression is presented in *Faust*, was expressed in its earliest and most dramatic form in the Book of Job. For years Jung had talked about it to his friends. It was talk of his in this regard that inspired H. G. Wells to write what Job meant to him in his *The Undying Fire*, just as Wells's *Christina Alberta's Father* was an elaboration of something Jung told him one night in his home in Regents Park in London. The latter was a case history of a schizophrenic patient and Wells gave some acknowledgement to Jung, unlike people all over the world in art, science, and philosophy who were increasingly inclined to borrow or steal from Jung what suited them but without acknowledgement, out of fear of the intellectualist disparagement that would tumble down on their heads if they did so. Froude, an unjustly neglected Victorian historian and essayist, had also been obsessed with the problem of Job. He answered his doubts ultimately by interpreting Job's meaning as an inspired allegory designed to show that worldly wealth and success were no proof of God's blessing on a life lived according to His commandments, as the Victorians were indeed overinclined to assume, but that those whom God loved most could be made to suffer most. That satisfied him for, of course, he has a vital point there but only a point. He leaves the "why" out of it.

Jung in all honesty could not do so and finally wrote one of his most subjective of all books—and one all the better and greater for it—as a dialogue with God on the drama of Job. Only a simple version of the main conclusion is possible here: Job proved that man found his greatest meaning in God's need of man's conscious awareness and freedom of choice between good and evil in order to deal with a cosmic shadow. Though God himself might be compelled to let the shadow, Satan, also have his say in reality, and so be compelled, as it were, for the moment to lend Satan a certain tactical support in the long-term strategy of the campaign for meaning in the universe, God counted on man not to submit to his Satanic shadow. And in order to let him win both battle and campaign, God delegates his most valuable of all powers, the power of his love, to do battle with man and Job against Satan and himself. Job in a sense is a prefiguration of Christ and, implicit in this divine alliance with love, there is an intimation of the future greater role of the feminine, the anima in its most evolved form from Eve to Helen and Helen into Mary and so finally into that personified in Sophia, as the wisdom of love. Most important of all, there is a significant and disturbing hint, which one must not overstress and yet cannot ignore, that man made whole through endurance in love of the shadow, is made so much more honourable and meaningful in his estate that he could ultimately surpass his Creator—a hint that makes the imperative of man's ethical obligations to what he knows and discovered increasingly of new power over nature more urgent and awesome than ever before in history.

It is not surprising, therefore, that nothing made Jung more impatient and at times angrier than the conventional and stubborn religious insistence that evil was only the absence of good, a fault in man alone, and a result of indulgence in the seven deadly sins. His language, which could be just as earthy as it was poetic, when he was roused in this profound regard was worthy of an inspired peasant and words like "shitbags" and "pisspots" would roll from his lips in sentences of crushing correction.

"Who the devil do they think put the serpent in the Garden of Eden?" he once exclaimed in talking about the fearful archetype of the shadow to me, and then suddenly laughed out loud at himself. "Did you notice how my unconscious intruded to point a finger at where the answer could be? Certainly not Adam. Maybe the devil, but certainly not man."

Perhaps he put his objections best of all in the most carefully considered, measured, and considerate fashion in a letter to Father Victor White, because he was fond of the man. Victor White had come to him for psychological understanding of his own religious beliefs. As so many others before him, he ultimately went away in the main with what suited his own preconceived beliefs and the latest modern ammunition for promoting them while rejecting the rest of Jung, on which the very illumination he took away depended. Jung, who longed for a serious, intelligent theologian qualified in depth to work with, had turned to him with unusual warmth, not surprising in one at the same time so lonely and so concerned for restoring modern people's capacity for religious experience.

Victor White was to turn on Jung later with, it seems to me, unnecessary violence and reprehensible disregard of what he owed him both as teacher and friend. At the time this particular letter was written he had already had a stab at Jung's broad back which Jung magnanimously overlooked, as he did other attacks and certain studied indignities inflicted on him by Victor White. Jung's *Answer to Job* at a first reading, if Victor White's immediate letter of appreciation can be taken at its face value, had both excited and uplifted him. But very soon he had second thoughts, began to decry the book in public, and became increasingly critical of Jung, not hesitating to call him naïve and ill informed on matters of theology, terms that were as undeserved as they were inaccurate. For if anyone were in a position to know the extent of Jung's theological knowledge, research and interest in religion, and his grasp of its history and implications for life past and present, it was Victor White. Yet despite this, Jung, up to the end, respected what had brought him and White together and understood Victor White's situation, committed as he was to a priority of prescribed faith, as much as the latter failed to understand his ultimate meaning.

Considerate as Jung was, however, his meaning and the quality of the temper of truth at work in the writing of the letter itself is clear as a sword of steel.

> This *privatio boni* business [the Catholic doctrine that evil is a privation of good] is odious to me on account of its dangerous consequences: it causes a negative inflation [overvaluation] of man, who can't help imagining himself, if not as a source of the [Evil], at least as a great destroyer, capable of devastating God's beautiful creation. This doctrine produces Luciferian vanity and it is also greatly responsible for the fatal underrating of the human soul being the original abode of Evil. It gives a monstrous importance to the soul and not a word about on whose account the presence of the Serpent in Paradise belongs!
>
> The question of Good and Evil, so far as I am concerned with it, has nothing to do with metaphysics; it is only a concern of psychology.
>
> As long as Evil is a μὴ ὄν [non-being], *nobody will take his own shadow seriously.* Hitler and Stalin will go on representing a mere "accidental lack of perfection." *The future of mankind very much depends upon the recognition of the shadow.* Evil is—psychologically speaking—*terribly real.* It is a fatal mistake to diminish its power and reality even merely metaphysically. I am sorry, this goes to the very

roots of Christianity. Evil verily does not decrease by being hushed up as a non-reality or as mere negligence of man. It was there before him, when he could not possibly have a hand in it. God is the mystery of all mysteries, a real Tremendum.

And there the final enigmatic, paradoxical truth was out. God was a reality man had to fear as much as to love; Old and New Testaments of the spirit did not abolish but complemented one another. Yet before one follows this final storm-bound perception further, it is important to stress my belief that this evaluation of the shadow in Jung's psychology is followed at its simplest and most immediate best in his letters, not only to Victor White but also to others, and to add that it is not surprising but indeed significant how Victor White was to go on from there to reject the reassertion of the feminine in Catholic doctrine. For the feminine soul in man is the go-between and guide to reconciliation of man and his shadow. That is why Jung attached such an enormous symbolical importance to the Vatican's proclamation of the new doctrine of the bodily assumption of the Virgin Mary into Heaven. For him at last in the highest dimension of reality and its greatest symbol, the masculine and some of the feminine were at one; the conscious will of the masculine in creation was increasingly being joined to serve the love of the feminine and a creation, no longer static but procreatively on the move again. It was for him a welcome sign that the Christian myth which mattered so much to him was still alive and breathing, that its content was not one of mere "historicity" but of an historical conception of a profound need in man still capable of growing in meaning.

White was among the foremost of Catholic intellectualists who pronounced the doctrine as a religious scandal, reading it literally, of course, and not symbolically as Jung did. The objection is all the more glaring when one considers that even symbolically only part of the feminine had ascended to heaven. The woman so exalted was the image of the feminine in man, the mother of the son of man, Dante's virgin mother, daughter of her son. Woman and her masculine self were still left stranded on the earth.

It was only after coming to terms with the role of the shadow in himself that Jung took upon himself the dangerous task of approaching its universal aspect. It was typical of him that he did this first as a living experience, exposing his imagination and all of his conscious self before all that was terrible, ruthless, and awful in the human spirit's experience of God. Out of these two sets of experience he emerged with an enriched awareness of the paradoxical nature of all reality, even that of the ultimate.

In this paradoxical pattern the image of God was both terrible and lovable. There the fear of God always was the beginning of all wisdom, and the love of God the only protection of the spirit that ventured in his presence. Fear and love were mysteriously joined to enable both man and God to achieve greater meaning. From that moment on, Jung saw the relationship between man and God in a way it has never been perceived, however mystically and intuitively it may have been pre-experienced.

He saw man and God, as it were, in partnership, the traffic between them no longer one-sided but two-way. Man was no longer at an almost intolerable receiving end but also at a giving end; he too now could contribute to the conscious reality of God as God contributed to his power to do so. Jung found man and his unconscious self, man in all four aspects of himself, the man and his feminine self, the woman and her masculine self, joined with God in a task of transcendental meaning.

Man was the chosen instrument for enabling life to answer the problem for which it had been invented. Life was a process of living an answer to a problem implicit in its creation. The suffering of man was meaningful because it reflected the suffering of its Creator. In this role, man might look as exposed as Job was to what appeared at times an almost capricious exercise of divine power. But even in his most miserable state, man was not alone, because Jung had clearly demonstrated that where man and God were encountered face to face, a vital, indescribable element of the greatest transforming energies at the disposal of this master pattern was delegated to intercede for man.

This was the long-rejected and despised feminine and its highest value of love. The history of man's experience of God had been a miserable, one-sided affair, a catastrophic, disaster-pitted dimension of history, precisely because this love of God and its averted feminine face allotted to man for his protection had been spurned.

No one in the history of man has worked harder to bring more light to the darkness that still surrounds our little day. No one has worked harder to push back, as it were, the frontiers of the mystery which encloses us. Yet no one at the same time has shown paradoxically so great a respect and reverence for the mystery. Indeed, Jung could not have worked to reduce the mystery of life half as well had he not done so utterly in a spirit of reverence and love. As a result one finds that at the end of his days, when he is ready to close his own account of what he had laboured to do in life, he leaves the last word not with these great new concepts of his but with a mystery which he confesses he is incapable of articulating, the mystery of love. And that love in the last analysis is a feminine mystery.

One of the few occasions I saw him moved nearly to tears is relevant to this mystery of the love before which he bowed his head and held his tongue. I repeated to him a dream told me by a remarkable woman when I went to say goodbye to her during an air raid in London in 1940; I was not to see her alive again. She said she had a friend once, an old lady, whose closing years were full of pain and sickness. Just before she died at a great age she told my friend of a dream that must be one of the dreams speaking to us from a condition closer to death than any on record. Like all dreams of greatest meaning from the collective unconscious, it was almost epigrammatic in expression. In her dream, all her pain and sickness were gathered together in a bed of roses and she knew that roses would always grow. And the rose was chosen by her unconscious because it is the image of the eternal of love, the Eros in life as only a woman can know it, and leads a man to discover as Dante did in the symbolism of the rose wherein he and Beatrice ascended to Heaven, and T. S. Eliot discovered when at last fire and rose in man for him were one.

Jung turned away when I told him of the dream and was silent a long while for him before he said, as if from far away, "*Ach, ja!* There is no end to dreams and their meaning." And then, I think because it meant so much, he teased himself and me, saying with a smile, "The dream is like a woman. It will have the last word as it had the first."

The essence of Jung's message, then, is that as far as the future is foreseeable the highest task of man once more is the old religious task of the redemption of Evil that he called the shadow. As shadow,

Evil was not absolute and final, but redeemable and through its challenge to be redeemed an instrument of enlargement of human awareness. In this transfiguration, the last word is with love. In the collection of essays *Modern Man in Search of a Soul* there is a sign of what his feelings, as opposed to his thinking, were about it. At the end of "Psychotherapists or the Clergy," he writes, "Who are forgiven their many sins? Those who have loved much. But as to those who love little, their few sins are held against them."

Jung was possessed by a capacity for love so great that it included also a love of all that life until now rejected, reviled, and persecuted. In all this he was more than a psychological or scientific phenomenon; he was to my mind one of the greatest religious phenomena the world has ever experienced. Until this central fact of his work and character is grasped and admitted, the full meaning and implication of Jung for the future of life is missed. But once this fact is grasped and admitted, the life of the individual who had experienced it can never be the same again, as I am certain the life of our time can never be the same again because of Jung.

However dark, disordered, and desperate this moment in which we live, the individual who finds himself in this way will, I believe, change the course of life in the direction of a greater wholeness of being, lived in greater awareness of the mystery of love. And since this love is so pre-eminently in the keeping of the feminine in life, and presides like an archangel over the spirit and passion of truth in Jung, this is perhaps the right moment to stress how it was confirmed by the numbers of truly remarkable women who rallied round Jung.

I remember as a young man going into northern Zululand because of a report that a great new prophet had arisen among the Zulus and I longed to meet him. When I found him at last, I was amazed that there was hardly a single man in his following but vast numbers of women. My guide, a remarkable Zulu himself and a highly educated person in the tribal as well as in the European sense, was not at all surprised.

"You can tell the greatest of new prophets among us from the numbers of women who flock to him long before the men have the courage to do so," he told me. And in time I saw the uncommon good sense of what he had said. More intuitive than men, women to this day, as in the early days of Christianity in Rome, are quicker to spot a revelation of new truth. The man who is the keeper of the rational conscious self in man—the Logos principle as Jung called it, or the Word as Saint John had it—needs a clear progression towards conviction by way of ideas and logic before he can see it. The woman in her role as chatelaine of love, the Eros principle, needs no such guidance and gets there first as if on wings of the heart. This to me is one explanation of why the numbers of women around and working with and for Jung were so great. But an even more potent factor than this was the fact that Jung was working ceaselessly to bring back into equal partnership with the man all that was feminine in life. So it was naturally right that the modern woman rather than the modern man should be the first to recognise what he was essentially doing.

Regrettably late as I came to know Jung, it was still soon enough for me to meet some of the most remarkable of this impressive circle of women colleagues and friends. His own wife Emma was still alive and taking an active part in the work of the Institute founded for the study of his psychology after the Second World War. I went regularly to her lectures on the myth and legend of the Holy Grail. She was an immensely sensitive, shy, solicitous, circumspect, and introverted spirit, and must have found public exposition of a task of such intimate concern extremely difficult if not painful. Yet she was dauntless as she was enduring and delivered her meaning with great precision, erudition, and understanding. At the same time, she was working as a lay analyst herself. I knew four of her pupils, all men, and even in the short time I was at Zürich I was amazed at the change in them. I gathered from them that she had a very "re-creative" way with men who had lost their own way with themselves.

I was to know her only as an elegant and generous hostess who kept herself very much in the background when her husband had male company. She knew better than anyone how he had lacked real masculine companionship in his life. Yet I remember an occasion also at Ascona where over the period of a fortnight my wife and I persuaded her and her husband to talk to us for the purposes of making a sound recording of their own spoken account of their work and lives. We were doing this, among other reasons, so that the BBC could broadcast a summary of it on Jung's eightieth birthday, which was to fall later in the year.

It was necessary to prerecord the summary because I was about to vanish for nearly nine months on an expedition into the Kalahari Desert. The BBC technician responsible for equipping me unfortunately did not know, or if he knew forgot to tell me, who would have to work the still rather crude recording machine of the day or that severe cold affected the quality of the sound considerably if not eliminating it altogether. Perhaps I should also have been put on my guard by the fact that when he heard why I wanted the machine he became strangely aggressive, obviously thought I was setting out on something reprehensible, and said so plainly, declaring that he had no time for such mystical nonsense since he himself was a student of the science of history and both a Marxist and an atheist. Oddly, from the start, Jung himself was convinced that the machine would not work.

"I warn you," he said with an ironic laugh, "things of this sort hate me. You might think they are inanimate but in my regard I tell you they are highly animate and even active and hostile. Don't say you've not been warned!"

Most of the time the cold was bitter and cruel and owing to it and my ignorance and inexperience, some seventy hours of Jung alone, speaking spontaneously about himself to my wife, were in large measure spoiled or lost in the recording. What we salvaged for the eightieth-birthday broadcast from London was a sad fragment of what had passed between us all. As far as Emma Jung was concerned, the recording was a total disaster and nothing of value retained. Yet the experience for me personally and the memory of an essentially feminine imagination put to a truly feminine use stay impressive, transparent and warm in my mind as the light in the window of a great house seen by a traveller at the end of a long day in the dark of winter.

And then, of course, there was Toni Wolff, of whom I have said almost all that can be usefully included here. I saw her most of all because my wife was working with her and we dined with her nearly every Sunday night. She was the most generous of hosts. She ran her own house as if there were a host implicit in its care and was a connoisseur of wine. She taught me all I know of the wines of Switzerland and, curious perhaps only to those who did not know her, a great deal about Portuguese wines, which I had despised up to then despite many more opportunities than she could have had to try them for myself. As I saw her, often at the end of a day or after a weekend spent with Jung at Bollingen, refreshed and uplifted, she was a stimulating and spiritual companion, in full command of the ceremonies of the house. She always had us fetched and sent home by car, for it was still a moment in post-war England when travel allowances were highly rationed. She knew this and despite our protests insisted on acting accordingly. She lived as she thought, behaving obedient to her awareness with the grace to match her own devout honesty of purpose.

Despite her native Bernese seriousness, she had moments of acute wit and exercise of a sense of humour that was enchanting. She, apart from Jung, was aware of how a sense of humour too had an instinctive unconscious root and a valuable role to play in providing the unconscious with a respect for proportion. I remember with what delight she told the story of a woman patient who tended to overidentify with Christ and who one night, she told her analyst, I believe it was H. G. Baynes, had written a letter to Christ, addressed to "Christ, Gethsemane." To her dismay the letter came back to her with the remark on the envelope, "Not known at this address."

She died suddenly and without ostensible physical warning. Jung saw her only two days before she died. Although he had had no conscious idea that her end was so near—he himself was far from well at the time—a dream of Hades some months before had made him uneasy in her regard. And there were recurring dreams too, which troubled him even before then, started by one of a great black elephant uprooting a tree. This, too, he realised, could be an image of death approaching to take away another to add to the many already dead who had mattered specially to him in life. He said little of his own feelings to others except to emphasise that her going, as far as he was concerned, left a gap which no one else could fill.

But there remained many others, like that aristocrat of spirit with her keen and piercing perceptions, Linda Fierz-David, whose work on Francesco Colonna's *Hypnerotomachia Poliphili*, *The Dream of Poliphilo*, shed new light on the inner motivation of spirit of the Renaissance and the pattern of its preliminary convolutions in the imagination of that singular Venetian monk who was its author. The dream for her, as she said herself, was "the symbol of the living process of growth which had been set going, obscurely and incomprehensibly in the men of his time, and made the Renaissance the beginning of a new era."

There was Barbara Hannah, who had come for a visit almost straight from an English cathedral close and remained to make her home in Zürich, where she lives to this day working as analyst and writer to make her own acute and astute contributions to Jung's work. If her essays on Stevenson, "R.L.S.," the analysis of his evolution as a writer and in particular of how his story of Dr. Jekyll and Mr. Hyde, inspired by a dream, is high drama of the conflict of man and his shadow played out in the Ludwig of Bavaria theatre in the hidden heart of each one of us, were her only contributions, it would have been enough. But of course, there was more work still to come.

How right she was to stay on in Zürich is confirmed for me by the fact that she never lost any of her essential Englishness in her Swiss translation. Her laugh was, and remains as young as it always was, full of a sense of fun and almost schoolgirl mischievousness. Her English capacity to laugh at herself remains intact and seems to be at her most active when her unconscious joins forces with it, as on one occasion when I went to see her. I found her laughing, saying, "You know, I dreamt about Neptune last night and would you believe it, I have just come back from a car accident in the Neptunestrasse. When will one ever learn?"

There is Aniela Jaffé, who had come to see Jung before the last war after a skiing accident that seemed too portentous to ignore. She told me that she went to see Jung for months and sat silent in his presence not knowing what to say or ask, so remote was the world of psychology to her. Jung would just go on patiently and calmly talking to her while sheer intuition that one day she would know what he meant kept her in her chair. And then one day she did know and knew to such an extent that she could set out on her own, explore what was nearest to her imagination, the area of psychic phenomena, write revealingly about it, and from there move on to her remarkable book *The Myth of Meaning* and her essays on other aspects of Jung's work. In addition, she found the energy and capacity, perhaps unexpectedly in someone ostensibly so delicate and vulnerable physically, to become Jung's secretary, co-author of his *Memories*, co-editor of his letters, and to perform many other tasks. During the time I was in Zürich, however, she was still secretary to the Institute and I got to know her well and learned to respect a spirit that owes its strength to the gentleness, precision, detail, and integrity of a truly feminine perception of reality.

There was Dr. Marie-Louise ("Marlus") von Franz, then the youngest of recruits to those formidable ranks, yet one of its greatest acquisitions. She was to collaborate most closely in a psychological sense with Jung and his wife in their last years. It was she who finished Emma Jung's work on the Holy Grail and did much of Jung's special research for him. A great natural scholar by instinct as well as by training, she has been able to carry on Jung's work now to an historical and archetypal depth unsurpassed by any co-worker of her sex.

There was also Jolande Jacobi, one of the members of the founding committee of the C. G. Jung Institute. In a world of profoundly introverted feminine personalities, she was the una-shamed extrovert. As such she was of immense value to them and, like all elements of value in so paradoxical a context, a problem both to herself and others in the most positive sense of the word. Also by temperament she belonged neither to the German complex of European culture nor to the English-speaking version. She was actually Hungarian, although she had worked in Vienna. She was Jewish but converted to Catholicism and had a special gift for analytical work with men. Through her own differences of temperament and approach she diversified and enriched the femi-nine contribution to Jung's work. Unafraid of the world and completely at peace with a fate which had so violently uprooted her from a culture she loved, she performed an invaluable service in establishing Jung's psychology in terms an extroverted world could understand. She spoke her astringent mind without fear or favour, perhaps at times too much as Jung was moved to warn her gently once, but as the years went by it was most impressive to me how her personality matured and rounded and real calm and benevolence of spirit emanated from her. She grew old with grace and art and became a centre round which the external world attracted to Jung's work in Zürich increasingly turned.

There was too, and happily still is, Cornelia Brunner, wife of one of Switzerland's most distinguished surgeons and for many years the respected head of the Psychological Club at Zürich. Her mastery of English enabled her to follow her instinct on the trail of the anima at work in the books of Rider Haggard and so provide a clear mirror wherein reflections of this profound, hidden process in men can be clearly and precisely seen. Her work and research into the life of Rider Haggard exceeds anything yet produced on him in the English-speaking world and demonstrates how negligent Rider Haggard's own countrymen have been in their assessment of his real achievement.

First under Toni Wolff's chairmanship and then under her own, the Psychological Club became a positive communal expression of colleagues, friends, pupils, and analysands. But it was no dead and perfunctory body sealed in academic and professional solemnity. Jung saw to it that its beginnings were as alive as he felt himself to be. Those meetings at the club could be as Dionysian as they were Apollonian and the last word of the profound lectures often lost in the sound of music and laughter that followed. The members would eat and drink well with taste and gusto and often dance their way towards a fulfilled goodnight.

There was Alice Lewisohn Crowley, co-founder and director of the Neighborhood Playhouse in New York, who also came on a visit and, like many other American women, remained to the end of her days. She took no active literary part in the work of the others but she was always a rare psychological presence in being, an indefinable but abiding influence more than a substance, who through the atmosphere she evoked became a rare and essential element in the feminine establishment of those days. Above all, she kept open house to the young who came to Zürich to study, and gave them a personal human centre of their own on which to turn and return.

I could go on multiplying the list but feel this is enough to illustrate the nature and quality of Jung's feminine following in Zürich at the time. Their unceasing work and care for the implications of analytical psychology, added to the efforts of women elsewhere as we shall see, constitute a unique feminine phenomenon. Both in sheer numbers as well as in quality of what was achieved, they created a new historical record and a breakthrough of the feminine into a field almost exclusively reserved until then for men, with rare exceptions that only went to prove the historical masculine rule of law.

Yet I knew how the outside world, far from appreciating its signifiance, made fun of the fact that Jung had so much feminine support. I remember how everywhere negative men prophesied that when Jung died Zürich would see such a dire harvest of feminine suicides as no city had ever experienced. Yet after Jung's death on the terrible blank morning after the afternoon of storm wherein he died, not one of those ladies cancelled an appointment but each and every one reported for duty as usual to their patients and students. They had not fallen out of the march when many a man had done and it is a convincing proof of both their quality and the stature of Jung that not one so much as faltered in step on the sombre march to his grave and on afterwards to a future where he was no longer present physically to guide them.

Finally there was one remarkable other woman, not in Zürich but nevertheless in Switzerland and out on a wing of her own at the Casa Gabriella in Ascona on Lake Maggiore. She was the Dutch lady, Olga Fröbe-Kapteyn, a profoundly introverted personality, sensitive, shy, and, with reason enough, not without fear of the external world. Yet she made of her shadow, her averted self, so positive a force that she created the Platonic institution of Eranos around her. She turned her home into a place where great scholars came annually from all over the world to talk to a select public on a common theme of abiding human concern. It was she who had gone to visit Jung in Zürich in the thirties and persuaded him to come to lecture at Ascona. As a result of his first experience there, those meetings at Ascona, the *Tagungen* as they were called, became an ideal platform for delivering what was new, active, and immediate at any given phase of the swift progression of his work.

When the last world war broke out and it looked as if Eranos might have to close down because the world could no longer come to it, Jung insisted with Olga Fröbe-Kapteyn, so she told me, that the meetings had to continue. Jung saw the mountains around Switzerland, he told her, as a kind of magic circle, a mandala, a protective movement of the earth itself, to provide a still centre where the search for meaning could be carried on in the midst of the storm of the madness of war around it. So Eranos went on and continues to go on to this day.

I hope someone will one day write a life of this moving and remarkable woman who, unaided and alone out of her own intuitive self, created Eranos. Her achievement seems to me all the more heroic in that she had no feminine community to support her or great man to whom to turn as her opposite numbers in Zürich had. In the Jungian Apocrypha, there is a legend that she discovered the magic circle, the mandala movement of spirit, or the Round Table of herself, by joining a circus as a young girl and riding, all spangled, on a white horse around the ring. I hope the legend is true because no symbol could have been more appropriate to the movement of her own seeking. It would be poetic justice if what was psychologically true of herself had been confirmed with such brave originality in the external circumstances of her life as well. And I know it was no idle accident that had made her build a great Round Table on the terrace of the lovely garden around the Casa Gabriella. There in the shade, overlooking the waters of the Avalonesque Maggiore, the speakers at those Eranos meetings would sit down together to talk, break their bread together, and drink the reddest of Italian wine. I, alas, never sat at the table with Jung as many others had done for years, but I have done so soon after his going and will always remember the quality and riches of the conversation it evoked.

This world of women around Jung even to this day has no clear intimation, I believe, of how rare and great a little universe it constituted. Its members could not, out of a natural modesty and respect for the reality of their own shadows, see the unique wood they planted because of the trees of themselves. But I never think of them without raising my hat to them. They loomed all the larger because the men around Jung, when I first met them, were so few. Dr. Ludwig Binswanger, the Existential psychoanalyst, who had been a steadfast friend to Jung all those long years, was about to withdraw from active participation; he had a remarkable head and a medieval face that was calm, rounded, and resolved, with a look of Gothic confidence and benevolence and a certain peace indelible upon it.

The main role of representing Jung as a man in the world had fallen on Dr. C. A. Meier. He was the head of the Institute and had been a close colleague of Jung's since long before the war. He was soon to leave the Institute and take up Jung's professorship at the federal Polytechnic Institute but had already, in addition to dealing with all the practical daily applied issues of Jung's psychology, performed a great historical service for it. A profound scholar of Greek and Roman antiquity, he had firmly traced the continuity of a Jungian theme back into the heart of the Greek world in its great mysteries of healing exercised at Epidaurus and Eleusis; hence his book *Ancient Incubation and Modern Psychotherapy*. He and Jung were to part immediate company after some years. I never knew or asked why, out of the respect for the silence both men felt compelled to keep on the subject.

I came to know Dr. Meier well over the years and to this day count him as a close friend. I have not once heard him complain or utter criticism of Jung about whatever it was that caused them to separate. But far more significant, he never personalised the cause as Freud had done. He never wavered in his attachment to Jung's work but carried it on in scientific fields for which only he had the technical equipment. As well as holding the professorship so ably that it has now been converted into a permanent chair instead of the temporary one it had hitherto been at the Polytechnic Institute, he established the Clinic and Research Center for Jungian Psychology in Zürich for further scientific Jungian research and treatment. He consolidated and expanded Jung's earlier scientific work in the association experiments, and has published in German two revealing books on dreams and the role of the unconscious in man, all as part of a multivolume manual of Jungian psychology. Since dreams and their interpretation had always been elements especially dear to him and for which he had a special gift, these books are indispensable for the understanding of the inner foundation of Jung's work and Jungian seeking. Yet at the time of which I speak, Dr. Meier tended to be an isolated masculine phenomenon.

The one other person of real stature who could also have supported him had long since returned to his native England. That was a doctor, Helton Godwin Baynes—"Peter," as he was known to his friends. He had been for years the man closest of all to Jung and uniquely equipped to establish a Jungian school in England, as his book *Mythology of the Soul* was to prove. He was a man of great intelligence and above all immense charm and feeling. Barbara Hannah was fond of saying with great affection, "He kept open heart like a grand hotel." That his pioneering effort occupied a grateful place in Jung's reflections was clear from a dream Jung had about him two years after Baynes's death in 1943.

"On the night before Germany's capitulation," Jung told me, "I had a dream I was a prisoner-of-war in a vast prison. I had no idea that peace was about to come in the world outside. But suddenly I heard the sound of marching feet as of a vast army approaching the prison. I looked amazed at the great iron gates shutting me in. Suddenly they were thrown wide open. I saw a long column of soldiers lost in the distance beyond, but at their head hurrying towards me came an officer in British Army uniform, waving his cap above his head excitedly at me. A voice said nearby, 'The Army of Liberation is here.' By that time the officer was near me and I saw he was 'Peter' Baynes."

Seeing how much the life of our time is a prisoner-of-war camp of two embattled aspects of itself, and how Jung fought to liberate it, the dream could hardly have been more to the point or more precise.

But even in England, Baynes's immediate supporters were women, though men of the calibre of Dr. E. A. Bennet, and later on Gerhard Adler, rallied to his work. The Zürich pattern held true there as well. Women like Irene Champernowne, who was unique in that she had done both a Freudian and Adlerian analysis as well as one with Jung by proxy of Baynes, saw to it that analytical psychology took firm root in England, and carried on Baynes's work in her establishment of the remarkable Withymead Centre. And, of course, there were many others as well—like Frieda Fordham, who wrote what I still think is the best handbook on Jungian psychology, and Winifred Rushforth, who founded the Davidson Clinic in one of the poorest districts of Edinburgh and gave analytical psychology a permanent root in Scotland. Then in America the importance of women in the crucial formative years of Jung's work was even more pronounced than either in Zürich or England. This was all the more remarkable because it was the interest of American scientists in Jung's earliest work that had brought him and Freud to America in 1909. But this interest declined after Freud's break with Jung and the consequences of Jung's confrontation with the collective unconscious were made apparent. Women like Frances G. Wickes, who tragically was deprived of her son in a fateful yachting accident and came to write with such profound insight about the psychology of the young, took over where the men left off for the moment. Her influence spread far beyond the frontiers of psychology into American art, even the dance and ballet of the New World. Her books testify to the height of a remarkable feminine achievement. She was a most impressive old lady when I met her, totally unembittered by loss of her son and by blindness, and went on working until her death in her nineties. She was indeed a great, rare, and perhaps the most charismatic of the women to follow Jung.

There was Dr. Esther M. Harding, an Englishwoman, who died in 1971. In America, where she went to settle, she made one of the greatest contributions of all in volume of work and depth of character. Her books on various aspects of psychology, literature, and history, seen from a feminine point of view, have far-reaching consequences for the nature and wholeness of human awareness. Close beside her was Dr. Eleanor Bertine—I speak only of those I knew personally—and many others like Elined Kotschnig and the gallant Martha Jaeger, both Quakers who laboured to carry Jung into the Society of Friends and make those indomitable "children and servants of the light" realise that the clearer the light the more precise the shadow.

To this day, American women help pre-eminently to maintain Jungian institutes and societies from East Coast to West, and from Montreal to Houston in Texas. Although the numbers of notable men have happily increased thanks greatly to the example of distinguished émigré initiates like James Kirsch and Max Zeller, the women still for me set the tone and maintain the growth. One final example from the unlikely world of Japan that cannot be ignored. A Japanese woman who trained in Zürich too has inspired one of the fastest growing Jungian schools of all, near the ancient capital of Kyoto and its thousand and one temples of Buddha and Zen. To put it in the terms of Jung's great dream of transition, the magnolia tree brought back from Europe is in flower again in the Far East and this interpenetration of spirit and traffic between East and West which I have mentioned is starting to become a two-way affair in great depth again. Without this mobilisation of the feminine in the world one could easily despair of any resolution to the clash of the opposites and the problem of the shadow which is basic to Jung's approach and the greatest challenge confronting our world.

I knew Jung, alas, only in the last sixteen years of his life and when I first met him this problem of the universal shadow was his greatest concern. I clearly remember him saying to me that the individual who withdraws his shadow from his neighbour and finds it in himself and is reconciled to it as to an estranged brother is doing a task of great universal importance. He added quickly that the future of mankind depended on the speed and extent to which individuals learnt to withdraw their shadows from others and reintegrate them honourably within themselves.

One of the paradoxes of the collective unconscious is that ultimately it abhors collective expressions of itself. However important collective expression in the world without may be as a defensive measure on behalf of a new-born and vulnerable value of the unconscious, ultimately what is sought is an individual realisation of the value. One sees an example of such a defensive collective expression in the movement known as Women's Lib. This movement is clearly intended to serve a new awareness of the importance of the masculine in woman. But it is only an archaic, defensive preliminary to a specific individual realisation of the feminine which the collective unconscious seeks.

Jung in his darkest hour after his break with Freud already had a clear, intuitive intimation of the importance of this irresistible drive in the collective unconscious. Long before the close of his own confrontation with his own unconscious he had coined the word "individuation" to describe it. If one wanted a slogan for what he stood for himself and sought for his patients in those days, it would be inscribed on a banner streaming in the wind as "differentiation and individuation."

But the importance of the individual in this role of making the collective specific was given another dimension in that hour of which I am speaking, when Jung saw the individual raised infinitely in worth and dignity as a working partner on the pattern of God. The greatest theological scandal of our time to my mind is not the fragmentation of the Christian churches but, as mentioned before, their failure to take up the work of Jung and the instruments he laboured so long to create on their behalf. He has placed in their unwitting hands the means of their renewal and creation as organs of living religious experience.

Yet the churches continue to exhort man without any knowledge of what the soul of modern man is and how starved and empty it has become. They have done nothing to inform themselves in a contemporary idiom of "The Dark Night of the Soul" to which Saint John of the Cross pointed so poetic and saintly a way. They behave as if repetition of the message of the Cross and reiteration of the miracles and parables of Christ were enough. Yet if they took Christ's message seriously, they would not ignore the empiric material and testimony of the nature of the soul and its experience of God which Jung has presented to the world. He had done his utmost to make them undertake the journey he accomplished so that they could know the reality of man's psyche and its relationship to God but to their everlasting shame and peril they ignored the call. Even William Temple, one of the most charismatic of archbishops of Canterbury since Becket, turned a deaf ear to Jung's desperate plea for a hearing.

" 'Please send me an intelligent young theologian,' " Jung begged him. " 'I will lead him into the night of the soul so that one of them at last may know what he is actually dealing with.' But nobody came.

"Naturally they knew it already, and much better," Jung commented wryly. "That is why the light [in the churches] has gone out." *

Although Jung never denied the historical reality of Christ and indeed stressed and restressed that only a real and specific person born in response to the greatest need of his time could have done what Christ had done, he thought Christ's meaning was of greatest immediate meaning as a life symbolically fulfilled in obedience to an overwhelmingly active symbol in all men to this day. He therefore traced an inborn and constantly recurring, hence also contemporary, pattern of Christ in the spirit of every man so that one could, in a psychological sense, declare with Paul that the Redeemer still lived. One of the most important statements Jung ever made, therefore, was his definition of what was meant in a twentieth-century way by the imitation of Christ.

He said quite plainly that the meaning of Christ's example was not that the individual should imitate the life of Christ blindly and make himself a pale, insipid copy of what that crucified person had been. The true meaning of Christ for him was that every individual should live out fully his own natural and specific self as truly as Christ had lived his unto the end to which he had been born, and this was only possible if man were reintegrated with the shadow over all in the despised and rejected aspects of himself and his time through intercession of the universal feminine in himself.

It was through the intercession of the feminine that Goethe had struggled to achive the redemption of the shadow of Faust. Jung knew this could only be done by uniting it with the eternal feminine

* Letter to Max Frischknecht, July 17, 1945.

in man which in its highest form he had called Sophia, as Goethe had done in *Faust*, and which was beatified in the person of the saintly Christian lady of a name that in its Greek derivation means "wisdom." Jung personified the evolution of the feminine in four self-evident ascending feminine models, of Eve, Helen, Maria, and Sophia, just as he saw four masculine patterns to support his own achievement in this rising scale of priorities: Lao-tzu, Mani, Buddha, and Christ—another illustration of how in him all streams of inner eventfulness met, no matter from what end of the earth.

"It is a gigantic task," he exclaimed once almost in despair, "to create a new approach to an old truth. The old way of interpreting has itself to be interpreted this time with the help of science. I do not combat Christian truth; I am only arguing with the modern mind."

I remember that when we were speaking of this once at Bollingen, there came to me again the line from Dante's *Paradiso*, "Virgin mother, daughter of your son."

It took on a completely new meaning. Biologically, of course, this great poetic statement makes no sense at all. Symbolically it could not be more meaningful. It is a symbol of Euclidean accuracy, because the Christ that was crucified was a creation of the feminine love which came from the master pattern in the collective unconscious in order to help man in his awesome task of serving the unconscious dominion consciously. It is a scientific fact that man has a biological birth through a woman of flesh and blood but a spiritual or psychological rebirth through a feminine self within. Man's biological birth provides him with the base material for creating something unique and individual of himself. This act of individual creation and re-creation within is done through the feminine fathered within by his own male spirit.

This is the contemporary meaning of the Immaculate Conception which troubled the literal spirit of post-Renaissance man so much, because he insisted on reading it physically instead of symbolically. Here one has a slight example from my own experience of what appears to be dead, dogmatic doctrine brought alive and meaningful back into the life of our time if it is reassessed and regarded in the light of the symbols that come from the collective unconscious to bombard our conscious selves night and day with the seeds of new being and meaning.

Yet Jung never bothered really to define precisely where he stood in terms of religion because the transcendental was ultimately beyond definition. But he did stress in a way no one could mistake how all-important his Christian heritage was to him and how he had worked scientifically to keep the door open in the imagination of his time for admission for the full meaning of Christ and—there was the trouble, the cosmic shadow that fell over the life—of the Son of man.

Even at work on the apparently remote, esoteric story of alchemy, he had a vision of Christ one night that stayed with him forever. In a bright light at the foot of his bed, with the intensity of a commanding beauty of a miraculous kind, he saw Christ on the Cross and his body as made of greenish gold—the combination of values in metal which was for the alchemists the expression of the life spirit that motivated the whole of the universe. That for him was proof almost enough of the universal importance of what Christ represented in the spirit of all men known by that or any other name or even without name at all.

For these and many other reasons I feel that Jung was the most deeply religious person I have ever met. He lived and worked out his religion in a way that made definition unnecessary if not redundant. Besides, it was never an arrested but a continuous and continuing process. There was no finality to it. Creation for him, I believe, was not ended on the last day of Genesis before the Creator rested. It was only the first commitment to a continuing act of creation wherein all life participates every second of night and day. The exposition and formulations in which it came temporarily to rest were only wayside inns of the spirit. It was moving on and on in everything he did. It accompanied him everywhere he went and its atmosphere was around him in the lowliest of tasks, like that of cooking food of his own unique invention.

He was a wonderful though utterly unconventional cook, and cooking in the house he built at Bollingen or just lighting the wood fire had a sense of ritual about them and gave out an air of such reverence that one understood why it was so important for men in the beginning to pour out a libation and sacrifice some of their food to the gods before they ate and drank or merely to say grace and thanks, as the Christian world did until recently: the two were in essence a tribute of the "whole" or "holy" spirit to the mystery of which it is the express messenger.

But just as he never rejected his cultural inheritance, he did not evade his own religious portions of it. The fortnight we spent with him and his wife on the shores of Lake Maggiore coincided with the moment when he was deeply involved with the meaning of Job in man and the consequences of the pattern of God in man. We would go walking in the sun that came right down to the dark waters of the lake and in the woods beyond, with Jung looking more than ever like a casual English country gentleman. I myself have never felt comfortable by the waters of Maggiore. It is for me sinister earth. At nights it is as if it still reverberated with the tramp of the invisible traffic of the Christian legions who were once delegated by the great father city of Rome to hold those narrow passes that led into the pagan heart of Europe.

I remember how we talked about this and the evolution of Christianity, how the Book of Revelation, which Calvin rejected as a dark and dangerous book, showed that the Christian dream did not end with the coming of Christ but that the search of which his coming was a consummation had still to be carried on into the Apocalyptic future of which John of Patmos had had such disturbing visions. For me the Christian vision, however final its relation to an abiding master pattern of the objective soul, had hardly begun in its unfolding. And it was when we came to this stage that Jung turned to me with a great laugh and said, "Of course, as you will have noticed, at heart I'm only a determined old Protestant of the left."

And of course this was true; he was a Protestant in the sense that he could not run spiritually to the shelter of some great mother church, however much he admired it and wished it well—as he did, for instance, the Church of Rome. He was a Protestant in the sense that he had to put his own individual conscience, the commandment of his own unique contract with life, above that of any doctrine or church. For those who needed a church he thought the Roman Catholic church with its roots in the pagan as well as Christian world, its ancient ritual, dogma, and symbolism, was the best available collective home. He thought it an immense pity that the leaders of the Reformation had dismissed the appeal of Pope Paul III to come to Trent in the sixteenth century under promise of safe conduct to try to reconcile their differences. He thought it scandalous that the Christian churches were so fragmented, and not only disunited but almost at war with each other, in the face of the growing peril threatening the Western spirit. But his concept of the

Protestant was that of a person operating as an individual and, however much prepared to honour the need of institutional religion, committed ultimately to following only the Pentecostal flame sent to guide the fearful disciples after the Ascension of Christ.

Religious revelation had not ended for him with Crucifixion, Resurrection, and Ascension but had barely begun, and he took the Book of Revelation, with which the Christian message is supposed to end, as only the beginning of a disconcerting call to resumption of religious searching with only what was once called the Holy Ghost as it manifested itself within him as his abiding light in the gathering darkness ahead.

But this in actuality was only part of the truth, because he worked really beyond the frontiers of even the boldest speculation and certainly outside the fortifications of any church. He was a born frontiersman and as such there were times when he would say to me, "I am only an old African for whom God is the dream."

He said this, of course, because one of the things that had impressed him about Africa was the fact that he found Africans drawing the same distinction in dreams as he did. They talked of "little" and "great" dreams, while he talked of dreams from the personal unconscious and from the collective unconscious. His voice was sad when he told me how an old African witch-doctor had once said to him that he no longer dreamt any "great" dreams because the English D.C. in his *boma* now dreamt them for him. I told him how the great African seer and prophet I had been to see as a young man implied something similar when he said to me, "People no longer talk of the First Spirit. His praise names are forgotten. They talk only of things useful to them brought by the Europeans."

Jung nodded and smiled before saying that of course, it must be far worse in Russia: it looked as if people were not allowed to dream any great dreams at night because the state was doing it for them.

Saying that, he became unusually sombre and silent and after a while stood still and pointed with his stick at a cloud in the sky that was swollen with snow like the sail of a great ship of war with wind, and said, "It is pitiful how ignorant we are of such things. Man everywhere is dangerously unaware of himself. We really know nothing about the nature of man and unless we hurry to get to know ourselves we are in dangerous trouble. I should have been a mathematician and a physician and God knows what else besides, perhaps even a musician, to do my task properly. I am appalled by the inadequacy of what I have done."

I took all this as another sign of his greatness, because only someone truly great could see the vast, unexplored prospect in front of him and experience the shrinking of his own measure of achievement in the full scale of his vision. I saw him as I have always seen truly creative pioneering spirits, as a kind of Moses who can lead millions to a new land of promise, which is our inherited image of greater being, but is forbidden to enter it himself, and that reference to music in particular had an association for me with the sort of burden of isolation Jung carried around with him all his life. It was only the second, and last, time he ever referred to music in conversation with me. I thought of Socrates' own sense of separation from the life which had condemned him, falling like a shadow over his remark not long before he took the hemlock that he regretted not having learned to play the lute.

I found this black mood of self-deprecation unexpected and almost unbearable, and protested all I could, but in vain that day. It was one of those occasions when one's own sense of his unfairness to himself was irrelevant because through it he achieved his warmest, greatest human stature. He was too aware of his own inadequacies to exceed his humanity. As a result he gave out a feeling of being known and belonging, and a sense of involvement in the unfolding of an expanding universe, that I have experienced only among the despised first people of my native country.

I remember him beside the black Maggiore water, pointing with his stick at another great cloud full of thunder and lightning which made one feel small and insignificant and saying in a voice low with awe, "It makes me shiver to think that such a cloud is unfolding and forming also in us and that we both partake with that cloud of what is being formed and unformed in this moment in time."

I told him he reminded me of how on a hot day in the southern desert of Africa I had wanted to go and speak to one of my favourite Stone Age hunters. He was sitting in the middle of a thorn bush, around which the sunlight crackled like electricity from a radio transmitter at the masthead of some ship. He was huddled in an attitude of the most intense concentration on the sand in the scrub with the shade of thorn, but his friends would not let me get near him, saying, "But don't you know, he is doing work of the utmost importance. He is making clouds."

And Jung laughed as only that desert maker of clouds could have laughed himself, and went on to talk at great length about the nature of time, and how a great many of our modern errors arose from our misunderstanding of the nature of time and our shallow attitude towards it. He had already written a book about it, outlining some principles towards a non-causal explanation of life and time.

He was compelled to do this by unexplained empiric evidence obtained in his work of a principle in life beyond cause and effect—how, for instance, in certain dreams the future already seemed to exist and was sometimes presented in precise detail and events occurred, as it were, long before any cause that could explain them was in being. Coincidences in his life and that of others, the Chinese experience of an inherent time sympathy in men, things, and events, the *mono-aware* of the Japanese I had learnt to appreciate in Japan through experience but found difficult to express, all challenged him to propose another exposition of its nature. His own intuitive attitude in this regard had been reinforced by his introduction through Richard Wilhelm to the Book of Changes. Told one day by someone that the Chinese had no science, he replied indignantly that they had already possessed one uniquely their own for thousands of years, a science based on a total acausal principle of approach, a profound observation and exploration of the pattern of meaning unfolded through time in the universe, utterly beyond and before our own conceptions of first cause and its effect. The *I Ching* was for him the greatest textbook of this classic Chinese science, which had constructed even its own machine for divining the meaningful context of any given moment of time, manifested through what we call sheer chance and coincidences. Through his own experiments with this Chinese "time machine," he was convinced of its efficiency as a measure of meaning in time, and confirmed in his concept of time as a continuous stream of dynamic energy of a character and drive peculiarly its own. Those were among the things he felt he had been unable to explore sufficiently and longed for physicists, mathematicians, and astronomers to take over and explore empirically.

Even so, the book *Synchronicity* which Jung wrote as a result of this and more is not so difficult as men make it out to be, but its importance on this particular day was the fact that as far as I myself was concerned, its message was that time is not merely the measure of our days. It is a reality in its own right as much as a dimension. It is an element vitally involved in the evolution of the human spirit. It has a character of its own which it communicates to life. Everything in life not only has its own but also a time-character which it shares with all other things existing at that unique moment. There is not an idea even that is free of it, and growth itself is possible only in so far as it corresponds to time and conforms to the overall character of what I had for years, intuitively and clumsily, called to myself "the great togetherness."

All living things, consciously or unconsciously, partake of that character in any moment of time. They share it no matter where they are. It is another great partner of man and in so far as it yields a scythe, it is only to cut what is provisional and perishable from what is permanent and imperishable, the false from the true. It carries a portion of the responsibility of living the answer for which life was created that would be unbearable if left to man alone.

The liberation of spirit implicit in such a concept for me is immense because it means that life is not a process of mere predictable cause and effect. Both cause and effect are aspects of something greater than either, and there is no real need for man to be merely an instrument, a prisoner in a chain-gang of action and reaction. What men call a cause is the raw material over which man out of his full rounded awareness exercises a freedom of choice, and can choose in harmony with time, to add something to the cause which was not there before, making it more meaningful than it was before. Between cause and its so-called effect there falls, as it were, a cosmic shadow and out of this shadow man can accomplish a transfiguration of his own, participating, however minutely, in an act of universal creation, and something effective that no cause all alone and purely out of itself could have produced. Above all, not only life and men on earth but meaning has its seasons; time and meaning in their interdependence themselves are profoundly seasonal, and only in loving bondage to the elemental seasons man was free. Here for Jung was the importance of astrology. It was not only an ancient effort at developing a psychology of its own by projection onto the stars and their courses but an effort to relate and read the meaning and character of man in terms of the quality of time. For him astrology had, as any study of the real Zodiac would show, nothing to do with real astronomy. The stars and planets were used only as mirrors to reflect inner psychological patterns. He could not follow it, alas, very far, because of the absence of empirical evidence to support its observations, but he emphatically thought, as he would put it to me with his love of slang, "It's on to something."

He took seriously too the intuition of the seasonal character of time born in Greece about two centuries before Christ. This was the concept of a Platonic year of about 26,000 years, a complete round of all time seasons, divided into months each of about two thousand years. Christianity was also in part the product of both such a season and a response of the spirit to its sense of the season. This season of the Christ and anti-Christ was approaching its end, he felt, and a new month, a new season was about to begin wherein the great opposites of light and shadow would face each other openly and the task of transcending them be completed without sacrifice of the Christian values which preceded it.

It is not surprising that having come to terms with the reality of the shadow not only in himself, his own time, but in the pattern of God, Jung felt more free than ever not to *do* so much as to *be* utterly within himself all that he had discovered and wanted life to become. An overvaluation of *doing* and a tendency to measure the importance of men exclusively by the importance of the functions they performed in the external world had long since struck him as part of the slanted character of his day. More and more he was concerned with men as they were in the quality and texture of their own being and less with the kind of things they did in the world, however impressive or powerful their role. Indeed, he knew already only too well the damage which that kind of obsessive doing inflicted on men and their societies unless it was an issue of the necessity of being in search of greater awareness and wholeness for their own inner sake. All round him he saw the fatal consequences of the power to do and act conferred on men whose being did not match the responsibilities of the functions entrusted to them. He was to say over and over again, as the Chinese of the Book of Changes and *The Secret of the Golden Flower* had done, that the right cause entrusted to the wrong man was disastrous. And as always what he preached was only uttered after he had practiced it himself. Accordingly his intuition, that faculty for seeing below the horizon of time and round the corners of life, had already prompted him to build by the lake at Bollingen, according to his own design, a house wherein he could just *be,* or perhaps "design" and "build" are a shade inadequate and overconscious for what came about as the result of thrust and organic growth in phases over more than a decade.

It is an interesting example, however much it arises by the way, of how intuition was really his own superior function. He himself always declared that he was a thinking, intuitive, introverted person and that his sensation function, this sense of the here and now, and his feeling function tended to be pushed down into an inferior position in his unconscious.

One does not doubt at all the introversion. Only introversion of the deepest kind can explain why outwardly his life was so uneventful and inwardly so packed and overflowing with an historic eventfulness. Nor does one question Jung's fears about the relative inferiority of this feeling function because he was so aware of it and worked so hard to compensate for its deficiencies.

I was amazed how often after visiting him I would suddenly get a letter in England which would say something to this effect: "I do think my behaviour the other day was really inexcusable. You must please remember that feeling is my inferior function and that if it had not been, I would have responded far more warmly to what you were saying. It was of immense value to me, please believe me, but for the moment I felt stunned. It is only now that the feelings I ought to have had then have surfaced." And not once did I know what he was referring to because I never recollected any failure of response of feeling in my own regard, which shows all the more, I believe, how much he was on his guard against an aspect that seemed insufficiently differentiated within himself.

By the time I met Jung, of course, he had worked so long and with such effect at his own individuation that it was not easy to say what "type" he was. He had always stressed that no man was wholly extroverted or totally introverted, nor were the inferior functions ever completely unconscious; these were all relative states. But what he did stress was that all men and women, particularly in the second half of their lives, if they were to avoid this swing from one opposite to the other in themselves, had to labour at differentiation, raising their inferior functions and making them equal partners of the superior. That was an elementary goal of individuation and of immense importance in redeeming one's shadow. Jung at that moment was, in those terms, too highly differentiated for anyone to define his basic type, as it were, just from appearances.

Yet I do quarrel with the position he gives to his powers of thinking, considerable though they were. The history of his life, to my mind, shows beyond doubt that he got himself wrong and that intuition was his superior faculty. Only a man of the most highly fortified and precise intuitions could have gone against the trend of a whole age, correct it in his own spirit, and maintain this course against the most formidable opposition, as Jung had done.

This intuition also prescribed relatively early on in his life that he would need a house and trees in isolation and silence by the water which all his life had meant so much to him. At his home at Küsnacht he had made a fortress from which he went out daily to function and work in the world. In this home where he lived with his wife and children, Jung *did*. But in the house of stone at Bollingen he could just *be*. This quality of sheer being in the fullest measure was his own preparation for the end to come and what might be beyond, and making his life in the final season a living testament of the measure of wholeness he had been able to achieve.

Significantly enough, he built this house with the utmost simplicity and to such a design that if, as he was fond of saying, a man of the sixteenth century came to it, he would feel utterly at home. He chose as a site a promontory of land some twenty miles outside Zürich on one of the least populated parts of the lake. It was a place where he had often camped and picnicked with his family. The photographs taken on these and similar occasions reveal things about the man that the writings, both his own and that of others, do not. They reveal things even that are ignored, anyway in my experience, in the recollections of those who knew him then. The writings and recollections are obsessed with Jung's work and his thought. In one way, of course, it is understandable, because of both the significance of the work and the great and immediate originality of the thinking. Fortunately, some striking record of his zest for living and his unfailing humanity is there in the hundreds of photographs of him in possession of various members of his family, although one would not think so from the selections made for publication so far. In those he is almost without exception pictured in the somewhat Olympian image of an unrelenting servant of science. But I have copies of photographs where he stands, complete with Alpenstock, with an air of boyish triumph on some peak he had just climbed in the Alps. I have others which show him dressed with vulgar abandon in aggressive knickerbocker or plus-four fashion, jauntily wearing a cap with a loud check pattern that would seem more appropriate to a bookmaker shouting the odds at a race-course than to the solemn, contemplative, far-seeing great man his official photographs make him out to be. I have others of him dressed like a stonemason, happily extracting the appropriate symbol locked up in yellow stone at Bollingen, or just sitting content in the sun slicing kindling wood, or busy chopping logs for the fire in the great open hearth of his medieval lakeside kitchen. But my favourite ones are those showing him at ease at the rudder of his boat, one or more of his young daughters, dressed enchantingly like apprentices to the great Dana Gibson himself, sprawling nonchalantly on cushions in front of him.

He had often sailed to this anchorage at Bollingen and it was as if some wind of the spirit naturally brought him there now and made him do his building just there. It was still a relatively bare place and he had to plant most of the trees which now surround the building, dense and high and which on nights of storm serenade the house and its occupants with harplike Druid music. But here the house was built, of course, in stone, which had always had such a special meaning for him. His first dialogue with something outside his lonely, introverted self, as we have seen, had been with the stone on which he happened to be sitting at the end of his father's garden in the vicarage at Laufen, where night and day silence was the sound of the Rhine flowing with infinite indifference over the rocks of the Falls beyond the castle walls. Here the sound was to be in different dimensions, first of all of course in the natural form of the lake water lapping almost against the foundations of stone, the wind, and a certain star-crackle in the frozen silences of some unclouded night in the deep of winter but then also, as if through the barrier of silence before and after his day, a distant sea murmur of voices of multitudes of being gone before and uncountable masses still to come were filtering through to swell the last chorale of this final orchestration of being for sheer being's sake.

Appropriately, right at the beginning there at Bollingen, through the means of stone he delivered himself of another proof of his commandment to himself that no matter how unfamiliar the form, all things had a character and meaning of their own and were not to be turned from one's door. When the foundations of the house of stone were being laid he arrived there one day to find that the builders had rejected a corner-stone as too large for their purpose. They were about to send it back to the quarry, amazed because with Swiss thoroughness they had meticulously prescribed measurements for the stone in the list of their requirements, but Jung would have none of it. There was a deep meaning for him in its appearance at such a moment. Not only the stone but the great "togetherness" seemed to demand of him some active recognition of the event.

He took the stone because he had a hunch it might be ideal for carving his own imagery of material that had come to him out of his confrontation with the unconscious and giving it an honoured position on a pedestal in the garden by the lake. To this day, though the colour of the stone has darkened and deepened with the patina of time subtly overlaid on the freshness of the material, the impact of Jung's work on it is still as immediate as it is authoritative. Indeed, the imagery and inscriptions in the stone seem to be an issue direct out of the nature and texture of the stone itself as much as a product of Jung's own imagination, and the result, therefore, of an unusual integrity of execution. He contemplated the stone for a long time, he told me, before he worked on it and only when an image came at him, as it were, out of the stone itself did he set to work.

On one side he carved an inscription in Latin taken from a great medieval alchemist, showing how for him this stone was more than a stone. On the face directed towards the terrace of the Tower he chiselled a kind of eye, a vision which the stone seemed to insist on focusing on him, and within the pupil, as it were, of this great eye the tiny reflection one sees of oneself within the eye of another, like the Telesphoros of Asclepius—the mythical pointer of the way in antiquity—and the child in man who fulfilled dreams and prayers. Below it, he carved an inscription in Greek composed of lines from Heraclitus, Homer, and the Mithras liturgy, beginning significantly enough with the words: "Time is a child—playing like a child— playing a board game—the kingdom of the child." Imagery and lettering in both Greek and Latin are chiselled with precision, confidence, and a devout hand that remain most impressive.

On the face towards the lake, he let the stone speak for itself in quotations from alchemy also inscribed in Latin. He followed this up by chiselling the names of his father's ancestors on stone tablets, which he placed in the courtyard of the Tower, and painted the ceilings with the main features from his own and his wife's coat of arms as well as those of his sons-in-law. So out of his own instinct and natural necessities he had given the illustrious dead who had preceded him collectively and individually what the prayer book calls decent burial—not an act of forgetting and entombment in oblivion so much as an enthronement in the deed of grace we call gratitude.

It was his private and personal affirmation in stone of the human being's continuity of responsibility for taking on the past and living it as an immediate *now* with increasing relevance to the future. It was his own version of the Chinese ritual of reverence for the spirit of our ancestors. The proof of its necessity and validity was that once the ritual was over he was at one with life as he had never been, and the Tower night and day seemed peopled by a greater family from far down the wellspring of the first century of man and he could see, Leonardo-like, life in the round forever coming into being, renewing itself and then not coming to an end so much as passing on, to make way for another version of itself not possible before.

Jung always held that one reason why modern man was so singularly poor in spirit was that he no longer lived a symbolic life. This stone saved from rejection which started this process I have described, once made into a memorial of the meaning and the magic lost in man's rejection of the symbols that would inform him of a deeper self, not surprisingly led him to make Bollingen a place built of other stones where even more than enacting the symbolism of himself, he could express it by just being it.

Only a very partial rendering of the extent to which he exercised his own symbolic self at Bollingen emerges from his writing, but he went to immense trouble to live it out in great detail. For instance, when in the course of the building a skeleton of a man was uncovered, Jung took pains to discover whose it was. When it was found to be the skeleton of a French soldier killed there in the course of the Napoleonic wars, he insisted on reburying it with full military ceremonial, appropriate to the day of the death of the person who had once invested the vanished flesh and blood. When a friend died, he carved a memorial for him like a small shrine in the walls of the house, covered with curtains so that it should not be exposed to any eyes except those who came to it prepared for it in the spirit which had prompted him. When his wife died, he designed a memorial in stone for her too, carved his own epitaph in it, and set it up where both sun and its reflection in the water of the lake could warm and illuminate it.

All round the building and in the walls are stone carvings of images of the unconscious which had a special meaning for him, or just quotations from the Greeks, Romans, or the obscure alchemists whom he had honoured as pioneers in his own field as well as heraldic patterns in vivid, immediate first colours of his senses, like badges of his questing mind. The walls of the bedrooms were all painted over with immense, brooding, winged personifications of the prototypes tried out first in the Red Book, but here they are far more authoritative and final.

He built the house itself in three stages, and in the last stage when already the trees he had planted were tall, and reverberating with the winds that came long-maned down from the Alps, the dark strands all streaming and the rush of its speed tearing from the branches a cry as though of Merlin clamouring to be released from his mound, he built high up a place for his own unique retreat and silent contemplation. He had often remarked how even in the poorest house in India there was some corner set apart where a man could go through the ritual of respect for the symbolism investing his life. This retreat became his own inner sanctuary, a kind of holy of holies within the natural tabernacle which Bollingen in some sort was for him, where he could communicate in the deeps of himself with life and time and whatever lay beyond its borders of death.

The old Zen Buddhists spoke of the importance of achieving action through non-action. At Bollingen, Jung sought it and achieved it moreover in a state of a silence of contemplation so great that one would not have been surprised if he had been able to hear the sound of one hand clapping, which is the Zen image of the ultimate in power of comprehension. Modern men have forgotten the art of growing old. They have devalued it into an inferior state they see as a decline and fall of the human spirit. They regard life merely as an orchard full of bright, thrusting young trees and forget that they have still to bear fruit which has to be harvested. Jung's old age was old in the classical sense, where the fruit of his experience was gathered, stored, and evaluated. It was no decline or crumbling away but a state of growth into death and beyond. As he grew older and further away from other men, the lonelier he became in a human sense, the more he discovered a kinship with natural things at Bollingen and through them made loneliness his home.

In that loneliness already he had made his peace with his own impending death. Life for him was greater than birth or death. During the Second World War he had nearly died, or rather, died to such an extent that he no longer wished to live. He had seen the world and himself as from far out in space, the earth like an ancient geographical globe underneath him, its map contours distinctly outlined. The vision was so distinct and so haunted him that many years later he wrote to a fellow scientist, described the view, and asked how high that would have put him out in space. The answer came back, "About a thousand miles." His own coming back from that height was another and deeper kind of dying to him which made his own personal death relatively unimportant. As a result he could comfort with authority those of his friends about to die—and they were to prove legion in number.

"Death," he wrote in February 1945 to Kristine Mann, one of those distinguished founder members in America of whom I have spoken and who was facing her own death sentence from cancer with indomitable courage, "is the hardest thing from the outside and as long as we are outside of it. But once inside you taste of such completeness and peace and fulfillment that you don't want to return. As a matter of fact, during the first month after my first vision I suffered from black depressions because I felt that I was recovering. It was like dying. I did not want to live and to return into this fragmentary, restricted, narrow, almost mechanical life. . . . Throughout my illness something has carried me. My feet were not standing on air and I had the proof that I have reached a safe ground. Whatever you do, if you do it sincerely, will eventually become the bridge to your wholeness, a good ship that carries you through the darkness of your second birth, which seems to be death to the outside. I will not last too long any more. I am marked. But life has fortunately become provisional. It has become a transitory prejudice, a working hypothesis for the time being, but not existence itself.

"Be patient and regard it as another difficult task, this time the last one."

By provisional, of course, he did not mean living life provisionally. He had the greatest scorn for such an approach. One's life had to be lived as an absolute commitment, as if it were not just a *now* but a *forever*. Only if one did that could one arrive at the moment of the great order of release and see it as provisional. And there at Bollingen what was provisional in his life receded from what was lasting and he felt strongly at one again with nature, the clouds, seasons, and those thoughts of God the trees had always been for him.

I have been back recently both to the house at Küsnacht and to Bollingen. Although I visited him repeatedly at Küsnacht and only rarely at Bollingen, and although Küsnacht is full of things to remind me of him and the library in which we so often sat and talked is lovingly preserved, he had gone for me in Küsnacht in a way he has not left Bollingen. There, in a house where I saw comparatively little of him, his presence still seems to me so near that one feels one only has to stretch out one's hand to touch it.

And these feelings are not just about some great marble solemnities but someone almost more human than anyone I have known. That was his greatness: being so human, with all the human capacity for error and distraction, he yet did so much with his fallible spirit that is everlasting. All these feelings of his greatness are accompanied by far too many intimate human snapshots of him to record here, like the day he went out to buy some fresh lamb chops and wrapped them in decorative paper and special ribbon to give to a little dog whose birthday it was. Since the dog had been given to him by an American, he wished it many happy returns and conversed with it in English because he thought that would appease a certain nostalgia for its place of origin he sensed in the small animal. Or again, on a birthday of his when, like an old Chinese sage, he noted how loudly the wild duck called and how at evening a cold wind came down from the mountains. He was human enough too to turn tail and run away at times from the letters which daily came cascading through his front door. He would tie string round great bundles of them and hide them as quickly as possible from his sight and pretend they had never come. Even when I was in his house at Küsnacht some three years ago, another bundle of letters appeared from behind some books on a library shelf through which we happened to be looking for an alchemical text.

And then, of course, there was always that laugh of his and the incorrigible look of mischief in his eyes that often accompanied it.

But perhaps most moving of all the many illustrations of how he never exceeded his own humanity is a remark from a letter to a pupil barely two years before his death: "In my case *Pilgrim's Progress* consisted in my having to climb down a thousand ladders until I could reach out my hand to the little clod of earth that I am."

All that I experienced and feel about Jung to this day seems to me to be focused and most comprehensive in our last meeting. As always, I made no notes of the meeting. I make no notes of my travels or journeys through life, nor do I keep any appointment book, but leave all to my head. Born as I was in Africa, I have a primitive memory, for my teachers in this regard were Africans who could remember the events and the men who made them for some thirty generations back in such detail that they could even describe the numbers and colours of each animal in their herds of cattle that were sacred to their ancestors centuries ago. If they had had written records, I am certain they would have had no such memories. So I keep no written records, lest my memory should leave me. Besides, I do not believe that forgetting is always a disaster. There is a positive aspect to it and it would be intolerable to remember all, so that the memory is equipped with this faculty of shedding the relatively unimportant and false we call forgetting. I remember, I believe accurately, the significant detail of our last encounter.

I had just come from Zermatt, where I had gone to climb the Matterhorn in the middle of the winter. Mountains have always meant more to me than meets the eye. I had been inflicted with a great longing to climb this mountain which because of its shape and name was some sort of metaphor to me and which, without deliberate punning, really was a horn that mattered especially to me. I climbed it a long way but I found the summit in that bitter season beyond my powers. I had to come down and go on to Zürich, feeling oddly deprived as a result.

I arrived at Jung's home just as someone was leaving. Jung, once the door was shut and I was safely inside, said to me, with a light of schoolboy mischief in his eye and a young smile that was a kind of reproof to himself, "I'm afraid I had to tell her that I really could no longer interest myself in which Jack went to bed with which Jill." And before that, Ruth Bailey, who had been a companion on his journey to Africa and who went to look after Jung and his household after his wife's death, told me that he had given an hour of his rapidly decreasing ration of time to a very young white hunter from Africa, a friend of hers. The young man was an incorruptible innocent of nature and rare observer of the birds and animals of the Dark Continent but no intellectual, and certainly uninitiated in the most elementary knowledge of psychology. At the end of the hour he had come down, as if dazed and somewhat dazzled, and yet exalted, exclaiming, "Thank God, someone at last who has nothing phony about him! He's a great man, Ruth, he's great! I wish to God we had more like him."

And when she saw Jung he exclaimed, "What an extraordinary young man! Thank you for bringing him to me. If only there were more like him."

But when we were alone at last, as always he asked me about myself before I could ask him about himself. I had to tell him among other things about my disappointment on the Matterhorn which, to borrow an adjective of his, looked the archetypal mountain to me. We talked about Whymper, his tragic descent after his conquest of the as yet unclimbed peak, and how not only he but the Italian priest and his party, climbing unbeknown to him on the other side, had also seen that strange cross appear in the sky over the abyss into which Whymper's guides and companions had just plunged to their death. Indeed, we talked about mountains at great length, from the Parnassus of the Greeks to the hills of the psalmist. He told me again how as an inarticulate boy, hardly capable of walking, in the garden at Laufen at sunset he had had his first view of the distant Alps. He spoke movingly of a sense of destiny evoked in him by the view, which in a sense he identified only years later when his father treated him to that excursion up the Rigi. He remembered again how there this evocation of destiny was confirmed and exalted by his view of the great circle of foam-covered mountains before him. It was, he said, the vital point of departure in his own spirit, amazing and singular, until he read an account of how the poet Petrarch, who, like Dante, in his Laura had a feminine spirit to lead him up and on, became the first man in European history to climb a mountain in the Alps.

If ever asked to fix a definite point at which the long reawakening of the Renaissance began, he would place it in that precise moment. It was a sign for him that after the protracted introspection of the Middle Ages the European spirit was coming out of itself and moving outwards into another opposite of extroversion. But para-doxically for him, in his own profoundly introverted spirit, that view of the Wilhelm Tell peak seemed a glimpse of a world within. And as he said that I felt, although to my regret I did not say it aloud then, "That day you climbed the Rigi too was a turning point in history, a turning point in the European spirit as well as the spirit of the world, a turning point towards the day when man shall be delivered at last from a disastrous swing of opposites and set free for an evolution of his life not divided against itself but served by his full self."

We went on then to talk about Dante, about the meaning of the smile on the face of the *Mona Lisa* and why Leonardo gave Saint John the Baptist the face of Bacchus, and a ritual murder in Kenya—all with more wealth of detail than I can record here but mentioned as signs of the unbelievable abundance and diversity of Jung's imagination. The smile on the *Mona Lisa*, for instance, was a "Sophia" smile, the smile of the eternal feminine transfigured into the ultimate of love as wisdom, knowing the secret of the everlasting creation and re-creation, aware that as men and events come and go, so they will return again and again to the end of time in new and more meaningful forms. Leonardo had caught her, as it were, with that last look on her face of medieval confidence and certainty of knowing and belonging which distinguished Gothic humanity at its best. The artist showed her as if watching this great outburst of Renaissance activity, the fleets of ships sailing out of ancient ports to discover new worlds, and men at work in laboratories, on societies and their structure in a way not seen for centuries, knowing its provisional necessities and at the same time knowing it would not and could not last. She was there like a great mistress and mother watching her own children at play, glad and sad that they would have to grow up and learn to make their way in their turn for another succession of the living spirit of life and its love.

As for Bacchus's face on the head of John the Baptist, symboli-cally nothing could have been more right. The revelation which Saint John came to announce so austerely came from a Bacchic element of the day. It needed that discipline of austerity of Saint John to contain the wild upsurge hinted at from within. It came from a profound change of focus in the underworld of the spirit of John the Baptist's Roman colonial day. We saw the same sort of thing going on round us, as for instance the way the young and even grown men like Huxley turned to drugs for their enlightenment. The account of the coming of Bacchus in the legends of antiquity was like a newspaper report of the drug traffic in our time, the drug then being wine, which in the first instance of its invention was regarded as a means of spiritual revelation and transformation.

It was a true parallel even to the extent that the authority in command, the King of Thebes, not only made no effort to understand the new phenomenon and its rapid spread but just cried for the application of more and more "law and order" against the recruits to the swelling followers of Bacchus. He ignored, as we have, that great inner eventfulness could be dealt with only from within and not merely by external reactions, least of all externals of sheer suppression. As a result, the king utterly failed in his task and was torn limb from limb by a frenzied crowd led by his own mother.

It was in this sense that Bacchus was the classical forerunner of a regrouping of irresistible unconscious forces and the wine that went with him an image of new vision and transfiguration, and not in regard to its negations as a representative of sheer license and indulgence, that Leonardo's association of him with John the Baptist was so prophetic and right.

We were in danger of repeating the mistake of the King of Thebes in failing to understand how great a shift there had been in the collective unconscious all over the world, how the season of time itself was changing. Unless we understood it soon, those who opposed the new Dionysian upsurge manifest in our time, as well as those who were its instruments and victims, would perish. These last, above all, seemed to be imperilled because they had forgotten the vital importance and validity of the ego in life. Egotism, like all "isms," was wrong but the ego itself had to stand fast in its own validity at the core of the conscious individual if consciousness were not to fail. It could no more be ignored or by-passed than the psyche could without disastrous consequences for all. The archetype of the persona, or the mask, which supported man in his relationship to the external realities, could not be rejected, however fashionable such a view. It might be accused psychologically of representing for man in his maturity everything that he and the world had thought him to be but which he in his individual searching retrospectively was not. Yet it had to be lived out if ever man were to grasp the importance of his own feminine psyche, which regulated and observed his relationship with his great objective collective unconscious. The two opposites had to be maintained and contained somehow. Our greatest immediate problem was to prevent one disastrous opposite from swinging over into another in the spirit of man to the eclipse of its predecessor.

If we stood fast and worked to bring our shadow into light, it had been empirically proved, somehow, sometime, man and his ego were transformed into something greater than both joined together. The ego, without loss of value and with immense enrichment of meaning, was enabled by a symbol grown from within to surrender itself to the greatest individual archetype of all, the self, which was there, as it were, in every person like the morning star mediating between the night and day in man. That self was, as far as one could define it, the end of the harsh road of individuation and the purpose of all one's seeking, for in that self one experienced the presence of the author of the mighty activity he called God. There one found clear reflection of the great mystery of the image of God.

This done, and only then, could one set out with the right instrument for taking on the turmoil, confusion, and sickness of the time. But to think one could gain self-knowledge and enlightenment from drugs like mescaline was almost the final depravity of the decline of the passion of the spirit into a flirtation with intellect, reason, and sensation. Drugs, of course, had their role in medicine and healing, but Jung viewed them with total distrust as a source of enlightenment. In the first place they disregarded the natural ethical accompaniment of their use. The view as from Everest which one gained lying in bed after taking the requisite drug was in terms of meaning totally different from the view of the man who had climbed the mountain the hard and dangerous way. Not only was the view of the one an hallucination but it was in terms of life "not earned," as the climber had earned his and as all reality had to be earned. Nor did it involve the drug-inflicted visionary with any moral commitment or exercise of conscious choice between error and accuracy of his vision. Besides, Jung added, he himself much as he knew of vision and the vista of the collective unconscious, did not know whether he had earned the right to know more of it.

He would be most uncomfortable to know more until he was

certain he had done his duty by what he already knew. That was one of the great troubles of our day; we had in our possession perhaps more knowledge and power resulting from our knowledge than ever before in the history of man, but less and less were we morally committed to our knowledge and its power. Life demanded that all knowledge should be evaluated and lived according to our best evaluation if it were not to destroy us. What did we think atomic power and Hiroshima were about if not a warning addressed to us from life what power without appropriate evaluation and obedience to our evaluation would do to us?

All this was summed up for me some years later, in perhaps the finest of the many poetic statements ever to come from him, in something he wrote about Huxley's *Doors of Perception*:

> If I once could say that I have done everything I know I had to do, then perhaps I should realize a legitimate need to take mescaline. But if I should take it now, I would not be sure at all that I had not taken it out of idle curiosity. I should hate the thought that I had touched on the sphere, where the paint is made that colours the world, where the light is created that makes shine the splendour of the dawn, the lines and shapes of all form, the sound that fills the orbit, the thought that illuminates the darkness of the void. There are some poor impoverished creatures, perhaps, for whom mescaline would be a heavensent gift without a counterpoison, but I am profoundly mistrustful of the "pure gifts of the Gods." You pay very dearly for them. "Quidquid id est, timeo Danaos et dona ferentes."
>
> This is not the point at all, to know of or about the unconscious, nor does the story end here; on the contrary it is how and where you begin the real quest.*

In his published works he contained himself within the discipline of a reverent empiricism. He never abandoned the resolution taken as a student that in talking to the world at large, he would do so no longer just out of intuition but out of intuition supported by facts. On occasions such as this meeting, however, his mind ranged far and wide and swift, and he speculated about possibilities of life and

* Letter to Father Victor White, April 10, 1954.

meaning not referred to or even hinted at in his work and seminars. On this occasion too we talked a great deal about the meaning of immortality and what faced life beyond death. We had discussed it many times before; he always said how impressed he was that even in the oldest of his patients, even in men and women he knew for certain were about to die, there was no sense of death in their objective psyche or in the heart of their collective unconscious. The objective psyche of man in an essential part of itself, he was convinced, behaved as if there were no death, as if it existed outside space and time and was therefore not subject to the majesty of death. He was impressed how old people lived as if there were no death. He urged one and all therefore to live on even to the last of his days as if the *now* were a great *forever*.

To me he said specifically that although one must not think the unthinkable, although one must never use the mind for a purpose for which it was never intended, something that was one of the outstanding hubrises of our time, we should always recognise what it was in one's imagination that gave one the greatest meaning. What gave one meaning should be one's greatest guide; one had to follow it always with all one's soul and heart and one's greatest awareness. If in the prospect of death the meaning was derived from a feeling that death was not the end, one had to follow that and live in terms of that feeling.

I had been much shaken once in that connection by an answer to a letter I wrote to him when his beloved wife Emma died. One knew, in more senses that one, how much more even than a wife and mother had died with her because of the recognition of the demands of the masculine in herself in her work on the quest of the Holy Grail. In that reply, in terms so moving and personal that I do not care to repeat them, he spoke of how he was faced now by a silence to which there was no answer.

My spirit went black because it seemed that he was denying his own precept of following the greatest meaning of his own intimation that the psyche existed outside space and time and beyond death. Some months later I was as relieved as I had been after that long pause when he was asked if he believed in God and he had said first, "I do not believe," before adding, "I know." He wrote to me that the silence had been broken by a dream in which he entered a vast and darkened theatre. He walked down the aisle between the empty rows leading to a stage, which was brilliantly lit. He came to the orchestra pit, which stretched like an abyss before him that he could not cross. There in the centre of the stage, more beautiful and free of care than he had ever seen her, was his wife.

Although not in great detail he refers to this dream in his *Memories*, like a portrait of his wife received from "the other side" as if it were specially commissioned for him, and adds something not mentioned in the letter to me. His wife's dress in this painting was made for her by the young seamstress, the psychic medium whose claim to speak with spirits had helped to make him aware of the end to which he had been born. It was as if that detail were an empiric dream intimation of some sort that his wife quintessentially lived on. So there is also another and wider significance to the return at this late hour in his dreams of the psychic young seamstress who had impelled his essential self on its natural course in his student years at Basel. It demonstrates both how his own interest in the question of life after death never diminished and how rigorous the scientific self-discipline which prevented him, despite the pressures of such an interest, from formulating a definite hypothesis about it. It was one thing to be convinced of a world of individual spirits, but another to produce objective proof either that they did exist or were not always mere personifications of unconscious, unlived elements of the human personality, as he had so often found them to be with his patients. How acutely the problem had exercised his probing mind is clearly illustrated for me by the manner of his recollection in old age of that fateful first visit of his and Freud to America for the Clark Conference of 1909.

The content of the papers delivered and all the discussions they provoked of such critical concern as they were to the two embattled men had sunk almost without trace into the sea of Jung's memory. No detailed recollection of the celebrated academics he met remained, with one or two exceptions. Of course his memory in this, as in all else he did, had a way of its own in measuring what was worth retaining. For instance, although not a fact or feeling of his meeting much later with Mountain Lake, an obscure chief of a despised and almost extinct Indian race, was ever erased, celebrity after celebrity of the high established American intellectual, social, and scientific scene was made to walk the plank in the course of his passage through the years. But on this first occasion in America, the most notable exception was William James, to whose stature and quality this was in no small measure a tribute. I have always felt that had it not been for the Atlantic in between, the two men could have been close friends and collaborators in spite of the gap in years, because at heart they had similar points of departure.

Among those Jung remembered in old age, William James seemed to stand out above all those many others with the precision and clarity of a silhouette against a sunset horizon. Apart from more formal meetings, Jung spent what he called two delightful evenings alone with William James, and warmed to the originality and immediacy of the man. From what Jung told me, as well as from what I have read, James shared considerably the family legacy of the gift of the artist which made his brother Henry so articulate and remarkable a writer. In both his writing and conversation William James had a capacity for expressing psychological findings and speculation with the grace, lucidity, and ease called art, and I myself if ever in need of a reminder of all this have only to think of the way he termed one of his basic concepts—"subliminal," which to this day is valid for me and expresses a nuance absent in both "subconscious" and "unconscious." James's clarity of mind and the total absence of prejudice accordingly impressed Jung greatly, all the more because James was so profoundly interested in the psychic, extrasensory, and particularly spiritualistic phenomena encountered in his work. Indeed at that very moment, James's work on the reality of the spirits with the celebrated medium Leonora Piper was making him increasingly suspect to contemporaries, even to their staunch host G. Stanley Hall, despite James's reservation: "I remain uncertain and await more facts, facts which may not point clearly to a conclusion for fifty or a hundred years."

So deep was the impression James made on Jung that he never lost contact with James's close friend James Hervey Hyslop, also a psychologist in his own right. The two of them once had a session together to survey the investigation of metaphysical phenomena. Hyslop himself was convinced of the identity of spirits in a life after death. Jung remained to the end in his scientific self closer to James's conclusion than the absolutism of Hyslop's belief but told me he had to concede to Hyslop that there was occasional evidence of a continuation of individual reality after death that could be better explained by some hypothesis of spirits than by the qualities and peculiarities of the unconscious. On the basis of his own experience, Jung still felt compelled to be sceptical in individual cases he encountered, since they were so often mere personifications of unconscious tendencies, but there were occasions when the spirit hypothesis seemed to yield better results in practice than any other.

The fact that in this concession to Hyslop's belief he appeared to go further than James himself had done is to be explained not only by the enigmatic variations on the basic theme encountered in his own research into the collective unconscious but by nature of Hyslop's own testimony.

This aspect of the matter is summed up best for me by something Jung told me, not long before he died, about Hyslop and James. I do not know if it is recorded elsewhere but I do not hesitate to do so here since it is little known and is such a striking illustration of how a psychological approach, particularly in this overexternalised hour, is valid only as an interest in life continuous and whole, presupposing as great a concern for a destination beyond death as it does for an origin before birth.

Hyslop and James, Jung told me, promised each other that whoever of the two died first would, if there were individual life after death, do all he could to give the survivor proof of it. Men like Rhine in work like his *Reach of the Mind* have since produced a host of examples of this kind but at that early hour in this century, the pact between the two friends was as rare as it was a moving demonstration of a call of duty to professional truth to be carried on after the dismissal we call death from the parade ground of life. It was evidence of how the lives of all three men in mere passing pointed to the importance of Michelangelo's observation in one of his most moving poems that the thought of death had preserved and sustained many men.

James died first and Hyslop, because of his conviction that somehow, somewhere, William James lived on, waited with growing dismay, Jung told me, for a proof that did not come. He waited for years and had almost despaired when one day he received a letter from Ireland, a country he had never visited. The letter was from a husband and wife who apologised profusely for perhaps intruding unnecessarily on his time. But they were, the letter explained, regular users of the planchette as a means of communicating with spirits, and for some months their experiments had been dominated by one who purported to be "a certain William James" and who insisted that they contact a Professor Hyslop, of whom they had never heard. He made such a "nuisance of himself" that they were finally compelled to make enquiries about Hyslop's identity and address and deliver this single message in the form of a question: "Did he remember the red pyjamas?"

Hyslop's first reaction was one of utter consternation, Jung said. He neither remembered any red pyjamas nor thought that James had honoured their solemn pact by so banal and trivial a communication. But in the days that followed he was increasingly impressed by the fact that no channel of communication could have been more objective and protected against subjective elements than the one chosen. And the moment the system of communication was fully honoured, he remembered in one lightning flash the red pyjamas as well.

As young men he and James had been sent on a grand tour of Europe. They had arrived in Paris one late evening some days ahead of their luggage, and were compelled to hasten out shopping for immediate necessities like pyjamas. The only ones Hyslop could find were what Jung called some "really fancy red pyjamas."

James teased Hyslop greatly about his "dubious taste" in night-wear for some days but soon the episode was forgotten, until resurrected by this intrusion on a planchette-scribbled message.

"Now, what in heaven do you make of things like that?" Jung asked me, and before I could say words to the effect that I had no comment, he added that he had never been bothered himself, as so many persons were, by the apparent triviality of messages "from the other side." If there were a life beyond death, it would be an idiom which we could not possibly possess in the here and now and as such utterly incapable of transmission in terms we could understand. What was surprising, therefore, was not the insignificant nature of these intrusions but that they should take place at all, implying, as this Hyslop experience did, that even in that extraordinary, transcendental state which a life after death had to be if it existed at all, nothing in our lives, however trivial or mean, had not played its part or been overlooked.

Besides, many of these so-called trivialities if looked at in this light were often not so slight and banal after all. If considered in terms of the imagery issuing out of the symbolic heart of reality and looked at as dream material imposed on men who were themselves stuff that dreams were made on, they made rare sense of a transcendental kind. Take the case of the red pyjamas. They were connected, in the case of James and Hyslop, with an incident on a journey to a world they had not been to before. They had arrived at a new stage of this journey, called Paris, ahead of their luggage, which is the image of the sheer impedimenta and inertia that retard the movement and change of life. What could reflect more truly the state of spirit of two men, particularly that of James, pushing on well in advance of the spirit of their day than such a journey and such an arrival?

As for the planchette reference to the incident, was there not a recurrence of the same image for the purpose of demonstrating how James had arrived at another stage even further in advance than before and, as popular image would have it, not died so much as passed on ahead? Surely the answer to this was in the fact that in the message the garments were pyjamas and moreover red. Pyjamas were a man's personal sleeping material, an image of the individual attitude to the night—above all to sleep, which always at all times and places symbolised death; red always was the colour of life. It is as if in this recurrence of the imagery of red pyjamas bought in advance of the baggage of physical existence in the here and now, James was saying to Hyslop that in this sleep called death he had only to look in his imagination they had called fancy and he would see that James lived on. No, far from dismissing manifestations such as these as trivial, there was cause for wonder and humility of mind and spirit before such apparent banalities and inspiration to look deeper into their origin of meaning. Certainly for Hyslop the message of the red pyjamas was conclusive and his belief and interest never again wavered.

All this went on while there was no sign that Jung's own death was near. He always had an enormous zest for life and it seemed to me then as great as ever. We ate delicious meals and he and his other guests also drank good and appropriate measures of wine and smoked with great enjoyment. Even at the age of eighty-seven he showed a glimpse of the Jung who, in the midst of the First World War and all its agonies, insisted that at the meetings of the Psychological Club its members should not neglect their Dionysian needs. This love of fun and the alert, thrusting mind, active as ever, seemed undiminished.

On the last day of all when I said goodbye to him, I found him sitting under a copy of the Holbein portrait of Erasmus, wearing a little black skull cap and with the light like splinters of glass around him, looking as if he might have been posed there by Rembrandt himself for his conclusive study of the perennial philosopher at work. The man, the attitude, the book in his hand, and the background provided the most complete visual and most precious rendering of Jung and what he represented among the many I recollect. The immense contribution Erasmus made to Jung's own spirit deserves and still awaits detailed evaluation. Jung was as aware as anyone of what Europe owed Erasmus for standing fast at a moment of great disintegration in the European spirit; he had belonged to the natural order of spirit of which Jung too was a companion of honour. But for the moment this, added to the little said about Erasmus in the beginning, must be enough and all that it is necessary to stress is that to the end Jung loved and reread him.

Just then Jung was looking through something Erasmus had written, of course in Latin. He was turning the pages as fast as someone reading a thriller. He excused himself for going on with his reading; one of his guests, he explained, wanted to know where he had got the Latin inscription carved in stone over his front door: "Called or not called, God shall be there."

He said, "Of course, I know it comes originally from the Greeks but I first came across it in Latin in Erasmus and I would like the exact quotation to give him."

And that is the focus of my last vision of him in Küsnacht, a vision that seems to confirm the religious essentials of all his seeking and such message as he lived for life; called or not called, God was always there, known or not known, despised or rejected, this master pattern theologians call God is there night and day in the collective unconscious of man, calling him to live and be his whole self.

It was a vision too of the confirmation of the importance he attached to continuity and the sense of history which the world has lost for the moment. It was a glimpse as though through a corner of a curtain lifted darkly in the deeps of his mind, to show how the future depended, not on the abolition of ancient values, the ancient truths of the spirit, but on their rediscovery and expression in a truly twentieth-century way. In making the past contemporary, the *now* forever, man found his greatest meaning and accomplished all wholeness that is true sanity and health in all dimensions of the body and mind.

He had never done anything which had not been a duty imposed from within. The life of a man, he was fond of saying, is an event which is completed in the here and now only through death. Psychologically, death was for him just as important as birth, and like birth an integral part of life, so the events of life could not be described until after death. That, among other reasons, is why he refused to write a detailed autobiography. It did not mean, as I have intimated, that death was the end for him and the last of the image of a self fulfilled.

There is clear implication in his writing and clearer affirmation in his conversation that the self achieved lived on at least as image and incorruptible core of new being. Death freed it only from what was false and provisional and sent it on indestructible in time to serve in another season of itself. The walls between birth and death, the known and the unknown, had always been no opaque barrier for his spirit but transparent as the windows of a house of many mansions amber with light at night. However solidly and empirically drawn his own frontiers were for us, one was always conscious of how for him they remained transparent with the light of new meanings pressing out of the dark against them. In particular one is conscious of how transparent with numinous light were the answers he found for the two great questions he had set himself at the beginning: "What is the secret of the human personality? And what is my own personal myth and the myth of my time?"

The secret of the personality was enclosed in the self, in the area where in the silence of one's own truth achieved and fortified by oneself, the "I" and the "thou" of life could converse with each other. The myth, of course, was that of the ancient quest of the Holy Grail, rediscovered and made modern and armed with scientific armour so that service of the feminine that is love was provided with the protection of the masculine that is the power of the word. How real and active this myth had become for him was as always revealed in dreams and for me most conclusively in one which had come to him years before, in India. In the midst of celebrations organised there in his honour, and bombarded as he was by the imagery though of another culture of a sort which always fascinated him, he yet had a dream which clearly asked him, "What are you doing here in such a scene with a culture not your own when your own Europe is sickening and in danger of collapse? Go home and do your own proper work with the common, everyday material given to you."

And this work, the dream said, was the resumption of his quest of the Grail. There on an island in the dream was a great castle, as there was once on that island his fantasy had created and encastled on the Rhine near his home. But in this dream it was a castle awaiting the coming of the Grail. Jung and some friends went out to look for it at sundown—at a twilight hour of the European spirit—since, though announced, it had failed to come. The scene became bleak and the nightfall bitter. Far away from the castle they found the island divided by a broad channel of the sea, a split of collective-unconscious proportions, and the Grail was beyond. One by one Jung's companions fell asleep, succumbed to that lack of awareness of which sleep is the fatal image, as it was in a garden in Gethsemane nearly two thousand years before. It was a cryptic dream, summing up what his own life had been and recording how often he had been abandoned by others as he was in the sleep of his companions. Undismayed, he stayed awake, took off his clothes, and prepared to swim the channel to find the Grail. This stripping is perhaps the most significant aspect of the dream, symbolising how he had unmasked himself of all pretensions and discarded all worldly presumptions and preconceived attitudes of the day to stand the man he was, naked as he was born, self-confessed and vulnerable as a child again, innocent and simple as Parsifal through self-confession of his own worldly inadequacies, before judgement in his confrontation with his own psyche and the vengeful tormented soul of his time. Only then was he fit to swim this great rift in himself, this abyss between the two great opposites, the gap in between his No. 1 and No. 2 personalities. And so at last the dream showed him prepared to cross over his own divide to a self that was more than the sum of himself, a Grail overflowing with light of the transparency of the ultimate mystery of creation.

I said goodbye to Jung with so much of this and far more than I can describe of turmoil within himself. As always with that innate sense of manners the French call *politesse de coeur*, he came with me down the path leading to the gate. He stood there for a moment, leaning perhaps more heavily than usual on his stick, and waved goodbye saying, in his schoolboy English, "I'll be seeing you."

But some weeks later Jung was dead. I do not know the medical diagnosis of the immediate cause and I really do not want to know, because it is irrelevant. I knew that he was dead because he had done his work and his life had come to its natural end. It may be true that many of those whom the gods love die young. Even then I believe that they do not die before they have done what the gods meant them to do, or that they die because it is only through dying that they can achieve the impact they were intended to have. But it is just as true also that those whom the gods love most live longest. In some mysterious way the length of their life is commensurate to the scale of the work they have to accomplish. They too tend not to die before that work is done. In that regard the length of Jung's life and the timing of his death is as compulsive as it is awesome.

He worked up to some three days before his death to finish some writing, on symbolism, I believe. He finished and said he was rather tired, and went to rest. The evening before he died, Ruth Bailey, to whom all who loved Jung owe such an immense debt for the way she took care of him, left him for a moment with his son.

Jung said something to this effect: "Quick, help me out of bed before she comes back or she'll stop me. I want to look at the sunset."

And he looked out of his window and saw the sun setting behind the Alps, and in this completed the full circle of his vision of life in the here and now. He was back in a moment that had never left him when as a child he had had his first view of the foam and spume of snow smoking over the blue swell of the storm-tossed Alps on the far horizon going red in the sunset. He was restored to that moment when he was in all that is symbolised by the Garden at our beginning. He was back in the garden at Laufen where, lying in his pram and looking at the sun dripping like crystal water from the green leaves, he was filled with a sense of wonder and utter belonging. The banishment and journey from that garden, more than fourscore years long, in the last view of the Alps was over, I believe, for otherwise he could not have gone so content back to his bed. And I say that because I know in myself and in many others beside whom I am insignificant, as well as from what he himself had told me, that in this pattern of departure and return I have mentioned, all our separation and traffic and travail in between our several beginnings serve only to enable us to see in a way we could never have any other way how departure and return are one and our home where we started from.

The afternoon on which Jung died a great thunder-storm raged over his house at Küsnacht, as if nature itself were mobilised to acknowledge the event. Just about the time of his death lightning struck his favourite tree in the garden.

One of the earliest rituals to reconcile men to the death of those dearest to them was to burn not only their bodies but all their most precious belongings with them. They did this so that through the fire, which brought light, what was imperishable in matter could be released from the perishable to accompany the spirit freed from bondage to flesh and blood on its journey beyond. The wood that makes the fire, the flesh and the blood that nourished the flame of the spirit, burned out, but fire and spirit flame and flare on. It is almost as if nature sent the lightning to perform this task for Jung. But not only did this happen in nature. It was as if in the dreaming and visionary unconscious of many who had known him, an awareness like a kind of witnessing of a great ship going down appeared to draw all sorts of portents and visions towards the vortex, like flotsam and jetsam on the sea marking the place of a *Titanic* sinking.

I myself had an experience of this which I have hesitated long to make public. I had sailed from Africa profoundly distressed by the condition of my native country. I was obsessed with forebodings of apocalyptic disaster. I did not recognise what my own people had become and they did not recognise me. As a result the sea and ships, which have always given me one of my greatest feelings of belonging and rest, utterly failed me on this occasion. I could not sleep. Even the strongest of sleeping-draughts were of no use to me.

And then one afternoon alone in my cabin, worn out and hovering in and out of an exhaustion near to sleep, I suddenly had a vision of myself in a deep, dark valley in avalanche country, among steep, snow-covered mountains. I was filled with a foreknowledge of imminent disaster. I knew that even raising my voice in the world of this vision could bring down the bulging avalanches upon me. Suddenly, at the far end of the valley, on one Matterhorn peak of my vision, still caught in the light of the sun, Jung appeared. He stood there briefly, as I had seen him some weeks before at the gate at the end of the garden of his house, then waved his hand at me and called out, "I'll be seeing you." And then he vanished down the far side of the mountain.

Instantly I fell asleep and slept for some eighteen hours. I woke next morning just as the sun was rising, and pushed aside the curtains of the porthole of my cabin. I saw a great, white lone albatross gliding by it, the sun on fire on its wings. As it glided by it turned its head and looked straight at me. I had done that voyage some fifty times and such a thing had never happened to me, and I had a feeling that the day before me was going to be utterly unlike any other day I had ever experienced. I had hardly got back into bed when my steward appeared with a tray of tea and fruit, as he always did, and handed me the ship's radio news. I opened it casually. The first item I saw was the announcement that Jung had died the previous afternoon at his home in Zürich. Taking into consideration the time and the latitude and longitude of the ship's position, it was clear that my dream, or vision, had come to me at the moment of his death.

But far more important than my own or other people's premonitions and visions were the last dreams experienced by Jung himself. Just before he died, he dreamt that he saw "high up on a high place" a boulder in the full sun. Carved into it were the words, "Take this as a sign of the wholeness you have achieved and the singleness you have become."

The symmetry of meaning conveyed in this dream is as complete as it is final. All Jung's life was a dialogue, a dialogue first with a stone, through stone with himself, a dialogue with all life, history, and time, continued and fulfilled through moulding, shaping, and carving its quintessentials in stone at Bollingen, and finally a dialogue with God himself, as if from the heap of ashes of himself and his time. Nothing could have been more fitting in the greatest process of question and answer in flesh and blood that life is than that the conclusion of the last dialogue of Jung accessible to us, his dialogue with death, was also in terms of sunlit stone, that stone which is so great an image of what is lasting and indestructible.

Hard on this he had another dream in which he saw a square and trees growing in it. The roots of the trees were intertwined with green and gold.

The square in itself is a symbol of wholeness and needs no voice to proclaim it. It is the wholeness that is consciously achieved and asserted in the flux and welter of appearances and things. The trees, of course, carry the image of life rooted in the authentic earth of the unconscious; the green and gold around the roots which nourish the trees are the image of the alchemical property of the ultimate in sublimation and transfiguration, as he had once seen them in that vision of Christ standing at the foot of his bed. It was as if the master pattern itself was saying to Jung at the very moment of transition and translation, "You have earned the freedom to move on. You have done your work and you have done it well."

That this is not just a fanciful and highly subjective reading of mine of the event of death in the life of somebody I loved, and to whom I owe much, was finally confirmed for me by another intrusion of the symmetry of meaning through a different sort of coincidence. I was making a film of the story of the life of Jung some years ago. The time schedule for the film had been determined nearly a year before we started filming. The final sequence on the last day of all was to be filmed in Jung's old house. We had worked all morning in his home and all day long the cameraman, producer, and myself, without mentioning it to one another, had an indescribable feeling that Jung was near to us. I heard the cameraman saying to an assistant, half jokingly at the time, "You know, I had a feeling as if Jung were looking over my shoulder all the time."

It was a dry, hot, blazing afternoon and we left the house at lunchtime to do some background filming in the afternoon in the oldest section of Zürich, intending to return for the filming of the final scene by his home at sunset. On our way from Zürich to Küsnacht to do so, suddenly out of the hot blue sky the thunder clouds tumbled without forewarning, as if in a great hurry. By the time we reached Küsnacht the lightning was flashing, the thunder rumbling, and the rain pouring down.

When the moment came for me to speak direct to the camera about Jung's death and I came to the description of how the lightning demolished Jung's favourite tree, the lightning struck in the garden again. The thunder crashed out so loud that I winced, and to this day the thunder, wince, and the impediment of speech it caused are there in the film for all to see, just as the lightning is visible on the screen over the storm-tossed lake and wind-whipped trees.

As far as I myself am concerned, confirmation of this kind is unnecessary enough to be almost irrelevant. But I am compelled to mention it because it would seem as if it is in some sort testimony of how that great spirit lives on and will continue to show the way towards the transfiguration of life until its uncompromised fulfillment at the end of history and time and both life and time, their mission accomplished, vanish in the ocean wake behind it and something more meaningful move into their place.